CHEROKEE IN CONTROVERSY

MERCER UNIVERSITY

MERCER UNIVERSITY PRESS

Endowed by

TOM WATSON BROWN

and

THE WATSON-BROWN FOUNDATION, INC.

CHEROKEE IN CONTROVERSY

The Life of Jesse Bushyhead

Dan B. Wimberly

MERCER UNIVERSITY PRESS | *Macon, Georgia*
2017

MUP/ H930

Published by Mercer University Press
1501 Mercer University Drive
Macon, Georgia 31207

9 8 7 6 5 4 3 2 1

Books published by Mercer University Press are printed on acid-free paper that meets the requirements of the American National Standard for Information Sciences—Permanence of Paper for Printed Library Materials.

ISBN 978-0-88146-607-2
Cataloging-in-Publication Data is available from the Library of Congress

For LaMarsha

Contents

Acknowledgments	ix
Preface	xi
Chapter 1: Background and Early Years	1
Chapter 2: Tennessee Ministry	20
Chapter 3: The Removal Crisis	50
Chapter 4: The Seminole Mission	71
Chapter 5: The Trail West	92
Chapter 6: Establishing a New Life in the West	119
Chapter 7: Ministry in the New Nation	162
Conclusion: The Legacy	190
Bibliography	201
Index	213

Acknowledgments

Several archival and personal sources have been significant to the research. Professor Daniel F. Littlefield, Jr. of the Sequoyah Center at the University of Arkansas at Little Rock made helpful suggestions. John Conner, a historian in Cleveland, Tennessee, provided beneficial information concerning local Baptist history and the early life of Bushyhead. Dr. J. M. Gaskin of Durant, Oklahoma, supplied a photo of the Bushyhead portrait. My wife, LaMarsha, deserves special recognition for other photos related to Bushyhead and computer advice.

Cherokee friends Bill Foster of Broken Arrow, Oklahoma, and Jack and Katy Vardeman of Bartlesville, Oklahoma, offered encouragement. Depositories accessed, to name a few, include the Oklahoma Historical Society (Oklahoma City); Tennessee State Library (Nashville); Gilcrease Museum (Tulsa); Southern Baptist Archives (Nashville); Arkansas History Commission (Little Rock); Special Collections at the David W. Mullins Library at the University of Arkansas at Fayetteville; McFarlin Library at the University of Tulsa; Western History Collections at the University of Oklahoma; Northeastern Oklahoma State University Library (Tahlequah); Center for Baptist Studies at Mercer University (Atlanta); Partee Center at William Jewell College (Liberty, Missouri); and National Archives at Fort Worth, Texas, and Kansas City, Missouri.

Preface

During a most crucial era, Jesse Bushyhead provided leadership to the Cherokee Nation. Born as the nineteenth century opened, Bushyhead played a multifaceted role. Early on he gained recognition as a Cherokee interpreter and translator, using his linguistic skills in legal disputes and delicate negotiations with United States authorities. He also utilized his knowledge to aid missionaries in Bible translation and interpreted for public worship. His conversion to Christianity was noteworthy because he became one of the first Cherokees to receive ordination to the ministry. Moreover, he was the pastor of at least two autonomous Cherokee Baptist congregations and aided in the establishment of several mission stations. But not only was he a spiritual shepherd, Bushyhead was a detachment leader during the forced removal on what has become known as the Trail of Tears. In this capacity, he was responsible for the safe conduct of over 900 emigrants from Tennessee to Indian Territory in eastern Oklahoma. After the journey, Bushyhead was a principal participant in the formation of the new Cherokee government, providing stability in the turbulent and often internecine struggle between factions. And although without legal training, Bushyhead served the new government as a chief justice of the Cherokee Supreme Court. Yet, during these challenges, Bushyhead also assisted missionary Evan Jones in establishing a vibrant Baptist presence among Cherokees.

The entrance of Bushyhead into early manhood coincided with divisive political, economic, and social developments among Cherokees. During the eighteenth and early nineteenth centuries, more conjugal unions occurred between whites and Cherokees. This resulted in mixed-blood offspring and caused tribal members to face issues of assimilation. In the past, historians have emphasized blood lines in an attempt to classify American Indians. As a result, two classifications have been apparent. Progressives, mostly mixed-bloods, desired to incorporate European-based lifestyles. These changes included Christianity, literacy, capitalism, and social practices. The other group, traditionalists, strove to retain age-old tribal culture. They favored customary tribal language, law, religion, political arrangements, and subsistence agriculture. Unfortunately, these categories have at times incorporated racist views. In *"Mixed Blood" Indians: Racial Construction in the Early South*, Theda Perdue ably underscores the dangers associated with insensitivity concerning mixed-blood versus full-blood designations. By using these terms, historians have implied that mixed-bloods were superior, simply because of their European ancestries. Such categorization, intentionally or otherwise, tends to denigrate Native peoples. In this work on Bushyhead, the author has remained aware of the dangers of cultural indifference. Yet it is impossible to study Bushyhead without reference to ancestry and culture. That is part of the narrative. After all, Christianity was a European import. And societal and linguistic links to Europeans provided the distinct advantage of ties to a global and increasingly industrialized economy. Yet much of Bushyhead's ministry was to Cherokees of non-European heritage. These included those who had chosen not to assimilate in terms of language and lifestyles. And by the time of his death in 1844, Bushyhead to some degree had transcended issues of assimilation; that is, he had garnered esteem from both assimilated and more traditional Cherokees.

A number of works have examined the changes encountered in the Cherokee Nation. This book looks at those issues but focuses more specifically on how these unfolding events and the trauma of removal affected Bushyhead and his family. In his personal life, Bushyhead mirrored some of the cultural, economic, and social changes. From a mixed lineage and possessing a degree of property, he identified more with progressives. But fluency in Cherokee and English allowed him to function in white society and also move among the councils of traditional tribesmen. Part of the assimilative difficulties centered on religion and politics. Those possessing blended lineages tended to consider education in white schools as essential for their children, especially when it came to an understanding of legal and business affairs. And in Cherokee country, schooling for tribal members was available only at mission schools. Throughout the 1820s and 1830s, Cherokees became more familiar with Christianity through Protestant mission schools. Although schools primarily reached more Europeanized Cherokees, some non-assimilated Native peoples also became Christians. But at times these conversions provoked ill will among some traditionalists, and shamans, those who clung to Native religion feared the erosion of influence. Feeling threatened by missionaries, shamans also accused missionaries of supporting removal. The conversion of Bushyhead to Christianity therefore placed him at odds with some traditionalists.

Another issue involved the political restructuring of the tribe. In 1827, the tribe adopted a written constitution modeled after the governing document of the United States. Once implemented, a centralized arrangement with separate branches made law and administered the government. Yet traditionalists, notably some of the older chiefs, resented the loss of the old, loosely federated tribal structure. But as Bushyhead rose to political prominence, many traditionalists looked to him for leadership in efforts to oppose removal. Entrusted with this responsibility, he had to bridge the gap between Europeanized and non-assimilated Cherokees.

Another source of friction developed within the ranks of progressives as they coalesced into upper- and middle-class groupings. Members of the upper class, linked by family kinship, often profited from businesses and significant amounts of property. In many cases, this property included African slaves. Through his wife, Eliza, Bushyhead had married into a slaveholding family. Although he was not among the most affluent of those from blended lineages, he owned slaves and reaped the rewards of a farm and orchard. These characteristics placed Bushyhead in the rising middle class. In his position, he could have felt chafed at being stymied by upper-class

Cherokees. A number of middle-class tribesmen, as examined in a following chapter, resented the upper class. It seemed to them that a minority had consolidated political and economic influence and restricted access to others. As a result, they felt blocked in their attempts to ascend to higher levels of political leadership. Partially because of this, they saw removal as a means to strip the upper class of power. They therefore cooperated with the United States government in this effort. In doing so, they favored the liquidation of tribal property in the Southeast and emigration to Indian Territory. But lineage alone did not always determine support for emigration. Some of those who lacked European ancestry, notably Major Ridge and others, favored removal. Some endorsed it for political advantages, but others viewed it as the only means to guard the tribe from debauchery and extinction. Yet most Cherokees, regardless of the degree of assimilation, staunchly resisted emigration.

Over time, the removal issue touched almost all Cherokees, including the Bushyhead family. Small bands of Cherokees voluntarily had been relocating across the Mississippi since the dawn of the nineteenth century. But in 1830 President Andrew Jackson, a Democrat, pushed through the Indian Removal Act. This legislation mandated the relocation of almost all Native peoples from the southeastern United States to Indian Territory. In 1825, Secretary of War John C. Calhoun had recommended the relocation of Native peoples still living east of the Mississippi to locations in newly created Indian Territory. The region composed most of modern Kansas, Oklahoma, and parts of Nebraska.[1] The area selected for Cherokees lay west of the State of Missouri and included part of the western domain of the Territory of Arkansas. One may assume that most Cherokees responded negatively. Most did, but the decision to emigrate was not always clear cut. And the Bushyheads were not united over this question. Bushyhead had friends and family members who, at times, fa-

[1] Arrell M. Gibson, *The American Indian: Prehistory to the Present* (Lexington MA: D. C. Heath, 1980) 312.

vored or opposed emigration. The decision became intertwined with family dynamics and relationships. Jack Walker, Jr., a charismatic brother-in-law, worked closely with United States agents to promote removal. In doing so, Walker became open to bribes. Considered by many Cherokees as a traitor, Walker fell at the hands of assassins. Yet Isaac, the occasionally errant brother of Jesse, at times partnered with Walker in business. Considering Bushyhead's middle-class status, he may have had reason to side with the pro-removal faction. Yet, as events developed, circumstances and acquaintances nudged him toward the anti-removal camp.

Another aspect of Bushyhead's life concerned religion and his denominational alignment. By 1830, he had joined the Baptists. A few years before, Bushyhead and some of his family had been converted under the auspices of a Congregational-Presbyterian mission near his home. As a gifted linguist and orator, Bushyhead was a valuable asset to the mission staff. It often took years for whites to become proficient enough to preach in an Indian tongue, so competent translators were essential to mission work among Native peoples as a whole. Had Bushyhead remained in the Congregational-Presbyterian fold, he likely would have been offered some type of enhanced leadership role in the local synod. So, what persuaded him to move from Congregational-Presbyterian ranks and affiliate with Baptists? Did he perceive that the Baptist mission board offered more opportunities, even a salaried position? Yet it may have been easier to remain among his original church fellowship rather than change, for once among Baptist ranks, Bushyhead became embroiled in denominational disputes involving local church support for missionary societies. Of course, it remained in Bushyhead's financial interest to side with ministers who saw the benefits of salaried missionaries and a more centralized denominational structure. But this was not an issue at the Congregational-Presbyterian mission. Finally, in the crucial period prior to removal, did Bushyhead become more involved in ministry as a façade to convince whites that Cherokee conversions manifested evidence of European civilization? And if so, perhaps state and federal governmental officials would reconsider removal. This question deserves attention, especially in light of his association with Evan Jones.

Jones had been active in Cherokee missions in North Carolina since the early 1820s. In this role, he worked tirelessly to resist the removal policies of Jackson. Even after other missionaries had left the Eastern Cherokee Nation, Jones remained and aided Cherokee principal chief John Ross in attempts to disseminate information and thwart removal. Yet certain political and religious aspects of Jones did not align with the views of many whites in the Southeast. For example, he did not support slavery. And as a salaried missionary from a centralized New England mission board, he may have seemed to be an outsider. Moreover, he was such a thorn in the side that some military authorities regarded him as cunningly subversive. And at times military and governmental authorities banished him from North Carolina, Georgia, and ultimately Indian Territory. Yet Bushyhead was the right-hand man of Jones, accompanying Jones on preaching tours and providing translation services. Without Bushyhead, it is almost certain that Jones could not have influenced Cherokees as much as he did, both politically and religiously. And later in Indian Territory, Bushyhead continued to aid Jones. But was Bushyhead no more than a malleable tool in the hands of Jones? But, again, did Bushyhead see Jones as primarily a means to resist removal? If so, did Bushyhead choose to cooperate more out of a sense of tribal preservation rather than religious convictions?

Another question focuses on the degree to which Bushyhead was willing to overlook, if not encourage, a bloody vendetta against Cherokee leaders who sponsored removal. During the latter part of 1837 and early 1838, Bushyhead participated as a team member in an ill-fated diplomatic mission to the Seminoles and an accompanying abortive trip to Washington. While in Florida, Bushyhead risked his life as he conveyed messages between General Thomas Sidney Jesup and hostile Seminole chiefs. But the mission proved fruitless, even to the point of casting aspersions of treachery on the Cherokee team members. In fact, Bushyhead and other team members never seemed to earn the trust of Jesup. And once the team had proceeded to Washington, government officials virtually ignored them. By the time the impecunious team left Washington, officials had approved only a pittance of monetary recompense. The embarrassing circumstances surrounding their travel home merely compounded the frustration.

Approximately six months after returning home from Washington, Bushyhead struggled through Kentucky as a detachment leader. Jesup happened to be visiting family in the region at the time. On one occasion, it seemed that Bushyhead made what Jesup considered to be an inflammatory comment. Bushyhead allegedly predicted deadly vengeance on those Cherokees who had cooperated with the United States in forced removal. And approximately nine months later in Indian Territory, assassins struck down three Cherokee leaders who had been complicit in forging the removal treaty. Of course, Jesup may have misunderstood the context of Bushyhead's words. Or perhaps Jesup allowed his past opinion of Bushyhead to color his report. Yet it raises questions regarding Bushyhead's involvement. Once he reached Indian Territory, there is no evidence that he participated in planning or executing the murders. Yet Bushyhead knew some of the assassins. So, how much he was aware of the planned murders and to what extent he attempted to prevent them still remains in question.

Although Bushyhead grew to adulthood in the midst of the above challenges, the most salient issue after removal was the establishment of a new government in the west. His life in the new nation was short, for he died of disease a little over five years after arriving. Yet he lived in turbulent times. This involved the merger of three Cherokee factions: Old Settlers, the Treaty party, and the Antitreaty party—that is, the majority group under John Ross.[2] Unity was diffi-

[2] The Antitreaty party has also been referred to as the National party or Patriot party. In this work I have chosen to use the term "Antitreaty party." See Daniel F. Littlefield, Jr. and James W. Parins, eds., *Encyclopedia of Amer-*

cult. Old grievances, rivalry over political leadership, and competition for thousands of dollars in government annuities fueled resentment. These differences often resulted in violent outbreaks. As unrest spread, it alarmed white settlers along the Arkansas border and threatened to erupt into a full-blown war. At this crucial time, Bushyhead helped to spearhead developments that ultimately preserved the Cherokee government. Yet Bushyhead, a Ross supporter, drew criticism. As chief justice, he delivered a death sentence to Archilla Smith, an enemy of the Ross faction, in a controversial murder trial. Under modern American jurisprudence, Smith did not receive a fair trial, for at one time before his arrest, according to one source, he had intended on killing Bushyhead. It is therefore easy to conclude that these circumstances could have prejudiced Bushyhead. Moreover, the court's denial of clemency may have provoked continued animosity. And on more than one occasion, his enemies targeted Bushyhead for assassination. Indeed, strife became so intense that political enemies brutally murdered Isaac Bushyhead.

Bushyhead's life also coincided with the national issue of slavery. By the 1830s, sectional controversy had become more pronounced. In the Northeast, the antislavery movement had coalesced into abolitionism. Abolitionist Baptists, influential in the denominational headquarters, became alarmed when they learned that Bushyhead, a salaried missionary, owned slaves. This news caused them to demand his resignation. In turn, some Baptists across the South reacted against their abolitionist brethren. They perceived the outcry as an attempt to force other Baptist ministers and congregations to bow to the dictates of a shrill minority. As a result, national Baptists split into separate denominations. They formed southern and northern wings, a division which foreshadowed national rupture and civil war.

ican Indian Removal (Santa Barbara CA: Greenwood, 2011) s.v. "Cherokee Removal," by Daniel F. Littlefield, Jr.; William G. McLoughlin, *Champions of the Cherokees: Evan and John B. Jones* (Princeton: Princeton University, 1990) 132.

In Indian Territory, the reaction against Bushyhead threatened to undermine Baptist work among Cherokees, for by this time, Bushyhead had become an esteemed leader in the eyes of many Cherokees.

Part of the slavery issue focused on Bushyhead's personal views of slavery. There is no evidence that Bushyhead owned slaves before his marriage. Yet part of his wife's dowry included a slave woman. And when Bushyhead left Tennessee in 1838, his expanded household included several slaves, possibly the children of this same bondwoman. In Indian Territory, he possessed at least two female slaves and a manservant. At some point after arriving in Indian Territory, it seems that Bushyhead had purchased the male slave. Although personally opposed to slavery, missionary Evan Jones provided a flimsy excuse to shield Bushyhead from criticism by abolitionists. Jones justified Bushyhead's participation as a means to evangelize other Africans; that is, Bushyhead's male slave was a preacher. Accordingly, Bushyhead had allowed his male slave considerable liberty to preach. But how much freedom did Bushyhead genuinely grant? Or did he strive to work within the system to make the best of a difficult situation? Yet it is difficult to ignore that, even in benevolent arrangements, slavery was still slavery, no matter how masked.

Issues of race and citizenship have accompanied the developing history of the Cherokee Nation. Two fine works, *Race and the Cherokee Nation: Sovereignty in the Nineteenth Century* by Fay A. Yarbrough and Celia A. Naylor's *African Cherokees in Indian Territory: From Chattel to Citizens*, explore the intricacies associated with these sensitive issues. Under pre-nineteenth-century Cherokee clan law, the position of Africans was insecure. Lacking membership in a clan meant that Africans possessed no citizenship rights, and the death of Africans would go unavenged. During the first two decades of the 1800s, Cherokee law allowed citizenship to the children of Cherokee mothers and African fathers. Yet reflecting racial attitudes in the antebellum South, attitudes toward Africans among Cherokees hardened. By

1824, the tribal legislature had banned marriage between Africans and whites or Cherokees.[3] These practices continued among Cherokees in Indian Territory. For example, Cherokee slave codes were harsh, and emancipated slaves did not fare much better. The presence and treatment of slaves in the Bushyhead household mirror this growing moral dilemma.

Even the events surrounding the death of Bushyhead stirred controversy. In summer 1844, he suddenly fell ill. Fortunately, he did not experience prolonged suffering. Yet, on the frontier, competent physicians were few. At first he received treatment from a missionary. Although the minister possessed some medical knowledge, he was not a physician. As the condition of Bushyhead worsened, two doctors arrived. But there was little they could do. In the wake of his untimely death, accusations surfaced among the missionary staff concerning the failure of the attending missionary to summon proper physicians sooner.

Although dissension surrounded him, a different picture of Bushyhead emerged in the early twentieth century. Historians such as Grant Foreman and others exalted Bushyhead and embellished his genealogy. Instead of a modest, if not humble, background, his revised lineage identified him as a grandson of the chief British Indian agent for the colonial South. Some assessments such as these painted him as nonpartisan and almost above reproach. Accordingly, he worked to bring healing and justice to his people in Indian Territory. He also endeavored to build a bridge to whites and evangelize Cherokees. In this role, Bushyhead seemed to be an almost docile peacemaker. Yet a closer look at Bushyhead reveals a more complex figure, for unfolding developments drew Bushyhead firmly into the Ross camp and influenced him to make difficult decisions. This book sifts the extent to which Bushyhead became involved in unsavory developments. Did he at times work for his own interest, or was he a tool

[3] Fay A. Yarbrough, *Race and the Cherokee Nation: Sovereignty in the Nineteenth Century* (Philadelphia: University of Pennsylvania, 2008) 7–11.

in the hands of John Ross and Evan Jones? On the other hand, to what degree did his enemies malign him?

Someone of Bushyhead's significance deserves attention. Yet, other than brief articles, an in-depth monograph has not been published. In 1887, J. S. Murrow, a pioneer Baptist missionary in Indian Territory, compiled a brief essay about Bushyhead. Privately published in 2015 as *Rev. Jesse Bushyhead: Cherokee Indian and Missionary*, the work is little more than a string of quotations from the articles of Evan Jones, which appeared in a Baptist periodical during Bushyhead's life. Unfortunately, few of Bushyhead's personal papers exist. If he left a journal, it has not survived. And there are no records from the congregations that he pastored. In fact, these churches dissolved after his death. The little remaining correspondence is found in Baptist periodicals or the papers of John Ross. Other than these, the historian has to sift through information available in other sources. These include Baptist associational minutes, pertinent documents of the Baptist Board of Foreign Missions and the American Board of Commissioners for Foreign Missions, presidential reports, government documents, military reports, and newspapers. Especially valuable were the letters and journals of Daniel Sabin Butrick and Evan Jones. I also have relied on the works of William G. McLoughlin for bibliographic references and information. Especially helpful were his *Champions of the Cherokees: Evan and John B. Jones* and *Cherokees and Missionaries, 1789–1839*. These books supplied information about Bushyhead's ministry and links to Evan Jones. Other invaluable sources have been the papers of John Ross, both the original manuscripts at the Gilcrease Museum and the two-volume set edited by Gary E. Moulton.

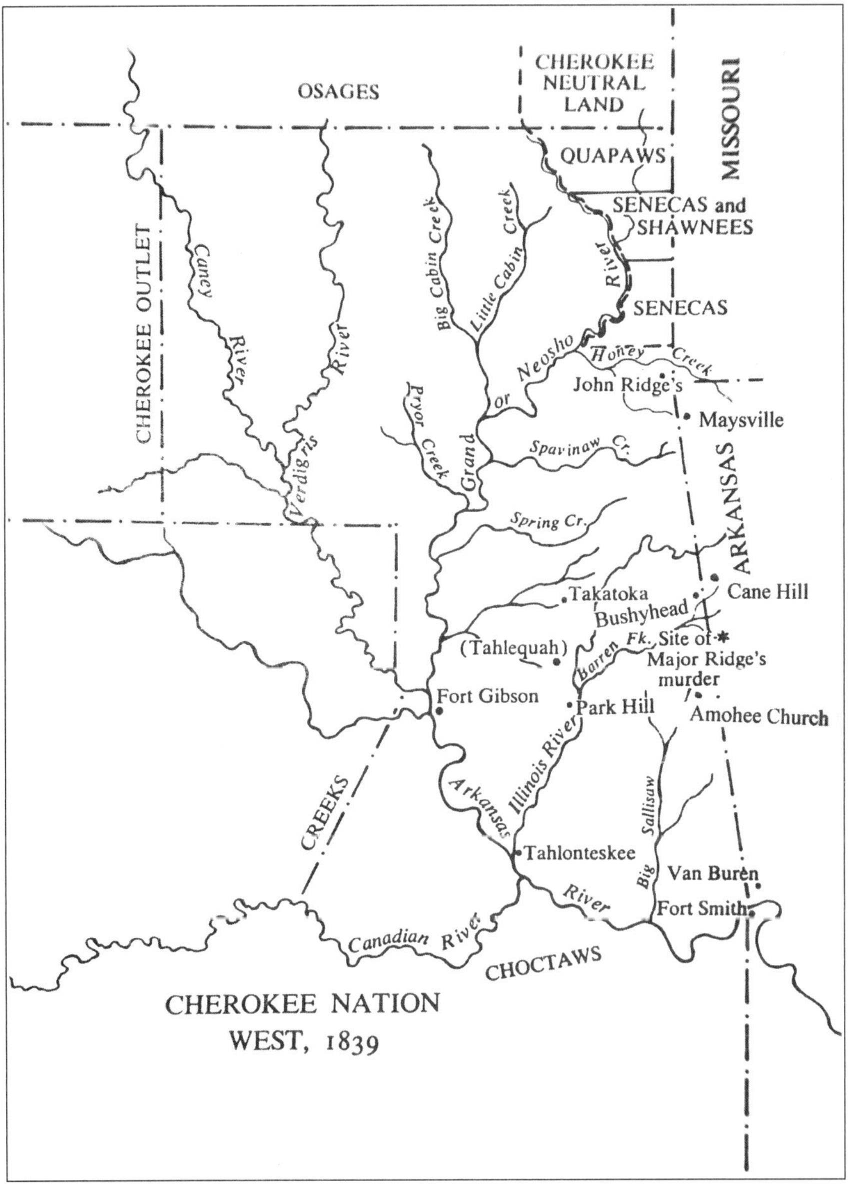

Western Cherokee Nation, modified from map on page 331 of *Cherokee Tragedy: The Ridge Family and the Decimation of a People* (2nd ed., rev.), by Thurman Wilkins.

Jesse Bushyhead monument at the Baptist Mission Cemetery in Westville, Oklahoma.

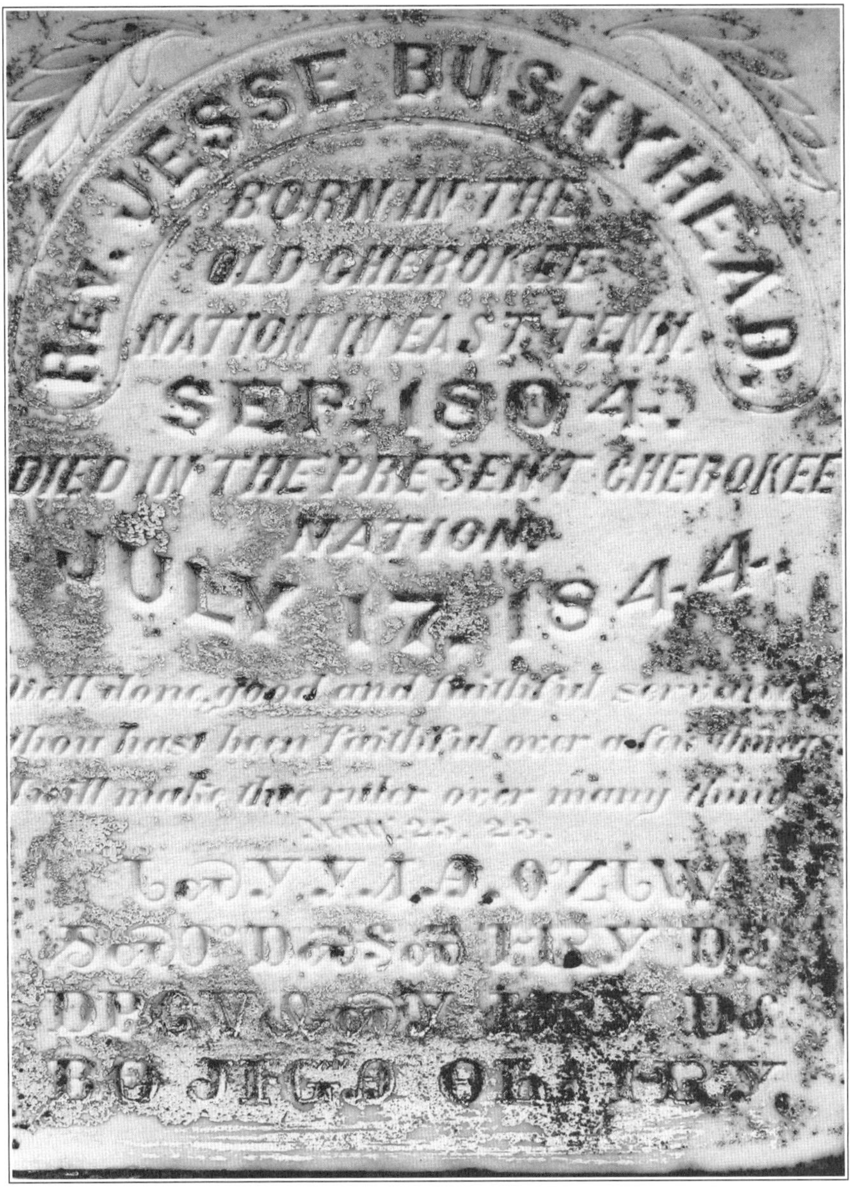

Detail of the inscription on the marker.
There is an inscription in English and in Cherokee.

The Old Baptist Mission located north of Westville, Oklahoma, and near the site of Bushyhead settlement, was organized by Evan Jones during the ministry of Jesse Bushyhead.

CHAPTER 1

Background and Early Years

In fall 1838, pines and sturdy hardwoods graced a scenic landscape in Bradley County, Tennessee. Organized in 1836, the county was in the southeastern part of the state and adjacent to the Georgia border. Located near the Tennessee River, the area benefitted from the river network that linked the area to the Mississippi Valley. Fertile soil and long growing seasons offered hopes of future economic development. But the peaceful surroundings stood in contrast to human disruption as thousands of Cherokees crowded into holding camps. There they waited in squalor while tribal leaders and United States agents came to terms over the details of their pending forced removal to the west. Jesse Bushyhead, often identified as "Bushyhead" in this work, was one of the Cherokees who played a central role in Cherokee affairs and resettlement.

The events in Bradley County were part of the larger scope of western expansion that followed the American Revolution and the War of 1812. During the revolution, many Cherokees had sided with the British. Aiding their British allies, Cherokee raiding parties attacked the American backwoods. Their raids extended from the Holston River in eastern Tennessee to Virginia, North Carolina, South Carolina, and Georgia. But the swift retaliatory response of American forces devastated Cherokee villages and destroyed crops. In eastern Tennessee, western North Carolina, and South Carolina, Cherokee resistance crumbled.[1] By 1777, defeat had persuaded older chiefs to

[1] Gibson, *The American Indian*, 253.

cede all tribal lands east of the Blue Ridge Mountains in North Carolina, South Carolina, and east of the Nolichucky River in Tennessee.[2] But some younger chiefs refused to countenance the loss of lands. Perhaps half the population followed the younger chiefs and settled along the Tennessee River between present Chattanooga and northeastern Alabama. The new settlements became known as Lower Towns, being farther south than tribesmen once had lived. Identified as Upper Towns, the older settlements were in North Carolina.[3]

In the 1780s, the United States government had little cash but counted on proceeds from public land sales to boost credit and pay debts. Taking advantage of this policy, squatters, speculators, small farmers, craftsmen, and businessmen jumped at the opportunity to acquire cheap acreage. Unfortunately for Cherokees and other tribes, American newcomers encroached on remaining tribal claims in North Carolina, South Carolina, Tennessee, Georgia, and northeastern Alabama. In 1785, American officials and Cherokees, seeking to delineate boundaries, signed the Treaty of Hopewell. Yet, under the Articles of Confederation, the form of national government at the time, the fledgling American government possessed little centralized power and virtually no national military. Thus, the Confederation government remained almost helpless to protect Indian lands.

With the ratification of the Constitution in 1788, the United States formed a more centralized government. But even after the implementation of the new structure, whites continued to chip away at Cherokee holdings in Tennessee and Georgia. Often this was accomplished through bribes to individual chiefs. Because Cherokee tribal government was an arrangement of loosely confederated towns, there were numerous chiefs and headmen, but few who claimed authority to speak for the entire Cherokee people. Using such fraudulent

[2] Ibid.

[3] William G. McLoughlin, *Cherokees and Missionaries, 1789–1839* (Norman: University of Oklahoma, 1995) 31.

means, whites often claimed that the cessions had been endorsed by a majority of Cherokees, although only a few may have participated. Under these circumstances, it became easier for whites to bribe individual chiefs into ceding tracts of land and claim that their acquiescence represented approval by a tribal majority.[4]

In 1805 and 1806, Lower Town chiefs ceded even more land to the United States, including substantial tracts in North Carolina, Tennessee, and Georgia. Yet Cherokees still retained northwestern Georgia, northeastern Alabama, southwestern North Carolina, and southeastern Tennessee. Wishing to annex this land as well, the American government opened talks with some Lower Town chiefs. In 1817, these negotiations resulted in another treaty. Under this agreement, Cherokees ceded much of East Tennessee. Known as the Hiwassee Purchase, the area encompassed land between the Hiwassee, Little Tennessee, and Big Tennessee Rivers. The Candy's Creek settlement, the home of the Bushyhead family, lay within the bounds of the Hiwassee Purchase. In exchange, the Cherokees received a promise for an equal amount of land in northwestern Arkansas. The treaty also offered an annuity to the Cherokee Nation and gifts to the heads of Cherokee families who voluntarily chose to relocate. As a result of increasingly diminished holdings, Cherokee leaders realized the need of a more centralized and unified political arrangement when dealing with the United States government.

Traditionally, chiefs and headmen of each town had advised their town councils and represented their constituents annually in national tribal council. Yet the decisions of the national tribal council had no binding effect on individual bands and towns. By the second decade of the nineteenth century, the national tribal council created a more centralized political structure with the creation of a standing committee. Although the standing committee was answerable to the

[4] John Ehle, *Trail of Tears: The Rise and Fall of the Cherokee Nation* (New York: Anchor Books, 1988) 72.

entire tribe, the committee had the authority to make decisions while the tribal council was not in session. In 1827, this system became even more centralized with the implementation of a written constitution. Modeled after the United States Constitution, the document provided for an elective chief, a national judiciary, and a bicameral legislature. Under this arrangement, Cherokees still held their general tribal council every October, but the legislative authority rested in the two elected representative chambers, the National Council and National Committee. Voters elected thirteen representatives to the National Committee and thirty-three delegates to the National Council. These bodies then elected the principal chief and his assistant. Moreover, all legislation had to be approved by both bodies as well as the principal chief.[5] Similar to the United States judiciary, there were eight district courts and a supreme court, the highest judicial entity. After removal in 1838, the Cherokee government underwent reorganization. Yet the basic constitutional structure adopted in the 1820s provided the form of government that continued throughout the nineteenth century.

Political changes also brought about social, economic, and religious changes. Political centralization created opportunities for the rise of tribal elites. These prominent men, often from blended Cherokee and European ancestry, were familiar with the legal and economic systems of whites. And as more whites entered Cherokee lands, the shortage of eligible white females often had resulted in unions between white husbands and Cherokee brides. Yet some Cherokees saw advantages to such cross-cultural arrangements, for the progeny of these unions provided business and legal support to the tribe as a whole. Of course, some full-bloods also obtained wealth and social prominence. But upward economic mobility especially marked some descendants of mixed unions. These included John Martin, Jo-

[5] John Howard Payne Papers, Ayer MS. 689, 8:106–107, Newberry Library, Chicago, Illinois [typewritten CD copy].

seph Vann, and brothers John and Lewis Ross. All of these had acquired significant business and property holdings as well as African slaves. Because of increased cotton cultivation, the demand for African slaves had increased. The 1825 census of the Cherokee Nation east of the Mississippi listed 13,563 citizens. In addition, there were 1,277 African slaves, roughly 9 percent of the national population.[6] In 1835, only 17 percent of the nation claimed white ancestry, yet 78 percent of slaveholders possessed some measure of white lineage.[7] And as property passed to children, successions often included slaves. Thus, the majority of slaveholders were whites or Cherokees with European ancestry.

Having more access to education and inherited wealth, mixed Cherokees also held other advantages. Because the 1827 constitution allowed the national legislature the right to demand bonds from certain officials, those who possessed a degree of wealth were more likely to seek elective offices. In essence, this practice limited the pool of officeholders to wealthier tribesmen of mixed ancestry who were able to pledge security for bonds.[8] Demographic and social challenges also influenced the spiritual attitudes of more affluent Cherokees. As whites began to travel freely through Cherokee country, unscrupulous white whiskey peddlers also appeared. As a result, violence, debauchery, theft, and deceit threatened to replace honesty, a traditional virtue among Cherokees. More and more, the old traditions and religion no longer seemed a firm anchor.[9] In light of these developments, many Cherokees realized that survival depended on learning to compete in a white society. This entailed knowledge of white culture, language, and means of subsistence. And the most available sources of

[6] *Missionary Herald* (1825), 355.

[7] Duane H. King, ed., *The Cherokee Indian Nation: A Troubled History* (Knoxville: University of Tennessee, 1979) 117.

[8] Theda Perdue, "The Conflict Within: The Cherokee Power Structure and Removal," *The Georgia Historical Quarterly* 73 (Fall 1989): 468–74.

[9] McLoughlin, *Cherokees and Missionaries*, 33.

educational opportunities were schools operated under the auspices of white missionary societies. In turn, missionaries welcomed the opportunity to expose Cherokee youth to literacy as a means of evangelism.

Missionary endeavors had sprouted from a religious revival among certain American Protestant denominations. Following the revolution, religion often had taken second place in the backwoods as Americans strove to launch a new nation and claim economic opportunities. But in 1800 and 1801, revival had erupted on the Kentucky frontier. Most well known was the camp meeting at Cane Ridge, Kentucky, where an estimated 10,000 to 25,000 gathered for spiritual renewal and socialization.[10] From 1800 through the late 1820s, intense religious fervor swept the frontier from Georgia to western New York. This revival, known as the Second Great Awakening, sparked Protestant denominations to evangelize and enlist converts. In the early 1800s, these efforts resulted in the organization of missionary and benevolence societies. These groups promoted evangelism, Bible distribution, tract publication, and Christian education.

Missionary endeavors also became entwined with the Indian policies of the national government. A product of the Enlightenment, President Thomas Jefferson believed in human progress. Over the course of a few generations, he felt that education and exposure to European civilization would prepare more settled Native peoples such as the Cherokees for citizenship. Government policy also became integrated with some of the goals of missionary societies. According to this arrangement, the government encouraged Protestant missionary societies to sponsor ministers and teachers among tribes at trading posts, Indian agencies, and mission stations across the frontier. These volunteers taught classes in rudimentary education and manual arts. The government also allowed missionaries to organize Sabbath schools and hold religious services. Hopefully, these efforts would

[10] Sydney E. Ahlstrom, *A Religious History of the American People* (New Haven: Yale, 1972) 365.

pacify the frontier and incorporate Native peoples into European civilization. And if successful, pacification promised to benefit the cash-strapped federal government by reducing the threat of wars and the necessity of maintaining a large military. Born around 1804, Jesse Bushyhead began life as the national government began to implement these policies.

Little is known about the ancestry and early life of Jesse Bushyhead. Family lore purports him to have been a grandson of John Stuart, a pre-Revolutionary Scottish merchant on the South Carolina frontier and later British superintendent of Indian affairs for the southern colonies. Such unions between Europeans and Cherokees were not uncommon. Before the early nineteenth century, fluid marital arrangements between European men and Native women characterized southern tribes. As superintendent, Stuart held an eminent position among Native peoples. Because of his prodigious amount of red or blond hair, tradition holds that Cherokees referred to Stuart as "Bushyhead." And likewise according to legend, Stuart fathered a one-eighth Cherokee son by Susannah Emory in an extramarital relationship. Susannah, one-fourth Cherokee, was the granddaughter of Ludovic Grant, a Scottish Indian trader in East Tennessee. Yet their son did not claim the Stuart surname, but instead received a Cherokee name, Oo-no-du-tu. The name denoted the hereditary thick mane of hair characteristic of John Stuart. In white society, he became known as "Old Bushyhead," or simply "Bushyhead." After her union with Stuart, Susannah married Englishmen Richard Fields. Following the death of Fields, she married Joseph Martin. Fields and Martin, as well as their descendants, were prominent in Cherokee affairs. As an adult, Oo-no-du-tu married Nancy Foreman, the daughter of a Scottish father and Cherokee mother. The firstborn of this union was Tas-ke-ket-chee, a five-sixteenths Cherokee, also known as Jesse Bushyhead.[11]

Stuart could have been the grandfather of Jesse Bushyhead. By the late nineteenth century, elements of the Bushyhead legend had appeared in print, but several aspects of the traditional lineage are difficult to reconcile with facts. First, the elder Bushyhead was born around 1777. Yet Stuart likely was not among Cherokees at the time of conception, for by the time of Oo-no-du-tu's birth, the Revolutionary War was in progress. By that time, Stuart, aged fifty-eight or fifty-nine, had moved to Pensacola, Florida, where he died 21 March 1779. Second, the appellation of "Bushyhead" or "Bush head" was not unique to Jesse's father. Rather, the name also appeared on lists of Cherokees in Georgia as well.[12]

Finally, Jesse Bushyhead almost certainly had more Cherokee ancestry than indicated in the Stuart lineage. In summer 1835, Jesse received an official governmental appointment as a census-taker. His assigned territory included his community. So, he personally supplied

[11] Emmet Starr, *History of the Cherokees and Their Legends and Folklore* (Warden: Oklahoma City, 1921; rep., Millwood NY: Kraus Reprint, 1977) 92, 577 (page references are to reprint edition); George Morrison Bell, Sr., *Genealogy of "Old & New Cherokee Indian Families"* (Bartlesville OK: By the author, 1972) 91–92; "Ludovic Grant," Bushyhead Folder, Special Collections, Oklahoma Historical Society Library. An article in the *New England Historical Register* by Samuel Drake in 1872 seems to be the source of the ancestral record. Grant Foreman, early twentieth-century Cherokee historian, sourced the Drake article in his explanation of the Bushyhead genealogy, and it has been accepted as fact by subsequent authors. See Grant Foreman Papers, Cherokee Notes, box 36, vol. 76, 777, Gilcrease Museum, Tulsa, Oklahoma. See the following sources for information concerning the Bushyhead lineage: John Richard Alden, *John Stuart and the Southern Colonial Frontier* (New York: Gordian, 1966) 169–71; Congress, House, Committee on Indian Affairs, House Document 285, *Memorial of the Cherokee Mediators*, report by Major Polecat and others, 25th Cong., 2nd sess., 7 (LexisNexis Academic, 2006) Serial Set ID: 328 H.doc. 285.

[12] E[lijah] Hicks to T. H[artley] Crawford, 23 May 1844, Letters Received by the Office of Indian Affairs, 1824–1881, National Archives M234, roll 88.

some of the data. It therefore seems that the information concerning his family would have been somewhat correct. Of course, the census often includes estimates of bloodlines for some heads of families. Yet the census indicated that Jesse was at least half Cherokee. But other sources suggested even more Cherokee heritage. In 1828, missionary William Holland recorded the Bushyhead siblings as three-quarters Cherokee.[13] Four years later, Evan Jones, Jesse's white missionary partner, described Jesse as a "full Cherokee." Finally, there was the facial appearance of Jesse. Although open to artistic interpretation, the only portrait of Jesse suggests a stronger Native lineage than five-sixteenths. In consideration of these observations, Jesse may not have been the grandson of John Stuart, however elevated that lineage may have seemed to later writers.[14] But at the same time, Jesse did possess some degree of European ancestry. And having a mixed lineage, he stood to establish strong ties to white society. Accordingly, this position gave him the advantages of a European education, fluency in Cherokee and English, and an understanding of the political and economic characteristics of both worlds.

Yet, unlike some with mixed ancestry, Jesse was not born into a wealthy family. However, he managed to accumulate a degree of wealth. From 1804 through 1816, the elder Bushyhead and Nancy

[13] William R. Snell, "Candy's Creek Mission Station," *Journal of Cherokee Studies* 4 (Summer 1979): 174–75.

[14] *Census Roll, 1835, of the Cherokee Indians East of the Mississippi and Index to the Roll*, National Archives, Washington, D.C., 1960; Gary E. Moulton, *The Papers of Chief John Ross* (Norman: University of Oklahoma, 1985) 1:344; Shirley Coats Hoskins, ed., *Cherokee Property Valuations in Tennessee, 1836* (n.p.: privately published, 1984) no pagination; *The Baptist Missionary Magazine* 12 (December 1832): 395; Cherokee Improvement Claims, Treaties of 1817 and 1819, Special Files of the Office of Indian Affairs, 1807–1904, National Archives, M574, roll 17, file 105; A Record Book of the Proceedings of the Supreme Court of the Cherokee Nation, 9 October 1829, Cherokee Supreme Court Minutes, vol. 1, 1823–1835, Cherokee Collection, 1775–1878, M-815, box 10, file 10,Tennessee State Library, Nashville.

Foreman had seven children, Jesse being the oldest. By 1818, the Bushyhead family was living on Mouse Creek near Cleveland, Tennessee, the future county seat of Bradley County. Earlier, the elder Bushyhead had relinquished land under the Treaty of 1817 and volunteered to emigrate west of the Mississippi River. But by 1819, he had changed his mind and decided to remain in Tennessee.[15] The 1835 census indicated the elder Bushyhead was a subsistence farmer with very few acres under cultivation. Yet, through marriage, Jesse managed to rise above the level of a subsistence farmer. In the early 1820s, perhaps 1822 or 1823, Jesse married Eliza Wilkerson. Eliza was also of mixed ancestry, the daughter of Edward Wilkerson and a full Cherokee mother. Her half-sister also was the wife of future Cherokee principal chief John Ross.[16] How much property Eliza brought into the marriage is unknown. However, she had fallen heir to a slave. In 1825, Jesse unsuccessfully brought suit in the Cherokee Supreme Court against Sarah Raincrow for the recovery of a slave girl named Jenny. Bushyhead claimed that Jenny belonged to Eliza by right of inheritance and had been illegally sold to Raincrow. But the court did not agree and ruled against Bushyhead. However, Eliza still remained a slaveholder, for the issue may have been resolved out of court. Eliza retained ownership of Jenny. And nineteen years later, Eliza still owned a slave woman who had been part of the estate of her father. Besides interest in at least one slave, Jesse and Eliza had access to other wealth. Over the course of their marriage, Jesse and Eliza acquired a sizable amount of property and had a large family.

[15] Cherokee Improvement Claims, Treaties of 1817 and 1819, Special Files of the Office of Indian Affairs, 1807–1904, National Archives, M574, roll 25, file 131; *Records of the Cherokee Agency in Tennessee, 1801–1835* (n.p.: 1990) 14.

[16] Mildred Whitmire, ed., *Noland's Cherokee Diary: A U.S. Soldier's Story from Inside the Cherokee Nation* (Spartanburg SC: Reprint Company, 1990) 94.

Jane, the first child of Jesse and Eliza, was born around 1824, the first of at least ten children.[17]

As the 1820s progressed, the presence of Jesse and his younger brother Isaac at court evidenced their increasing involvement in business and tribal affairs. In October 1827, Jesse and Isaac each received $6.75 for nine days' service as witnesses before the Cherokee Supreme Court in a case concerning damage to glassware. In 1828, the National Committee awarded Jesse $25 for services rendered, presumably involving translation, clerical, or courier work. In October 1829, Jesse again received compensation for providing testimony before the Cherokee Supreme Court in the case of *Betsy Walker v. David Vann.* On 3 June 1830, Jesse, along with Thomas and James Foreman, announced the cancellation of their guaranty pledges on behalf of Samuel M'Junkin. Evidently, M'Junkin, likely a non-Cherokee, had sought a permit to engage in some type of business in the Cherokee Nation. Because M'Junkin had disappointed Jesse and the Foremans in some manner, they refused to post bond for him.[18] In October 1832, James Foreman sued Jesse and Isaac for an unpaid loan. The tribal high court ruled in favor of Foreman and ordered the defendants to pay $16.75 to the plaintiff.[19] Less than two years later, Foreman became accused in the murder of John Walker, Jr., the former husband of Jesse's oldest sister.

During his youth, Jesse became influenced by missionaries. And it was partly due to them that he rose to prominence. From 1740 through 1799, Anglican, Presbyterian, and Moravian ministers had proclaimed Christianity among the Cherokees. But Cherokees had

[17] Bell, *Genealogy*, 91–93, 536–37; Carolyn Thomas Foreman, "Aunt Eliza of Tahlequah," *Chronicles of Oklahoma* 9 (March 1931): 43; Payne Papers, 7:64–66. Unmentioned in Bell's work is a son of Jesse and Eliza who died in 1837.

[18] *Cherokee Phoenix*, 19 June 1830.

[19] *Record Book of the Proceedings of the Supreme Court of the Cherokee Nation*, Cherokee Supreme Court Minutes, vol. 1, 1823–1835; *Cherokee Phoenix*, 19 November 1828.

shown little interest.[20] Part of their apathy resulted from the failure of missionaries to establish permanent mission stations and schools. However, this changed in 1801. In that year, the Moravians, a German pietistic denomination, planted a permanent mission at Springplace. The site was about fifty miles southeast of Chattanooga and near the home of wealthy and influential Cherokee chief James Vann.[21] Yet even the Springplace mission failed to win many converts. Unfortunately, the Moravians preferred to evangelize through preaching and proved slow in establishing a school. But prominent Cherokees maintained interest in educational facilities even though difficulties persisted. One of the challenges was enlisting Cherokee-speaking teachers. This failure caused Cherokees to doubt the expressed purposes of missionaries. Instead of welcoming missionaries, some Cherokees remained wary. They feared that missionaries had entered Cherokee lands only in order to exploit economic opportunities. As a result, negative sentiments toward Moravians enabled Presbyterians to seize an opportunity. In order to gain official approval from the Cherokee national leadership, Reverend Gideon Blackburn, a Presbyterian from Maryville, Tennessee, made tribal leaders an attractive offer. He promised to establish several schools and provide students free room, board, and clothing.[22] This appealed to Cherokees.

In February 1804, Presbyterians opened their first school on the Hiwassee River in southeastern Tennessee, about sixty miles northwest of Springplace.[23] But there were several negative aspects of Presbyterian mission schools, which soon became apparent. First, a particularly glaring failure concerned the numerical imbalance in student populations concerning gender and lineage. More males than females

[20] McLoughlin, *Cherokees and Missionaries*, 35.
[21] Ibid., 47.
[22] Ibid., 54–56.
[23] Ibid., 53–57.

enrolled, and mixed-bloods outnumbered full-bloods. There were several reasons for the lopsided figures. In order to overcome the lack of Cherokee-speaking instructors, school officials stressed the enrollment of English-speaking Cherokee students. Hopefully, English speakers would be able to translate for their non-English-speaking classmates. Second, the three to four years of attendance required for non-English speakers to become familiar with rudimentary English did not encourage consistent attendance. Third, fathers did not push daughters to enroll. If there were expenses associated with schooling, it became more essential for sons rather than daughters to learn the skills necessary to compete with whites. Although some mixed-lineage girls attended, the purpose of their schooling differed from males. Their instruction centered on the domestic skills needed to make them desirable as potential mates for upwardly bound husbands.[24] Finally, it seems likely that influential mixed-ancestry tribesmen, as in the case of James Vann, used their prestige to sway government and church officials into locating schools near mixed-blood communities rather than enclaves of full Native peoples.[25] As a result, mission schools contributed to an overbalance of educational opportunities to those of mixed lineage. And this advantage favored this class as potential tribal leaders and holders of wealth.

One of the most significant missions was Brainerd. Near the Chattanooga home of John Ross, the mission operated under the auspices of the American Board of Commissioners for Foreign Missions (ABCFM), a New England missionary society supported by Congregationalists and Presbyterians. A school opened at Brainerd in March 1817.[26] In November 1823, newly wedded missionaries William and Electra Holland, both New Englanders, arrived at Brainerd. By that time, the missionary staff had become interested in organiz-

[24] Ibid., 57–58.
[25] Ibid., 47.
[26] Ibid., 110.

ing another school at Candy's Creek.[27] The prospective site was about twenty-five miles northeast of Brainerd and half a mile west of present-day Cleveland. Candy's Creek also was near the Bushyhead settlement. In early June 1824, Holland, John Arch, a Cherokee interpreter and convert, and two other Brainerd personnel journeyed to the Bushyhead settlement. Invaluable to the Brainerd staff, Arch had been accompanying missionaries on preaching tours and assisting in establishing schools for over four years.[28] The residents of the Bushyhead settlement impressed the missionaries as being "so far civilized" as to "be benefited" by a school.[29] Encouraged by promising opportunities, Holland soon received permission from denominational superiors to open a mission. In July 1824, Holland wrote to administrators at the American Board from his new station at "Bushy Head's District, Cherokee Nation, near Calhoun, Ten."[30] In February 1825, the Hollands opened a school and, the following September, formally organized a church. The following month, Holland listed the name of the mission station as Candy's Creek. Moreover, he reported his secular appointment as postmaster of Candy's Creek, Cherokee Nation Tennessee.[31]

Candy's Creek, a close-knit community, offered a fruitful spiritual harvest, for no permanent missionary had ever resided in the settlement.[32] Several of the local families either were related by mar-

[27] J. E. Ellsworth to Jeremiah Evarts, 3 June 1824, American Board of Commissioners for Foreign Missions Papers (ABCFM), 18.3.1, vol. 13, item 313. ABCFM documents accessed on microfilm at the Oklahoma Historical Society Library (OHSL).

[28] Rufus Anderson, *Memoir of Catherine Brown: A Christian Cherokee of the Cherokee Nation* (Cincinnati: Morgan, Fisher and L'Hommedieu, 1827; rep., n.p.: Our Christian Heritage Foundation, 2012) 71–72 (page references are to reprint edition).

[29] Ard Hoyt to Jeremiah Evarts, ABCFM 18.3.1, vol. 13, items 107–109.

[30] Snell, "Candy's Creek Mission Station," 164.

[31] Ibid., 165.

[32] *Missionary Herald* (1828): 353.

riage or lived in close proximity to each other. These included the Bushyheads, Bigbys, Fieldses, Foremans, Hares (also spelled "Hair"), and Springstons. Because of the dual denominational alignment of the ABCFM, both Presbyterian and Congregationalist personnel ministered at Candy's Creek. At first, the mission reported modest gains. In January 1828, there were ten congregants, but the following year the membership totaled seventeen.[33] The school also made modest progress. By 1 January 1828, the school roster totaled thirty-eight students. But attendance posed a challenge, for only fifteen "scholars" regularly attended classes. And the school had enrolled only four full Cherokees.[34]

In spite of limited initial success, the missionaries had a favorable influence on the Bushyhead family. Along with Holland, visiting missionaries included Samuel Worcester and Elizur Butler, men so significant to Bushyhead in later years.[35] During the removal period, Worcester and Butler resettled in Western Cherokee Nation and remained acquaintances of Bushyhead until his death in 1844. Nine Bushyhead students, including three of Jesse's siblings, two of his children, and four nieces and nephews, at some time attended classes. It is almost certain that at least half of the students in January 1828 were Bushyhead cousins.[36]

In the next four years, the school experienced growth. On 30 September 1832, Holland reported that a total of eighty-four students had attended "for any considerable length of time."[37] And although small, the mission church also received additions. Holland included George Bushyhead, a younger brother of Jesse, among a list of stu-

[33] *Missionary Herald* (1829), 345.

[34] Snell, "Candy's Creek Mission Station," 175.

[35] James Franklin Corn, *Red Clay and Rattlesnake Springs* (Cleveland TN: Author, 1959) 71.

[36] Bell, *Genealogy*, 170; David Keith Hampton, *Cherokee Mixed Bloods* (Lincoln AR: ARC Press, 2005) 236.

[37] Snell, "Candy's Creek Mission Station," 183.

dents who had "professed religion & in general lived exemplarily."[38] But a particularly faithful convert was Stephen Foreman, a half-brother of Jesse's mother. In his upper teens when the school opened, Foreman, one-half Cherokee, was one of the school's first students. He made rapid academic progress and soon became employed as the principal interpreter at the mission. By 1826, Foreman had begun to prepare himself for the ministry.[39] The station also became an artery for the dissemination of Christian literature. One of the publications most surely was the *Missionary Herald*, a journal of the ABCFM. In 1826, Holland was able to use his position as postmaster to enlist subscriptions for religious newspapers. One of the early subscribers was Jesse Bushyhead.[40]

Much of the reason for increased attendance at Candy's Creek was a growing interest in Christianity. In 1828, Holland had noticed an "unusual desire in the members of this church for a revival of religion."[41] In August, the "hopeful conversion of five Cherokees, all heads of families," occurred. Four of the converts, "after examination," became scheduled for admission to membership in November. Accordingly, on Sunday, 9 November, three adults, including the father of Jesse, "were admitted to the privileges" of the church.[42] On the same day, eleven children received baptism. Yet not all adult converts remained with the mission. On 20 August 1829, Holland mentioned two "persons of whose piety we have had some evidence…have recently united with a Baptist church in this vicinity. Both of these have attended our meetings, and received most of their religious knowledge from missionary instruction."[43] Holland did not list the

[38] Ibid., 183–84.

[39] Ibid., 167.

[40] Ibid., 166.

[41] *Missionary Herald* (1828), 353.

[42] William Holland to Jeremiah Evarts, 26 November 1828, ABCFM 18.3.1, vol. 5, item 222.

[43] *Missionary Herald* (1829), 345.

names of these converts, but it is almost certain that one was Jesse Bushyhead.

As the 1830s dawned, some of the most influential Cherokees, mostly from mixed lineages, had embraced Christianity. Of course, mixed ancestry did not always determine acceptance of Christianity, for several Cherokee preachers and interpreters in Baptist ranks were full-bloods. Yet conversions had another result. The successful proliferation of the Christian message challenged traditional belief systems and lifestyles of full-bloods and at times stirred resistance to Christianity. Mission-educated mixed-bloods at times rivaled full-bloods for traditional leadership roles. Also, missionaries opposed the practices of conjuring, so much a part of traditional Cherokee culture. Opposition to conjurers posed a social and economic challenge to this special status, for conjurers, those able to use magic and charms, received respect and pay for their services. Missionaries also preached against attendance at traditional ball plays, where team members participated partially nude and gambling and drunkenness were common.[44] In some cases, open hostility to Christianity developed, even at Candy's Creek. As early as August 1825, missionary William Chamberlain indicated strong opposition among some residents. Chamberlain reported "some rejoicing in hope others seriously enquiring & others pursueing [*sic*] the pleasures of sin with all their might."[45] In 1829, Holland even reported "determined" resistance from one of the most influential families of the community.[46]

In the 1820s, the introduction of missionary efforts and the whittling away of Cherokee land coincided with political challenges. Threatened with encroachment, Cherokees had made rapid steps toward acculturation. The institution of an elective national legislature,

[44] McLoughlin, *Cherokees and Missionaries*, 217–30.

[45] William Chamberlain to Jeremiah Evarts, ABCFM 18.3.1, vol. 4, item 43.

[46] *Missionary Herald* (1829), 345.

a high court, and a written constitution demonstrated the change. In 1828, advances in literacy appeared when the *Cherokee Phoenix*, the first Cherokee-language newspaper, came off the press. George Guess, also called Sequoyah, had developed a phonetic alphabet. Known as a syllabary, this development made possible the transcription of Cherokee. Easily learned, this form of written communication resulted in a fairly high level of literacy among both more- and less-assimilated Cherokees. But such upheavals posed challenges. White Path, leader of the full-blood faction, opposed political change, missionaries, and acculturation. He feared loss of political power at the hands of certain economically and socially well-positioned Cherokees. In February 1827, White Path called for a rival minority assembly to resist the implementation of a written constitution. This act challenged authority and provoked unrest. As a result, the Cherokee Nation edged toward anarchy, and rumors of slave revolts circulated. Fortunately, in May 1827, the election of a legitimate national legislature defused the crisis.[47] But several among the majority also had shown opposition to missions. Most of the Moravian, Congregationalist, and Presbyterian missionaries had come from New England, and some slaveholding Cherokee national leaders had come to resent the intrusion of New Englanders. This sentiment especially targeted the overly pietistic manner of Moravians and the antislavery stance taken by missionaries supported by the ABCFM. Furthermore, the recent threat of slave insurrections only exacerbated these sentiments. Thus, by the late 1820s, full Cherokees and some with blended ancestry still harbored coolness or manifested opposition toward evangelistic efforts.

It was during this very difficult time that Jesse Bushyhead, the husband of a slaveholder, rose to prominence in religious and political circles. And on a national level, events transpired that changed the Cherokee Nation forever. A major issue was removal. Accordingly,

[47] McLoughlin, *Cherokees and Missionaries*, 214–27.

Bushyhead became caught up in the controversies that accompanied change. And over almost the next twenty years, relocation to Indian Territory, the unorganized areas of west of the Mississippi became much of the focus of Jesse and Eliza.

CHAPTER 2

Tennessee Ministry

Lawlessness was common in early Bradley County. The county court docket included infractions such as breaking and entering, liquor sales, gambling, illicit sexual intercourse, assault, public fighting, swine stealing, and indecent exposure. In the latter case, the defendant had been seen "riding though Cleveland with his shirt off and gun in hand."[1] Immorality in Candy's Creek already had challenged the patience of missionaries. The temptations of white society, especially the sale of alcohol, also made it more difficult for Cherokees to remain faithful to the expectations of missionaries. Even prior to the founding of the county, the free flow of liquor around Candy's Creek had concerned William Holland and other residents. On Sunday, 26 February 1832, supporters met at the courthouse in Cleveland to reorganize the inactive temperance society. Holland rejoiced that forty to fifty members had enrolled in the chapter.[2] Yet interest in temperance also dovetailed with Cherokee attempts to thwart white encroachment. The Saturday following the temperance meeting, the United States Supreme Court decided *Worcester v. Georgia*. The ruling declared a Georgia law unconstitutional. The Georgia statute essentially had barred the Cherokee Nation from its rights to legal existence. The high court's favorable decision fed Cherokee hopes that

[1] Charles A. Sherrill, ed., *Bradley County, Tennessee Circuit Court Case File Abstracts, 1836–1860* (Cleveland TN: Cleveland Public Library, 1988) no pagination.

[2] *Missionary Herald* (1833), 241.

the federal government had come to support political independence for the Cherokee Nation. However, the federal executive was yet to respond to the ruling, and John Ross admonished Cherokees to avoid provocative actions against whites. This restraint included avoiding alcohol and drunkenness.[3]

In addition to the interest of missionaries at Candy's Creek, Baptist clergymen also had become interested in the spiritual condition of Bradley County and the surrounding region. Some Baptist outreach among Cherokees had begun in Georgia before 1799. But the main impetus in American Indian missions came after the War of 1812, when peace made conditions on the frontier more favorable. In 1815, the newly formed, New England-based Baptist Board of Foreign Missions (BBFM), the missionary arm of the loosely federated Baptist Triennial Convention, solicited support from Baptist churches throughout the United States. The Triennial Convention was the national denomination entity of Baptists. It was so named because its delegates, representing Baptist bodies throughout the United States and its territories, met every three years.

But not all Baptists favored support for the Triennial Convention or its mission board. Traditional Baptist polity stressed the autonomy of local congregations. Yet this emphasis often conflicted with attempts to establish more centralized administrative agencies. The strain also reflected growing sectional controversy—that is, the developing political and economic competition between frontier and northeastern states. Until the organization of the Triennial Convention, cooperative Baptist work often had been carried out through the efforts of local churches. Although autonomous, these congregations voluntarily cooperated through associations. Associations, usually composed of from around ten to several dozen churches over two to three counties, provided fellowship and doctrinal guidance to member

[3] Robert V. Remini, *The Life of Andrew Jackson* (New York: Penguin, 1988) 216; Moulton, *The Papers of Chief John Ross*, 2:242–43.

congregations. But some Baptist ministers resented the loss of congregational autonomy. These Baptists, mostly in the backwoods of North Carolina, South Carolina, Georgia, Tennessee, Kentucky, Indiana, and Illinois, feared that the Triennial Convention placed too much control in the hands of New England ministers. Also, hyper-Calvinistic tenets led some congregational leaders to condemn missionary societies as infringements on divine grace. In their minds, such organizations usurped the role of God in the calling and conversion of sinners.[4] Thus, when it came to missionary outreach to Cherokees, Baptists responded differently. Those favoring missionary societies contributed funds to centralized agencies for the support of missionaries and support personnel. But others concentrated on local church outreach and refused to take collections for mission work carried on outside the confines of local congregations. Soon this difference became so shrill that it sometimes fractured churches and associations.

Yet there were some early efforts in the Southeast to advance cooperative outreach. In 1815, Baptist churches in northern Georgia initiated mission work through the Sarepta Association. And in 1817, the Baptist Board sanctioned the Reverend Humphrey Posey to begin mission work among Cherokee settlements in the southwestern region of North Carolina. One of the mission stations was at Valley Towns near modern Murphy. Several settlements, known as "towns," along the Valley and Hiwassee Rivers composed Valley Towns.[5] In 1821, the shorthanded Posey requested volunteers from the Baptist Board at Philadelphia to aid in establishing a school.

[4] James W. Moffitt, "Early Baptist Missionary Work among the Cherokees," *The East Tennessee Historical Society's Publications* 12 (1940): 16–18; Dan B. Wimberly, *Frontier Religion: Elder Daniel Parker, His Religious and Political Life* (Austin: Eakin Press, 2002) 16–20.

[5] John P. Brown, "Eastern Cherokee Chiefs," *Chronicles of Oklahoma* 16 (March 1938): 5.

On 11 December 1821, a missionary team of approximately two dozen adults and children arrived after almost three months on the road. The newcomers included Evan Jones, an immigrant from Wales; and his wife, Elizabeth. In spite of noble intentions, life at the remote Valley Towns mission proved difficult at best. Illness, harsh weather, isolation, fiscal challenges, and the apparent lack of converts discouraged workers. Most missionaries, including Posey, abandoned the arduous frontier life. Few remained to sacrifice the lives of their families, yet Evan and Elizabeth Jones chose to stay. Although Elizabeth died in 1831, Evan devoted over fifty years to Cherokee missions. No other white Baptist missionary influenced Cherokees in North Carolina, Georgia, Tennessee, and, later, Indian Territory as much as Jones. His duties involved pastoral leadership, evangelism, and organizing churches and schools. Equally important was his role in publishing materials and overseeing the translation of the Bible into Cherokee.[6] And it was Jones who formed a close bond with Bushyhead, providing the Cherokee minister with opportunities for ministry and church leadership.

Cherokee traditions stressed superstition and afforded a degree of esteem to shamans and conjurers. But Cherokee concepts of a Supreme Being, Satan, or places of eternal reward or punishment bore little semblance to Christian theology. For example, any belief in an afterlife entailed an ill-defined shadowy existence. Some Cherokees may have had an inchoate belief in a celestial deity but tended more to honor and fear the spirits of slain animals. It was therefore necessary to seek the services of conjurers who might appease the spirits. If not, the spirits posed to threaten and harm the slayer with sickness, death, or other misfortune. In this sense, palliative services also benefitted conjurers with offerings from their clients. Yet their religious roles did not assure conjurers with leadership positions in govern-

[6] McLoughlin, *Cherokees and Missionaries*, 152–54; McLoughlin, *Champions of the Cherokees*, 17–31, 443.

ment. If they rose to national prominence, it was not due to religious activities, but recognition acquired through political skills.[7] Bushyhead surely was familiar with conjurers, but it is unknown when he was first exposed to Christianity. His mother may or may not have embraced Christianity before the missionary efforts at Candy's Creek. But his father received baptism in 1828, about the time of Bushyhead's conversion.

Bushyhead likely affiliated with Baptists in summer 1829. Jones confirmed this in a letter written from Valley Towns on 7 September 1832:

> We have a native brother on a visit with us, named Jesse Bushyhead, who lives about 75 miles west of this place. He became convinced of his duty with regard to baptism, about three years ago, by reading the Scriptures alone; the professors of religion in his neighborhood being all Pedobaptist, and he unacquainted with Baptists, and they with him. Hearing, however, of a Baptist meeting about twenty miles distant, he went there, told them the exercises of his mind, and was baptized.[8]

Yet Bushyhead may not have been so "unacquainted" with Baptists as Jones indicated. Although Bushyhead's direct personal affiliation with Baptists did not occur until 1829, he likely had received some exposure to Baptists. In 1823, John Timson, a mixed-blood Cherokee, became the first baptized convert at Valley Towns. Soon Timson was assisting Jones in interpreting and preaching. This allowed Jones to itinerate in areas outside of Valley Towns. Moreover, some contacts existed between Jones and the area near Brainerd. As early as 1824, Jones had made at least one trip to northern Georgia and reported interest among Cherokees concerning Christianity. In October 1825, Jones expressed sorrow that John Arch, a full-blood

[7] John Phillip Reid, *A Law of Blood: The Primitive Law of the Cherokee Nation* (DeKalb IL: Northern Illinois University, 2006) 22–24.

[8] *Baptist Missionary Magazine* 12 (December 1832): 394–95.

Cherokee interpreter, and well known at Valley Towns, had died. It is almost certain that this was the same convert who had been instrumental in establishing the Candy's Creek mission. And the previous summer, Jones spoke to a meeting of the Hiwassee Association, composed of churches from white settlements in McMinn County and future Bradley County. In August 1824, some of these ministers had journeyed to Valley Towns to participate in the ordination of Jones. In 1828, Jones and Timson, fearing competition from Methodist circuit riders, made a preaching tour along the North Carolina and Tennessee border.[9] So, it is plausible that Bushyhead indirectly had heard about Baptist work through the activities of Timson or Jones.

Bushyhead formally affiliated with Baptists through baptism into the membership of the Macedonia Baptist Church, about twenty miles from Bushyhead's home. This likely occurred at the Macedonia meetinghouse on Camp Creek in Rhea County.[10] Because of the practice of immersing converts, Baptists often constructed houses of worship near bodies of water. From the description of Jones and other sources, it seems that the minister who baptized Bushyhead was Elder Burrow Buckner.[11] Buckner, a self-supporting farmer-preacher, had moved into the Hiwassee area about 1827.[12] Having been baptized

[9] J. E. Ellsworth et al. to Jeremiah Evarts, 3 June 1824, ABCFM 18.3.1, vol. 3, item 313; *Missionary Herald* (1826), 7; McLoughlin, *Champions of the Cherokees*, 42, 46, 64; Robert G. Gardner, *Cherokees and Baptists in Georgia* (Atlanta: Georgia Baptist Historical Society, 1989) 108–109.

[10] John B. Conner of Cleveland, Tennessee to Dan B. Wimberly, telephone interview, 19 August 2006; Bettye J. Broyles, *Churches and Schools of Rhea County, Tennessee* (n.p.[Dayton?]: Rhea County Historical and Genealogical Society, 1992) 115.

[11] Ordained and licensed Baptist ministers on the frontier often went by the title of "Elder," believing "Reverend" was not scriptural and characterized non-Baptist ministers.

[12] Daniel Buckner to R[obert] S[amuel] Duncan, 17 September 1875, Partee Center for Baptist Historical Studies, William Jewell College, Liberty, Missouri; Big Pigeon Church Minutes, 1787–1874, transcribed by Glen R. Bayless,

into the fellowship of Macedonia, Bushyhead soon became active in congregational affairs. On Friday and Saturday, 24–25 September 1830, he served as the sole representative from the Macedonia church at the annual meeting of the Hiwassee Baptist Association. The Chestua Baptist Church in Monroe County, Tennessee, approximately fifty miles from Cleveland, hosted the meeting.[13] The participation of Bushyhead meant that he almost certainly spent several nights away from home. And because the Macedonia congregation was small, he may have borne some, if not all, of his travel expenses.

But membership in a congregation twenty miles from home posed problems, even though services were held over the course of one weekend a month. Congregations usually expected members to attend faithfully. Thus, regular attendance meant that Bushyhead had to spend considerable time away from home. Desiring to establish a congregation closer to home, Bushyhead interested Buckner in organizing a Baptist congregation nearer to Bushyhead's home. Soon after the baptism of Bushyhead, Buckner began holding worship services once a month in the Candy's Creek area. It seems almost certain that Bushyhead hosted the assemblies in his own home. After several prospective members had expressed interest, Burrow Buckner and his brother Daniel, also a Baptist minister, conducted the organizational service of the Achaia Baptist Church sometime around May 1831. At the heartfelt and solemn occasion, Daniel preached and Bushyhead interpreted for Cherokees in attendance. After the organizational process, the church observed communion, known among Baptists as the Lord's Supper. The occasion was joyful as the diverse communicants came together as a church body. Daniel described the communicants as "full blood Indians, white and black men, half breed and

Stokely Memorial Library, Newport, Tennessee, 43–47 (page references are to transcribed typewritten copy).

[13] Minutes of the Hiwassee Association (1830) (n.p.: F. S. Heiskell, 1830) 1.

quarterroon [*sic*], all pertaking [*sic*] together emblems of the broken boddy [*sic*] and shed blood of our adorable Savaiour [*sic*]...."[14]

Shortly after, the congregation affiliated with the Hiwassee Association and flourished under the pastoral leadership of Burrow Buckner. Approximately sixteen months after its organization, church membership totaled seventy-three, thirty-five of which were recent converts. The membership of the church continued to evidence racial and ethnic diversity. The congregation consisted of sixteen whites, nineteen Cherokees, and forty Africans.[15] The large proportion of Africans indicated the number of slaves owned by recent white newcomers and local Cherokees.

Achaia soon eclipsed the Congregationalist-Presbyterian mission at Candy's Creek. In December 1831, Holland, his wife, and fifteen Cherokees comprised its entire membership.[16] In light of spiritual apathy, Holland had made recent attempts to boost low attendance through a four-day series of special services known as a "protracted meeting." The services resulted in the addition of one Cherokee woman and the baptism of her child. Yet overall numerical increases were few, and spiritual vitality waned. In March 1833, Holland lamented the "low interest" in "religion" and lack of additions.[17] The spiritual ebb of Holland's mission and the success of Achaia may have been a factor in the appointment of Stephen Foreman as minister at Candy's Creek in 1834. Foreman had received licensure to the ministry on 25 September 1833 and was ordained a year later.[18]

[14] Buckner to Duncan, 17 September 1875.

[15] *Baptist Missionary Magazine* 12 (December 1832): 395; Minutes of the Hiwassee United Baptist Association (1834) (Athens TN: John M. Gibbs, 1834) 1.

[16] *Missionary Herald* (1832), 78–79.

[17] *Missionary Herald* (1833), 241.

[18] Journal and Letters of Stephen Foreman, Cherokee Minister, Part III, 14, 20 [typewritten copy] at Western History Collections, University of Oklahoma.

Foreman had an advanced education, an attribute frontier Baptist ministers often did not possess. He had attended the Union Theological Seminary in Virginia and was fresh from two years at Princeton Theological Seminary. Thus, Foreman possessed the necessary academic and linguistic skills to revive the flagging mission.[19] And although aligned with another denomination, Foreman was a lifelong support to Bushyhead in ministry and affairs of state.

Bushyhead's involvement at Achaia served to draw Cherokees, but the fruitfulness of Achaia likely came as a result of several factors besides Bushyhead. The pastoral leadership of Burrow Buckner, a southerner, likely attracted southern whites more than the New Englander Holland. Because most Congregationalist ministers hailed from the Northeast, they were more negative toward slavery. And this antislavery sentiment did not appeal to most southern whites. Of the forty or so African members at Achaia, most, if not all, were surely slaves. As most slaves did not enjoy freedom of travel, blacks at Achaia almost certainly accompanied their masters. Yet very few Africans attended the Candy's Creek mission. The membership patterns also reflected the economic characteristics of Holland's congregants as compared to the membership of Achaia. The few Africans at Candy's Creek meant that its members may not have had the desire or resources to purchase and support slaves.

The growing Baptist presence among Cherokees heightened the need for interpreters. Early on, Bushyhead had evidenced the promise of being an invaluable asset as an interpreter. His linguistic skills benefited Achaia and extended to Baptist work in North Carolina and Georgia. The procurement of Cherokee interpreters and preachers, either lay or ordained, had been one of the keys to the long-term success of the Valley Towns mission. The Cherokee language was complex, with a heavy stress on inflections and often void of Christian

[19] Ross Foreman, "Reverend Stephen Foreman, Cherokee Missionary," *Chronicles of Oklahoma* 18 (September 1940): 231.

theological concepts. The translation of concepts such as sin, baptism, heaven, hell, soul, salvation, and grace proved difficult.[20] Missionary Samuel Roberts, reporting from Valley Towns in 1822, lamented, "I have seen but two full Cherokees that know English enough to understand the plainest passage in the Bible."[21] The comment of Roberts underscored the great difficulty that whites had in mastering the language well enough to deliver sermons. Even Jones, familiar with Welsh, Latin, Greek, and Hebrew, required almost ten years to acquire the necessary fluency to preach in Cherokee.[22] Fortunately for Jones, in 1822, the board hired the mission's first part-time interpreter. A short time later, Timson received an appointment as the second interpreter. And between 1830 and 1832, the Baptist Board added three more interpreters.[23]

Word of Bushyhead's ministry soon reached national missions administrators. In 1832, an article from Jones appeared in the *Baptist Missionary Magazine*, the national mission organ of the Baptist Board. Jones wrote, "He [Bushyhead] devotes every Saturday and Sabbath to instructing his people in the way of salvation, and has frequent meetings at other times."[24] Jones added that Bushyhead had spoken or "exhorted" at Valley Towns in September 1832. Speaking at a series of weekend services, Jones recorded that Bushyhead preached "quite an intelligent and interesting discourse, which was listened to with much attention." On Saturday, 8 September, he preached twice, and once the following Monday. Jones described the sermons as "impressive" and "affecting."[25] Because of his increased participation in area church affairs, it seems that the Achaia congregation had licensed Bushyhead—that is, formally authorized him to

[20] McLoughlin, *Champions of the Cherokees*, 35.

[21] *Latter Day Luminary* 3 (July 1822) 213.

[22] McLoughlin, *Cherokees and Missionaries*, 157.

[23] McLoughlin, *Champions of the Cherokees*, 45, 91.

[24] *Baptist Missionary Magazine* 12 (December 1832): 395.

[25] Ibid.

preach under the supervision of an ordained minister. This occurred sometime before June 1833. This was significant because licensure was the next step toward ordination.[26] In April 1833, the Reverend Heman Lincoln, treasurer of the Baptist Board, visited Valley Towns and also heard Bushyhead preach to a large audience of Cherokees. Although under painful circumstances, the meeting resulted in attempts of the national board to supply Bushyhead with financial support.

The meeting of Bushyhead and Lincoln occurred as a result of an event that almost wrecked the ministry of Jones. In October 1832, Cynthia Cunningham arrived at the mission from Cleveland, Tennessee, for a visit. Cynthia was an unmarried sister of Pauline Jones, the second wife of Evan. Unknown to the mission staff, Cynthia was also about six months pregnant. On the night of 7 January 1833, Cynthia secretly gave birth and died the next night from complications. Upon preparing her body for burial, women attendants discovered a dead infant at her feet under the bedcovers. But it appeared as if the infant had been born alive. The behavior of Jones further exacerbated this tragedy. Already gossip had circulated about the circumstances surrounding the abrupt marriage of Jones and Pauline.[27] Eliza Jones had died on 5 February 1831. But in early August 1832, Pauline and Jones celebrated the birth of their first child. For some unknown reason, Jones had failed to inform the Baptist Board of his second marriage or the birth of a child. Some therefore felt that the marriage was too hasty and was an attempt to conceal premarital sexual relations between Jones and Pauline.

[26] Among Baptists on the frontier, licensing granted formal recognition of a preacher by a local church. It allowed him to preach under the supervision of the church, usually the pastor and deacons. It did not require any formal theological education. The next step usually was ordination, which permitted the licensed minister to preach beyond the supervision of a local church. Ordination also gave him authority to baptize and administer communion.

[27] McLoughlin, *Champions of the Cherokees*, 98–101.

When Jones learned of the deceased infant, he kept the information from local Cherokees. Fearing the loss of their support should he become associated with scandal, Jones suggested a secret burial at night. But women missionaries advised against such an interment and continued to prepare for a day burial. In preparation for burial, the aides placed Cynthia and her child in the same coffin but concealed the small body from view. Yet Valley Town Cherokees soon learned of the circumstances and expressed shock. Moreover, two Cherokee interpreters refused to translate for Jones until the matter underwent investigation. Their lack of cooperation thus made it impossible for Jones to conduct services for several weeks. And the circumstances immediately placed Jones under a cloud of suspicion among local whites as well. Possibly desiring to obtain the mission property, local whites accused Jones of murder. Consequently, North Carolina authorities arrested Jones and his wife, charging Jones with murder and Pauline for complicity. Jones and Pauline stood trial in Franklin, North Carolina, on 8 April. Although the court acquitted them, the decision did not mean Jones had the confidence of area ministers, local Cherokees, or the Baptist Board. News of the Jones scandal soon reached administrators of the Baptist Board. The board thought the accusations serious enough and sent Lincoln to investigate. In order to settle matters, a church council assembled at Valley Towns on Wednesday, 17 April. Some of the council members were Lincoln, Burrow Buckner, and Bushyhead.

The council exonerated Jones, but his future ministry nevertheless remained in the balance.[28] It was in the wake of these traumatic developments that Lincoln became associated with Bushyhead. Lincoln felt it imperative to appeal to the Cherokees for their continued support of Jones. In a very emotional service, Bushyhead interpreted while Lincoln addressed a Cherokee audience. Accordingly, Lincoln possibly promised the Cherokees more support, including funds to

[28] Ibid., 101–11.

improve the school building and for Native Cherokee ministers. Jones recorded the event:

> Mr. Lincoln addressed the assembly in a short speech; but so fully charged with Christian philanthropy and holy unction, that the whole audience were greatly affected. Brother Bushyhead attempted to reply in English, on behalf of the Cherokees, but was so overcome that he could utter but a few broken sentences, accompanied by the sobs and tears of the whole assemblage.[29]

Moved by the piety and devotion of Bushyhead, Lincoln soon took action. No doubt before he departed Valley Towns, Lincoln discussed opportunities for financial support with Bushyhead, for without Bushyhead, the effectiveness of Jones among the Cherokees still remained in question. On 18 April, Lincoln arrived in Boston. Soon after, the board recommended the hiring of Bushyhead as interpreter/missionary "so soon as negotiations for the purpose can be completed."[30]

Over the coming months, Bushyhead continued his involvement with Jones and Valley Towns. In October 1833, Baptist missionary Leonard Butterfield rode from Valley Towns to the home of Bushyhead, where he attended a "protracted meeting." Due to unfavorable weather and the Cherokee national tribal council being in session, attendance was light. Nevertheless, Butterfield commented on the warm reception extended to him by Cherokees worshippers. He reported even "a more intimate acquaintance" than at Valley Towns.[31] While at the meeting, Butterfield hoped to enlist Bushyhead in participating in a series of services at Valley Towns on the following 14 and 15 December. It is unknown if Bushyhead complied with the request, for Bushyhead's growing family demanded

[29] *Baptist Missionary Magazine* 13 (June 1833): 227.

[30] Ibid., 13 (August 1833): 322.

[31] Leonard Butterfield to Lucius Bolles, 10 December 1833, American Indian Correspondence, 1800–1900, American Baptist Historical Society (ABHS), FM-98, Mercer University, Atlanta, Georgia.

more of his time when, on 17 March 1834, Eliza gave birth to Caroline Elizabeth Bushyhead.[32]

Yet, by the following May, Jones had invited Bushyhead to move to Valley Towns for the purpose of aiding in a translation project. Operated by Samuel Worcester, the Cherokee press at New Echota, Georgia, the Cherokee national capital, had ceased publication on orders of state authorities. Because Worcester had printed Cherokee materials for Jones, this deprived the Baptist missionary of a key ministry tool. In turn, Jones considered requesting Cherokee authorities to move the press to Valley Towns. If this occurred, Jones desired Bushyhead's translation skills.[33] Of course, there were other interpreters such as Timson, but it seems that Bushyhead was better equipped as a translator.[34] Realizing distance and travel proved problematic, Jones had requested $40 from the Baptist Board to pay for the construction of two cabins at Valley Towns for Bushyhead.[35] Yet Jones was not able to obtain the press.

Although Bushyhead did not move to Valley Towns, he continued to aid Jones when possible. On 30 September 1834, Butterfield informed the Baptist Board about another "protracted meeting of four days" at Valley Towns, which had concluded the previous day. Bushyhead again served as exhorter and interpreter. In order to attend the services, Bushyhead had left an annual associational meeting in Rhea County, Tennessee, five days earlier in order to arrive before the services opened. Butterfield was disappointed at the results and reported very little evidence of conversions. He also complained that more visiting ministers had not appeared to help with ministerial du-

[32] Bell, *Genealogy*, 93.

[33] McLoughlin, *Champions of the Cherokees*, 131–32.

[34] James W. Parins, *Literacy and Intellectual Life in the Cherokee Nation, 1820–1906* (Norman: University of Oklahoma, 2013) 31.

[35] Evan Jones to Corresponding Secretary, 20 May 1834, ABHS.

ties. However, he mentioned that Bushyhead and a Presbyterian "brother," almost certainly Stephen Foreman, had rendered aid.[36]

The early ministry of Bushyhead coincided with a crucial period in the Cherokee Nation. Under the 1817 treaty, removal had been voluntary. Yet uncertainty over forced emigration remained. In 1828, another treaty only exacerbated anxiety. Under this agreement, Western Cherokees in northwestern Arkansas exchanged their land for territory in present-day Oklahoma. The treaty also provided incentives for Cherokees east of the Mississippi. The government promised each emigrating family a small amount of material inducements and compensation for moving expenses and abandoned property. Writing from Candy's Creek in 1828, Holland mentioned local anxiety over removal. Fifty families already had enrolled for removal. Even some of Holland's congregation anticipated departure for Arkansas and waited for instructions.[37] Some of Bushyhead's siblings also accepted the offer. In 1831, George Bushyhead volunteered to relocate, and in December 1833, his sister Nancy Bushyhead signed papers indicating her intent to leave for Indian Territory. The following May, George and Isaac Bushyhead arrived in Indian Territory. They were among 6,000 Cherokees who had emigrated by 1835.[38]

But in 1830, the government replaced voluntary emigration with forced exile, and removal seemed even more certain. During that year, the Indian Removal Act provided for an exchange of Indian lands in the East for territorially unorganized areas west of the Mississippi. It

[36] Leonard Butterfield to Lucius Bolles, 30 September 1834, American Indian Correspondence, 1800 1900, ABHS, FM-98; Robert Sparks Walker, *Torchlights to the Cherokees: The Brainerd Mission* (New York: MacMillan, 1931; rep., Johnson City TN: Overmountain Press, 1993) 313 (page reference is to reprint edition).

[37] William Holland to Jeremiah Evarts, 26 November 1828, ABCFM 18.3.1, vol. 5, item 222.

[38] Ehle, *Trail of Tears*, 131; Gibson, *The American Indian*, 300; Jack D. Baker, trans., *Cherokee Emigration Rolls, 1817–1835* (Oklahoma City OK: Baker Publishing, 1977) 14, 35, 49.

likewise made the United States financially responsible for removal assistance and expenses. And it promised compensation to emigrants for improvements on eastern lands. The government soon initiated plans for removal of Southeastern tribes. By fall 1830, Choctaw and Chickasaw tribes had signed removal treaties. Creeks and Seminoles followed in 1832. Yet Cherokees still hoped to avoid removal, for their previous treaties had not mandated forced removal.[39] Moreover, unlike other tribes, they had not signed a treaty relative to the Indian Removal Act.

The conversion of Bushyhead coincided with this anxiety. Not only did conversion to Christianity evidence European acculturation, it also made available spiritual solace in an unsettled time. The New Testament provided examples of divine personal aid, pardon, personal change, social justice, and equality. Against a backdrop of anxiety, Christianity offered hope not found in the old Native religion. Thus, Christianity promised to become a significant force in Cherokee revitalization, especially when it was preached and interpreted by Cherokees in their own language.[40] And the emphasis of Baptists and Methodists on emotional oratory reflected Cherokee tradition, for Cherokee audiences often granted Native preachers and exhorters the honor due to eloquent public speakers in traditional Cherokee society.[41] But some listeners did not extend a positive reception to Bushyhead or his message. Some Cherokee traditionalists resisted Christianity. And because of denominational controversies over missions and church autonomy, many area white Baptist ministers also opposed the ministry of Bushyhead.

By the mid-1830s, efforts to organize a state convention had divided Tennessee Baptists. Some Baptists feared that the convention

[39] Robert V. Remini, *Andrew Jackson and His Indian Wars* (New York: Penguin, 2001) 237, 248–51.

[40] McLoughlin, *Cherokees and Missionaries*, 161.

[41] Ibid.

was an extension of the Triennial Convention and another attempt to usurp the roles and the local associations and churches. Also, participation in temperance societies became an issue for many white southerners. Although Baptist congregations in the South encouraged sobriety, the temperance movement often had been associated with New England reformers, including abolitionists. At first, efforts against slavery had focused on the humane treatment and gradual emancipation of slaves. But by the early 1830s, New England antislavery societies began to push for the total abolition of slavery. Yet many white southerners feared that abolitionism fostered slave insurrections, racial miscegenation, social chaos, and economic loss. Thus, temperance societies in the South fell under the negative scrutiny of southerners.

The issues of temperance and support for the recently organized Tennessee State Convention placed Bushyhead in an uncomfortable position. Bushyhead favored temperance for spiritual and political reasons. In the past, whites had used liquor as an incentive to induce chiefs to sign land-grab treaties. And conversely, removal provided some whites with a veiled excuse to protect tribes from whiskey-induced debauchery and extinction. Risking disapproval, Bushyhead and Thomas Foreman, a fellow Baptist and half-brother of Stephen Foreman, advanced the temperance movement. By November 1834, the temperance society in the Candy's Creek area had increased to 119 members, "though warmly opposed" by local Baptist ministers.[42]

In 1833, a church in the Hiwassee United Baptist Association had asked the body for guidance concerning church support for temperance societies. The following year, associational delegates convened at the Good Hope Meeting House in Rhea County. The meeting opened on Friday, 19 September, and adjourned the following

[42] William Holland to David Green, 15 November 1834, ABCFM 18.3.1, vol. 8, item 128; W[illia]m Holland's report to ABCFM, 1 January 1828, Journal and Letters of Stephen Foreman, Part III, 1.

Sunday. A total of seventy-seven messengers represented twenty-four churches. One of the items on the agenda addressed the issue of church support for temperance societies. Bushyhead was the only delegate from Achaia—and likely one of the few pro-temperance society ministers—at the meeting. At the meeting, a five-man committee voiced the official opinion of the association and urged personal temperance from church members. Yet the committee also firmly recommended that "our churches, ministers and members, not…join the temperance society."[43] Bushyhead must have felt disappointment. Nevertheless, he did not immediately withdraw from the association. Before the meeting adjourned, he volunteered, along with twenty-three other ministers, to fill vacant pulpits of member churches for the coming year. In so doing, Bushyhead agreed to hold at least one service at the Tennessee Church, meeting the fourth weekend in November.[44] But 1834 marked the last year that Bushyhead served as a delegate to the Hiwassee Association. By that time, the association had taken a more decided stand against the Tennessee Baptist Convention and missionary and temperance societies. Sensing that these sentiments hindered missionary outreach, and faced with the looming possibility of removal, Bushyhead focused even more on a Cherokee ministry.

On Saturday, 5 September 1835, Bushyhead and twenty-two other Cherokees formally organized an autonomous Cherokee congregation known as the Amohee Baptist Church. For purposes of outreach, a congregation under the pastoral care of a Native speaker appealed to Cherokees. Also, a separate Cherokee church was a political statement. Hoping to avoid forced removal, the organization of Amohee provided another example to whites of advanced Cherokee

[43] Minutes of the Hiwassee United Baptist Association (1834) (Athens TN: John M. Gibbs, [1834]) 1.

[44] Ibid., 3.

civilization.[45] The congregation met at a building constructed at the farm of Bushyhead on Mouse Creek. Considerable effort already had been expended to erect a 35x35-foot, "comfortable" log-hewn meetinghouse with flooring. The builders rushed to have the structure finished before winter.[46] The Amohee congregation likely chose to meet at the Bushyhead farm for two reasons. It was not unusual for frontier Baptist ministers to host services at their homes. But the location also saved investing in another parcel of land, which might undergo confiscation if removal occurred For the following year, Bushyhead lamented that whites had taken away "meeting-houses and camp-meeting places" and places of worship.[47]

Jones no doubt had encouraged Bushyhead to gather the Amohee fold, for Jones journeyed from Valley Towns to provide ministerial aid in the constitution of the church. Cherokee ministers John Wickliffe and Danonolee accompanied Jones. Following its organization, the Amohee members chose Bushyhead as pastor. This was in keeping with a fairly restrictive aspect of Baptist polity. It only allowed ordained ministers to serve as pastors. This meant that sometime between June 1833 and the organization of Amohee, Bushyhead had been ordained. The day after the formal organization, the church assembled for Sunday worship. As part of the service, Bushyhead baptized "one female" before a "large congregation of solemn spectators." Following this rite, the congregation observed communion. And at the close of the events on Monday morning, the audience listened to "a serious discourse."[48]

Having overseen its formal organization, Bushyhead quickly made overtures indicating a desire to align Amohee with an associa-

[45] John B. Conner, "Materials Toward a History of the Baptists of Cleveland, Tennessee," 22, unpublished manuscript courtesy of the author.

[46] Evan Jones, 8 September 1835, American Baptist Foreign Mission Societies Records, 1817–1959.

[47] *Baptist Missionary Magazine* 16 (August 1836): 202.

[48] Ibid.

tion other than Hiwassee. The Friday following the congregational organization, the Sweetwater Association convened with the Friendship Church in McMinn County. Daniel Buckner, a strong supporter of centralized mission societies, was influential in the Sweetwater Association and may have had invited Bushyhead to attend. Bushyhead visited the gathering as a guest minister. During the meeting, the delegates invited Bushyhead and two other visiting ministers to preach on Sunday, September 13. The guest preachers did not disappoint their audience, for they expounded "with apparent good effect to a numerous congregation."[49]

Yet the Amohee Church never formally affiliated with the Sweetwater Association or any other association in Tennessee or North Carolina.[50] This was not necessarily because of disinterest. Part of it may have been related to the anxiety associated with continuing concerns over removal. Another reason may have been related to associational politics. Due to his support for the state convention and missions, Daniel Buckner had alienated some local pastors. In 1834, Buckner, acting as an official correspondent of the Sweetwater Association, had accused members of the Hiwassee Association of harboring "the spirit of domination & intolerance."[51] His harsh words resulted in a strong reaction from ministers in the Hiwassee Association. This growing controversy may have discouraged Bushyhead from seeking membership in the Sweetwater Association for Amohee. And it was another example of how Bushyhead had become caught up in the strife of white society.

[49] Minutes of the Fifth Session of the Sweet-Water Baptist Association (1835) (n.p.: Monitor, [1835]) 3; Conner to author, 2 June 2012.

[50] John B. Conner to the author, telephone interview, 19 August 2006.

[51] Minutes of the Hiwassee United Baptist Association (1834) 2; Minutes of the Fourth Session of the Sweet-Water Baptist Association (1834) (Madisonville TN: Tennessean, [1834]) 2; Minutes of the Fifth Session of the Sweet-Water Baptist Association (1835) 2.

The dissension soon resulted in divisions in the Hiwassee Association and the Achaia congregation. In 1836, both of these entities finally split over the convention issue. In 1832, the membership of Achaia had numbered seventy-three. But after the division, only fifteen pro-convention members remained, the other members choosing to separate from the church. This split likewise reflected the schism in the association. The pro-convention faction of the association numbered four small churches.[52] Yet twenty-two churches, the bulk of the association, remained with the anti-conventionists.[53] Of course, Bushyhead chose to stay with the pro-convention faction. Because he had chosen to accept funding from the Baptist Board, churches affiliated with the anti-convention faction would offer few, if any, opportunities for preaching. Writing in 1837, Burrow Buckner lamented the cold state of religion in Bradley County and the lack of missionary outreach. However, he mentioned the Achaia and Amohee congregations. The veteran minister commended "little Achaia…and a Cherokee church pastored by the Reverend Jesse Bushyhead" for being the only Baptist churches in the county that cooperated with missionary societies.[54]

From the time of the organization of Amohee until removal approximately three years later, Bushyhead maintained an effective ministry amidst increasing political involvement. In 1835, he won election to a seat in the National Council.[55] By that year, the Treaty and Antitreaty factions had become entrenched. The Antitreaty party, still led by John Ross and his supporters, opposed removal. Major Ridge

[52] *Baptist and Reflector*, 15 June 1837, 90–91; Minutes of the Minority of the Hiwassee Association of the United Baptists (1836) (Madisonville TN: Johnston & Edwards, [1836] 1.

[53] Minutes of the Minority of the Hiwassee Association of the United Baptists (1836) 1.

[54] William R. Snell, *Cleveland the Beautiful: A History of Cleveland, Tennessee, 1842–1931* (Cleveland TN: First American National Bank, 1986) 40.

[55] McLoughlin, *Champions of the Cherokees*, 92.

led the opposition faction known as the Treaty party. Major Ridge was an influential chief who had once opposed any unauthorized cession of Cherokee lands. Other leaders were John Ridge, the son of Major Ridge, and two of the elder Ridge's nephews, Stand Watie and his brother Buck. In his early life, Buck became better known by the name of Elias Boudinot. By the mid-1830s, the Ridge faction viewed removal as the most advisable way to save Cherokees from disaster. Although the Ridge-Watie-Boudinot family claimed closer ties to pure Cherokee lineage than Ross, they blamed Ross for politically manipulating tribal members. They felt that Ross allies such as Lewis Ross, John Martin, and Joseph Vann had accrued too much wealth and power. In their eyes, removal promised to merge Eastern and Western Cherokee governments and dilute the power of the Ross elite. Such a development offered Ross opponents hope and opportunities to rise economically and politically. But if removal efforts failed, the Treaty party feared utter ruin for the Cherokee Nation. The ensuing results potentially included the inevitable seizure of land, ensuing economic devastation, and possible military action. Yet stiff resistance to removal remained, for the great majority of Cherokees, including full-bloods, sided with the Antitreaty party.[56] Fearing the loss of property and political influence, Bushyhead, head of a small slaveholding family with modest holdings, sided with Ross.

As discussed more fully in a following chapter, momentous events surrounding the negotiation of a removal treaty transpired in fall 1835. In October, several thousand Cherokees convened at the Red Clay campgrounds for the annual tribal assembly. The legislative branches of the Cherokee Nation also used this opportunity to convene. While periodic negotiations between Cherokee emissaries and the Jackson administration occurred in Washington, Red Clay had become the temporary council ground of the Cherokee Nation instead of tribal headquarters at New Echota. Effective 1 June 1830,

[56] Perdue, "The Conflict Within," 467–91.

the Georgia legislature had prohibited the Cherokee government from functioning in Georgia except for the purpose of ceding land.[57] In order to thwart Georgian intervention, Cherokees began conducting their tribal assembly at Red Clay. Located just north of the Tennessee-Georgia border, Red Clay was about twenty miles from the home of Bushyhead. Nevertheless, United States officials attended and hoped to persuade Cherokees to approve a removal treaty. While these developments unfolded, John Ross handpicked a delegation of twenty Cherokees to travel to Washington, D.C., and negotiate with the government. Bushyhead was one of the delegates.

Bushyhead was absent from home for six months and six days, returning in June 1836. While in Washington, Bushyhead served as the unofficial spiritual leader of the delegates. Writing to the *Baptist Missionary Magazine*, Jones commented on the upstanding behavior of Bushyhead and the "brethren" while they had been away in Washington. His words portrayed Bushyhead and other delegates as dedicated Christians in the midst of a perceived corrupt Jackson administration. "I hope all our brethren, who were on national business at the seat of government, have returned without losing their relish for spiritual things. I am glad to find that they maintained, at their boarding house, daily devotional exercises, with the reading of scriptures."[58]

But Bushyhead also kept the Amohee congregation in his thoughts. On 3 May 1836, he wrote a letter, printed several months later in the *Baptist Missionary Magazine*, about the condition of his pastorate. In his absence, Cherokee preacher Beaver Carrier had held services and reported increased interest toward the gospel. Another correspondence mentioned the names of six converts while

[57] William R. Snell, "The Councils at Red Clay Council Ground, Bradley County, Tennessee, 1832–1837," *Journal of Cherokee Studies* 2 (Fall 1977): 344.

[58] *Baptist Missionary Magazine* 16 (October 1836): 255.

Bushyhead had been absent.[59] Through his correspondence, Bushyhead meant to inform the Baptist Board and defend his absence from ministerial duties. It also had political overtones. As discussed more fully later, by the time Bushyhead returned home, the Treaty of New Echota had been ratified by the United States Senate. The document authorized the removal of Cherokees from the Southeast. Yet hope remained that readers might yet exert political leverage on Washington to repeal or ameliorate the treaty.

Upon his return, Bushyhead learned that the removal crisis posed a challenge to missionary outreach. The Jackson administration had increased pressure on the Antitreaty party to desist opposition to removal. And during summer 1836, United States troops began entering the Cherokee lands. On 5 July, Brigadier General John E. Wool received orders to expel the Cherokees by force if necessary. Wool waited at Athens, Tennessee, for the imminent arrival of twenty-five to thirty companies of militia.[60] Later that month, Wool and his men arrived at Valley Towns. When Wool made his mission known to Jones, the missionary flatly refused cooperation. In doing so, Jones violated the relationship between the federal government and mission station supervisors. Mission schools often received federal funding. Under this arrangement, the Civilization Fund Act of 1819 required white missionaries such as Jones to act as Indian agents. Because of the obstinacy of Jones, the detachment commander ordered the missionary to leave North Carolina. Without permission from the Baptist Board, Jones and his family moved to Four Mile Branch, a short distance from Amohee. Locating near

[59] *Baptist Missionary Magazine* 17 (February 1837): 45, and 16 (August 1836): 202.

[60] Brigadier General John E. Wool to Secretary of War Lewis Cass, 5 July 1836, Letter Books, Special Collections, McFarlin Library, University of Tulsa, Tulsa, Oklahoma, handwritten copy.

Bushyhead's residence, Jones hoped to begin a school and enlist the aid of Bushyhead in translating the New Testament.[61]

Faced with military intervention, it became difficult for other missionaries to remain among the Cherokees. Some such as Worcester chose to exit the Southeast and continue their work among tribesmen in what was commonly known as Arkansas Territory. Because Baptists had been more successful sponsoring Native preachers and interpreters, Baptists remained the only denomination among the Eastern Cherokees still winning significant numbers of converts. But for several reasons, some Cherokees had formed a negative image of Baptists, for the Baptist Board received support from southerners who favored removal. Fearing loss of offerings, the agency did not wish to become embroiled in political controversy. Furthermore, the board had supported the ministry of Isaac McCoy, a Baptist missionary ministering to Native peoples in Indiana. In 1823, McCoy had favored the resettlement of Native peoples from east of the Mississippi to colonies in the West. Because of this, some Cherokees believed the board also endorsed forced removal. For example, Georgia Baptist missionary Duncan O'Bryant enrolled for emigration. In late March 1832, O'Bryant and his family departed northern Georgia with a party of Cherokees bound for Arkansas Territory. Some of the emigrants were members of his congregation. O'Bryant may have meant well, but his actions partially undermined the missionary efforts of other evangelicals. During the following year, Joseph B. Adams, a missionary sponsored by the ABCFM, visited O'Bryant's former area of ministry. Adams recorded that some Cherokees bitterly criticized O'Bryant for deserting Cherokees. In their minds, conversion to Christianity essentially repudiated ancient Cherokee traditions and evidenced support for emigration to Arkansas.[62]

[61] McLoughlin, *Champions of the Cherokees*, 150.

[62] Ibid., 154–55; Robert G. Torbet, *A History of the Baptists*, 3rd ed. (Valley Forge: Judson, 1973) 528.

In light of these challenges, Bushyhead and Jones undertook steps to strengthen Cherokee Baptists around Cleveland. On the first weekend of the month, from Friday, 2 September 1836, through the following Monday, Bushyhead held a "series of meetings" at his home. In preparation for the meetings, he had arranged seats and a "temporary pulpit" in his 60x22-foot log barn with a "good floor." Normally, his congregation would have met at the Amohee meeting-house. The likely reason for holding services in the barn was the availability of more seating. Bushyhead and Jones likely felt that the recent foreboding developments demanded the immediate dissemination of information to as large an audience as possible. In spite of downpours on Saturday and Sunday, some fifty to seventy persons gathered at his farm. On Saturday, three converts—one male and two females—presented themselves for baptism. One of the females was a daughter of former chief Charles Hicks.[63]

But in Georgia, some Cherokee Baptists wavered. The exodus of O'Bryant and other missionaries continued to threaten the influence of Bushyhead and Jones. Full-bloods began to listen more attentively to the Native conjurers who remained stoutly opposed to Christianity. Encountering this challenge, Jones and Bushyhead attempted to counter their influence. Bushyhead considered the rumors of Baptist duplicity false and "boldly assailed the reports, as slanderous...."[64] In light of these developments, Bushyhead and Jones also felt it necessary to visit twenty preaching stations in the outlying areas of northern Georgia. There also was a political reason for their visit. Bushyhead had been present on 15 February 1837 when Wool had addressed an assembly of Cherokees at New Echota. The general remained on horseback while Bushyhead stood on a stump and inter-

[63] *Baptist Missionary Magazine* 17 (February 1837): 44; Hoskins, *Cherokee Property Evaluations in Tennessee, 1836*, no pagination.

[64] *Baptist Missionary Magazine* 18 (January 1838): 17.

preted.[65] Wool informed the audience that military force would be used if Cherokees did not remove by June 1838. And already a few uncooperative Cherokees had been arrested near Ross's Landing at Chattanooga.[66] In 1835, the Georgia militia had seized the *Cherokee Phoenix*. This move shut down the publication and inhibited the flow of information concerning developments related to removal. The need for communication between anti-removal voices afforded Bushyhead and Jones the opportunity to serve as messengers to outlying areas.[67] These occurrences served as added catalysts to prompt Bushyhead and Jones to depart on an extensive preaching tour.

In spring and summer 1837, Bushyhead and Jones made two exhaustive preaching excursions through northern Georgia. From 16 March through 31 March, they rode at least 250 miles. Bushyhead interpreted but also preached eleven sermons. After concluding services at their last stop, Bushyhead and Jones set out to cover fifty miles in order to arrive home in time to conduct services at Amohee on Saturday and Sunday. The following June, the missionary partners repeated the same tour but preached at even more points. They often rode twenty or more miles a day and, on some days, preached multiple times.[68] Bushyhead arrived home on Tuesday, 27 June, and three days later penned a letter to *The Baptist*, a denominational organ published in Nashville. His letter provided an account of his journey. It also urged readers to accept the "scripturality of missionary institutions, for we the Cherokees almost altogether owe our knowledge of our Savior to that source."[69] Then in mid-July, Bushyhead left the banished Jones in Tennessee and journeyed to Valley Towns, where he ministered for at least six days. The three tours certainly bore fruit.

[65] Lewis Ross to John Ross, 18 February 1837, Penelope Johnson Allen Cherokee Collection, box 1, folder 24, Tennessee State Library.

[66] Ibid.

[67] McLoughlin, *Cherokees and Missionaries*, 324.

[68] *Baptist Missionary Magazine* 17 (August 1837): 202–205.

[69] *The Baptist*, 1 August 1837, 114.

In addition to numerous seekers, a total of forty-six converts received baptism.[70] Yet word of the March visits of Bushyhead and Jones also alarmed government authorities. United States commanders became apprehensive that the two were provoking resistance. And shortly before their June tour, authorities ordered the arrest and immediate deportation to Arkansas for itinerants such as Bushyhead and Jones caught interfering with removal.

But Cherokees still hoped for a compromise treaty. President Martin Van Buren, Jackson's chosen successor, had taken office in March 1837. Cherokees hoped that Van Buren, a New Yorker, would prove more cooperative than Jackson and remain open to additional negotiations. Jones offered encouraging news as proof that Cherokees still harbored hope. In March 1837, some Cherokee parents still were submitting applications for their children to attend local mission schools. And at Valley Towns the following June, Bushyhead and Jones left their hearers "with the pleasing hope, that in this place many more will be rescued from the slavish chains of sin."[71]

On Monday, 31 July 1837, some 3,000 to 4,000 Cherokees again assembled at Red Clay to discuss the New Echota Treaty. For over a month, the national legislature debated official business in the council house situated at the top of the hill. When the council was not in session, worshippers assembled in the council house for morning devotions and evening preaching. Strains of familiar hymns, sung in harmony from a Cherokee hymnal, floated over the campground. Most of the white Protestant missionaries in the Cherokee Nation also attended. Availing themselves of these guests, the crowds welcomed preaching. Missionaries delivered sermons each evening and conducted prayer services each morning. Bushyhead evidently felt the heavy weight of responsibility. If negotiations failed, he was keenly

[70] Ibid., 278.

[71] *Baptist Missionary Magazine* 17 (June 1837): 204, and 18 (January 1838): 17–18; Moulton, *The Papers of Chief John Ross*, 1:468–69.

aware of the ominous results. On this occasion, as in many accounts, Jones described the actions of Bushyhead through the lens of a Baptist missionary. Yet it seems that Bushyhead manifested a genuine deep burden for his people. During the next several days, Bushyhead interpreted for Jones and Presbyterian missionary Daniel Sabin Butrick. Butrick earlier had served at Brainerd and been active in the Candy's Creek mission. During the sermons, Bushyhead, a large man with a resonant voice, evidenced his pulpit skills. In Cherokee tradition, these vocal traits commanded respect. When interpreting scripture, he punctuated the end of each verse with a deep guttural accent meant to emphasize the serious nature of the words.[72] While interpreting one sermon, Bushyhead spoke with energy punctuated by sweeping gestures. But when the sermon turned to the crucifixion of Christ, emotion overcame him. He wept, and his voice quivered. The emotion of the moment also spread to the congregation. Later the same day, Bushyhead preached in Cherokee. According to Jones, Bushyhead became overpowered by emotion and had difficulty maintaining his composure.[73]

From 1829 through 1837, Bushyhead had embraced Christianity and evidenced a successful ministry. His linguistic and oratory skills had gained him the reputation as perhaps the best interpreter in the Cherokee Nation. And he had gathered an independent Cherokee church, a congregation as autonomous as any non-Cherokee Baptist church in the area. His support for missionary societies and conventions had garnered funding and national recognition from the Baptist Board. His abilities also had allowed him the opportunity to represent the Cherokee government as a negotiator in Washington. Of course, there is the possibility that Bushyhead became a minister as a means

[72] *Baptist Missionary Magazine* 18 (April 1838): 94; George W. Featherstonhaugh, *A Canoe Voyage up the Minnay Sotor* (London: Richard Bentley, 1847), quoted in Carolyn Thomas Foreman, "An Early Account of the Cherokees," *Chronicles of Oklahoma* 34 (Summer 1956): 150–51.

[73] *Baptist Missionary Magazine* 18 (April 1838): 95.

to achieve the respect and economic opportunities afforded traditional Cherokee conjurers. Yet this seems unlikely, for in many cases, his growing prominence and association with Jones had resulted in opposition from conjurers and some whites. Thus, there may have been an easier path to recognition other than the ministry. And even after he began ministerial duties, he could have resigned at any time. Yet he chose not to do so. As these developments transpired, the tribe faced the ominous choice of virtual extermination or removal. In the process, Cherokees became divided and embittered as the Treaty and Antitreaty factions jockeyed for control. And Bushyhead increasingly became involved in the controversy.

CHAPTER 3

The Removal Crisis

As removal loomed, Bushyhead encountered political, personal, and familial challenges. One concern involved Bushyhead's brother-in-law, John (Jack) Walker, Jr. Walker, a prosperous and charismatic mixed-blood, was the son of Major John Walker. Major Walker was an influential chief who had signed the 1817 treaty. For his efforts, Major Walker had received $3,425 from United States agents.[1] The junior Walker, following the example of his father, also reaped personal economic advantages through cooperation with the United States. In 1827, the younger Walker had aided government agent General John Cocke in an attempt to garner support. In so doing, they entreated tribal leaders Elias Boudinot, John Ridge, and John Ross to agree to a removal treaty. Although deliberations bogged down, Walker realized the value of venality in facilitating such a sensitive and volatile issue. He thus requested $2,000 from Cocke. Justifying his request, Walker crassly admitted an "Indan [*sic*] will do nothing without pay."[2] Walker's machinations also required trustworthy aides. Accordingly, he had recommended Bushyhead to Cocke as a courier at a $3 per diem rate. Walker considered Bushyhead "a man I would recommend before any other."[3] Bushyhead evidently accepted Cocke's offer. On 17 September 1827, Cocke paid Bushyhead $36

[1] Remini, *Andrew Jackson and His Indian Wars*, 127.

[2] John Walker to John Cocke, 26 August 1827, Oklahoma Trail of Tears Association Collection (OTOTA), box 1, file 56, doc.4, Sequoyah Center, University of Arkansas at Little Rock, photocopied.

[3] Ibid.

"for twelve days service in carrying a [letter] of Invitation to the Chiefs Headmen and Warriors of the Cherokee Nation."[4] Cocke also paid Isaac Bushyhead, presumably for similar services.[5] In addition, Cocke acknowledged payment of $1500 to Walker, John Ridge, and Boudinot for influencing "the Indians to sell their land to the United States."[6]

Besides the removal issue, Walker also had business and personal connections to the Bushyhead family. In 1827, Jesse and Isaac had served with Walker as witnesses in the Cherokee court case of *Peggy Morgan v. Arch[ibal]d Foreman and Joseph Spears.*[7] And at some point prior to 1831, Walker had become the consort of Jesse's sister, Nancy (Nannie) Bushyhead. From this union, at least two children were born and possibly more.[8] But by 1831, Walker had married Emily Stanfield Meigs, daughter of wealthy and influential whites Timothy and Elizabeth Meigs and granddaughter of former United States Indian agent Return J. Meigs.[9] In 1825, tribal law had limited marriage arrangements to one man and one woman. Regardless if only one or both were Cherokee citizens, the law still applied. Yet tribal traditions concerning divorce had been loose. The cessation of conjugal cohabitation usually was enough to effect divorce. Essentially, husbands and wives had the right to separate and dissolve unions at any time.[10] Because Walker and Nancy were citizens of the Cherokee Nation, they had been joined under Cherokee custom. And at the time of their

[4] John Cocke Papers, 1827, OTOTA, file 56, doc. 15, Sequoyah Center.

[5] Ibid.

[6] John Cocke Account Book, 1827, OTOTA, box 261, file 6, doc. 7.

[7] A Record Book of the Proceedings of the Supreme Court of the Cherokee Nation, 1823–1835.

[8] David Keith Hampton, *Cherokee Mixed Bloods* (n.p.: ARC Press, 2005) 236.

[9] John Morgan Wooten, "Chief Jack Walker," John Wooten Scrapbook, Chattanooga (TN) Public Library, M-54; "Chief Jack Walker Marker Rededicated," *Cleveland Daily Banner*, 10 September 1973.

[10] Yarbrough, *Race and the Cherokee Nation*, 27.

union, the legality of their conjugal arrangement remained outside the parameters of Tennessee state law. Yet it is highly probable that Emily's parents did not condone their daughter sharing her husband with another woman. So at some point, Walker separated from Nancy. The 1835 Cherokee Census listed "Emily Walker" as living near the home of Jesse Bushyhead. In his wills, dated 1830 and 1831, Walker included Emily and their three children. He also provided $500 for "a young woman by the name of Nancy Bushyhead from former circumstances." Walker commended Nancy for "her true and faithful attachment toward me which I have been so much compelled to abuse."[11] Jesse Bushyhead served as one of two witnesses at the signing.

Yet any remorse over Nancy did not prevent Walker from continuing his roguery. Walker, a well-liked acquaintance of President Jackson, used Jackson's influence to pursue personal financial gains. Although not an official tribal emissary, in fall 1832, Walker requested that the United States government defray his expenses for a planned visit to Washington. Upon arrival, he aimed to lobby for removal. Furthermore, Walker made an additional offer to Colonel Hugh Montgomery, the Cherokee agent stationed at the Charleston agency across the Hiwassee River from Calhoun, Tennessee. Walker proposed that Washington bear the costs of "a few of our men" to make an exploratory visit to "the western country."[12] Writing to influential Cherokee William Rogers on 18 December 1832, Walker invited Rogers to accompany him on a visit to "Ol' Hickory." Before his anticipated departure, Walker urged Rogers, a Ross man, to visit his farm. In a private setting, Walker hoped to "lead your family into my

[11] Will of John Walker, Jr., John Walker, Jr. File, Cleveland (TN) Public Library, typewritten copy.

[12] John Walker, Jr. to Hugh Montgomery, 12 November 1832, Letters Received by the Office of Indian Affairs, 1824–1881, National Archives, M234, roll 75.

views."[13] Word of the friendship between Walker and Jackson elevated the eyebrows of certain Cherokees, for any unauthorized emissary such as Walker stirred suspicion as delicate negotiations over removal proceeded. On 29 January 1833, fifty-one Tennessee Cherokees suspecting treachery on the part of Walker signed a petition of protest. They directed the protest to Secretary of War Lewis Cass. Isaac Bushyhead personally circulated the petition. Several Bushyheads signed the document, including Jesse, Isaac, George, and their father.[14]

In the face of this opposition, Walker proceeded with his Washington visit the following February. He quickly conducted his affairs there and was back on his Tennessee farm in April. Also by this time, economic developments had persuaded Isaac Bushyhead to reconsider his stance against removal. Beginning in 1830, the Jackson administration had withheld annuities to Eastern Cherokees, the part of the tribe still remaining in the Southeast. Jackson meant to use their resulting impoverishment as leverage in removal negotiations. Yet, by spring 1833, removal talks had made little progress, and many of the poorer Cherokees suffered destitution. Isaac cleverly saw an opportunity to profit from their misfortunes. Possibly with Walker's assent, Isaac and a white man peddled goods such as tobacco, salt, and cloth on credit. Although his customers lacked money, Isaac accepted their trade certificates in return for merchandise. In turn, he hoped for Montgomery's cooperation in redeeming them at the agency.

On 26 April, Walker noted Isaac's bent for business. Writing from Hopewell Farm near Cleveland, he noted, "...here is an evidence of self interest, being the principle by which the Indian acts, as well as the white man, there are many that would make this [removal]

[13] William Rogers to John Ross, 1 February 1833, John Ross Papers, folder 78, Gilcrease Museum.

[14] John Ross and others to Lewis Cass, 25 February 1833, Letters Received by the Office of Indian Affairs, 1824–1881, National Archives, M234, roll 75.

a matter of speculation if the government would allow it."[15] In the case of Isaac, Walker's assumption concerning a profit motive proved true. For nineteen days after Walker penned his letter, the names of Isaac, Walker, and twenty-four other Cherokees appeared on a petition to the National Council in session at Red Clay. The appeal urged the council to make the preservation of the Cherokees first and foremost in their deliberations. In this case, the concern over tribal salvation was a tongue-in-cheek appeal for removal. Also numbered among the petitioners were Elias Boudinot, Major Ridge, John Ridge, Stand Watie, David Vann, Elijah Hicks, and John West.[16] All remained leading proponents of removal. Thus, the politics of removal increasingly was becoming a family issue among the Bushyheads.

From 1832 through 1834, the Ross party blocked removal efforts through their control of the national Cherokee legislature. But by the August 1834 meeting of the national legislature, the crisis had reached a boiling point. During these sessions, removal advocates drew fury from the council. Thomas Foreman, a backer of John Ross and, by this time, another ministerial associate of Bushyhead, publicly decried a removal proposal of Major Ridge as duplicitous. According to Foreman, Major Ridge had encouraged Cherokees to hold dear their land rights but simultaneously had negotiated land sales.[17] Angry at such double-dealing, anti-removal supporters circulated a petition signed by 130 citizens of the Cherokee Nation. The document urged the ouster of leaders such as Ridge for cooperating with the Jackson administration.[18]

[15] John Walker, Jr. to [Benjamin F. Currey], 26 April 1833, Letters Received by the Office of Indian Affairs, 1824–1881, National Archives, M234, roll 75.

[16] Petition to Committee and Council, 15 May 1833. Letters Received by the office of Indian Affairs, 1824–1881, M234, roll 75.

[17] Gary E. Moulton, *John Ross: Cherokee Chief* (Athens: University of Georgia, 1978) 57.

[18] Snell, "The Councils at Red Clay Council Ground," 347.

Walker also was present at the 1834 council. As tempers flared, Walker felt targeted and feared for his life. His concerns were justified. The 1827 Cherokee Constitution had specified that only the National Council had the right to sell tribal lands. This policy aimed at preventing individual Cherokees or parties from negotiating land deals without tribal approval.[19] In 1828, the national legislature had strengthened the prohibition and revived an old tribal law. Under its provisions, anyone who sold land without tribal sanction faced death.[20] As the sessions continued, Walker learned that James Foreman, a Cherokee in attendance, was planning to assassinate him. On 23 August, Walker, accompanied by a white friend, decided to leave the Red Clay council grounds and head for home. His fear of personal peril proved genuine. About eight or ten miles from Red Clay, Anderson Springston and James Foreman hid by the road. As Walker approached, Springston delivered a musket blast. The assassins then fled. Suffering from loss of blood and a severe wound to the right side of his chest, Walker rode three miles northeast of Cleveland to his and Emily's residence. He lingered there until his death on 11 September. Yet the killing only added more tension to the volatile situation. While Walker lay on his deathbed, rumors implicated John Ross with responsibility for the attack. Old Hickory soon responded to the hearsay. From his estate near Nashville, Jackson hastily penned a letter to Major Benjamin F. Currey, the federal agent charged with enrolling Cherokees for removal. Jackson ordered Currey to deliver an ominous warning to Ross. Jackson promised to hold Ross and his "council" personally responsible for the murder of any removal supporters.[21]

[19] Andrew Denson, *Demanding the Cherokee Nation: Indian Autonomy and American Culture, 1830–1900* (Lincoln: University of Nebraska, 2004) 23.

[20] Rennard Strickland, *Fire and the Spirits: Cherokee Law from Clan to Court* (Norman: University of Oklahoma, 1975) 77.

[21] Payne Papers, 1:141; John Morgan Wooten, "Chief Jack Walker"; Ehle, *Trail of Tears,* 271; *State v. Anderson Springston and James Foreman*, East Tennes-

Not only did the murder outrage Jackson, the ensuing trial of Springston and Foreman challenged Cherokee sovereignty under Tennessee law. In 1833, the Tennessee legislature had passed laws extending state authority over Cherokees in cases involving larceny, rape, and murder.[22] Tennessee authorities quickly moved to bring Springston and Foreman to justice. Under the jurisdiction of the McMinn County Circuit Court, a grand jury assembled at Athens. The jury indicted Springston and Foreman on Saturday, 1 November 1834, and the trial opened the following Tuesday. State-summoned witnesses included Jesse Bushyhead, Nancy Bushyhead, and their mother. The testimonies of the Bushyheads were important to the case. They resided near Walker's home and had been closely linked with the victim. They also were related to Springston. A half-blood in his early twenties, Springston was a first cousin to Jesse. And less than seven years before, Springston had been a schoolmate of two of Jesse's younger siblings at Candy's Creek.[23] The witnesses, accompanied by neighbors, traveled approximately twenty-four miles to Athens. The trip occurred scarcely over a month after Jesse had returned from a preaching tour to Valley Towns.[24] The state appointed Bushyhead and Charles Vann as "sworn interpreters" for the benefit of non-English-speaking witnesses. The proceedings lasted several days and

see Supreme Court, box 245, Tennessee State Library; 1835 Cherokee Census; John Spencer Bassett, *Correspondence of Andrew Jackson* (Nashville: Carnegie Institution, 1931) 5:288.

[22] Congress, Committee of the Whole House, House Document 286, *Memorial of the Cherokee Representatives, submitting the protest of the Cherokee Nation against the ratification, execution, and enforcement of the treaty negotiated at New Echota, in December 1835*, 24th Cong., 1st sess., 22 (LexisNexis Academic, 2006) Serial Set ID: 292 H.doc 286.

[23] Snell, "Candy's Creek Mission Station," 174–75; Bell, *Genealogy*, 92, 451; The 1835 Cherokee Census reported seven Cherokees at the home of Nancy Bushyhead. See 1835 Cherokee Census, microfilm at Chattanooga Public Library.

[24] Leonard Butterfield to Lucius Bolles, 30 September 1834, ABHS.

required the Bushyheads to remain in Athens. A local businessman billed the court for six days' lodging for Jesse and his sister and four days for their mother.

On Friday, 7 November, the court handed down an inconclusive decision. Because Springston and Foreman were Cherokee citizens, the defense argued that the state circuit court lacked jurisdiction. This difficulty resulted in the case being transferred to the Tennessee Supreme Court. The next session of the high court was set to convene in Knoxville in July 1835. Accordingly, the circuit court ordered the accused transferred to a Knoxville jail.[25] Yet Springston and Foreman never stood trial. On 21 April 1835, missionary J. C. Ellsworth reported from Brainerd Mission that the two had escaped and returned to their homes. The jailer had offered a $100 reward for their apprehension and return. But it seemed that the escapees had little to fear. Prospective bounty hunters either were afraid of retaliation or were aware of popular support for Springston and Foreman. Also, interest in the case had prompted John Ross to secure considerable funds for their legal defense. Ellsworth wryly noted that no one seemed "anxious to secure the reward."[26]

While events involving Springston and Foreman unfolded, emigration more closely affected the Bushyheads. In February 1834, delegations from the Treaty and Antitreaty factions were in Washington to discuss removal. But by that time, George and Isaac Bushyhead were preparing to travel west. The two brothers arrived with their families in the Western Cherokee Nation in May 1834.[27] Yet Isaac remained only a short time and then returned to Tennessee. But while away, he had gathered information about Texas. Already John Ross had been in contact with Joaquin Maria del Castillo y Lanzas, a

[25] *State v. Anderson Springston and James Foreman*; Marybelle W. Chase, trans., *Records of the Cherokee Agency in Tennessee, 1801–1835* (n.p.: 1990) 53.

[26] Papers of American Board of Commissioners for Foreign Missions (ABCFM) 18.3.1, vol. 8, item 106; Ehle, *Trail of Tears*, 272.

[27] Baker, *Cherokee Emigration Rolls, 1817–1835*, 49.

high-ranking Mexican diplomat posted to the United States, concerning the relocation of the Eastern Cherokees to Texas.[28] And if removal occurred, Jesse evidently also was interested in settling in Texas rather than Indian Territory. Already a significant number of Cherokees had settled in East Texas, the result of a slow drift from east of the Mississippi. Moreover, a possible home in Texas held promise for future Cherokee emigrants. In 1834, Texas remained a province of Mexico and outside the jurisdiction of the United States. But support was growing among newly arrived United States citizens in eastern Texas for Cherokee settlement. In 1823, Texas Cherokees had appealed to the Mexican government for land titles in East Texas. The Mexican government rejected the request, but later some newly arrived American settlers in Texas favored grants to Cherokees.[29]

If Jesse had pondered supporting removal, he reconsidered. Certainly, the influence of Evan Jones, the murder of his former brother-in-law, and negative reports from Isaac were sufficient reasons. Indeed, the reports from Isaac were so critical that Currey accused Isaac of purposefully spreading misinformation in order to interfere with the ongoing treaty process. In order to defend himself against Currey's calumny, Isaac penned a letter to Jesse on 13 August 1835. The correspondence detailed his grievances against government policy toward Cherokees in the west. Isaac accused the government of being tardy in supplying payment to emigrants and insisted that most of the recently arrived Cherokees had lost half of their wealth in the process of relocation. Moreover, white encroachment among the Western

[28] Moulton, *The Papers of Chief John Ross*, 1:334–35.

[29] By November 1835, revolution against Mexico was brewing among Texas Anglos. American settlers who led the provincial government, the Texas Consultation, promised to honor Cherokee land claims in East Texas in exchange for Cherokee support in the coming war with Mexico. See Robert A. Calvert and Arnoldo De Leon, *The History of Texas* (Arlington Heights IL: Harland Davidson, 1990) 85.

Cherokees went unchecked, for whites remained outside the reach of Cherokee law. And further failing to honor its promises, the government had withheld education funds. Finally, government-supplied rations of corn and beef had been unsatisfactory, the cattle being "as wild and as unruly as the buffaloes in the western prairies."[30]

While Jesse and Isaac exchanged information, separate delegations from the Treaty and Antitreaty factions had been negotiating a removal treaty in Washington. John Ross headed the Antitreaty delegation. Ross, a savvy politician, knew that his personal reputation, political future, and the destiny of the Cherokees remained in the balance. Banking on a Whig party victory in the 1836 presidential election and a more sympathetic chief executive, Ross used the negotiations as a delaying tactic. In a meeting with Jackson on 5 February 1834, Ross made an offer that Jackson was almost certain to refuse. Ross proposed that Cherokees retain a remnant of tribal lands in North Carolina, Tennessee, Georgia, and Alabama, some of which white settlers had already occupied. Moreover, Ross hoisted an excessive sum as recompense for remaining Eastern Cherokee lands. He demanded $20,000,000 plus indemnities for past damages. Seeing through the ruse, Jackson demonstrated a strong negative reaction. In essence, he threatened to cease negotiations entirely. Sensing a need to keep talks alive and deflate any alternate proposal from the Treaty party, Ross agreed to accept any price that the Senate offered. Yet, when the Senate proposed a $5,000,000 buyout, Ross found himself backed into a corner of his own making. He therefore attempted to circumvent the agreement. Ross insisted that all future negotiations receive approval from the Cherokee national legislature sitting in council. Of course, under the influence of Ross, the national legislature would reject the government offer and allow Ross a means of escape.

[30] Isaac Bushyhead to Jesse Bushyhead, 13 August 1835, Payne Papers, 3:195–96.

Jackson and Cass recognized the dodge. They then proceeded to negotiate the Senate's terms with the Treaty party delegation headed by John Ridge. The Ridge delegation signed the treaty draft on 14 March 1835 and left for home. With treaty in hand, Ridge planned to submit it for tribal approval. The proposal offered $4,500,000 for land in the East in exchange for 800,000 acres worth $500,000 in Indian Territory. In addition, the United States promised to provide emigrants with travel provisions and compensation for incurred losses. With these carrots, Ridge felt that the force of Jackson and some political maneuvering would overcome the Ross faction.[31]

Throughout the year, Treaty and Antitreaty factions jockeyed for position. They carefully implemented strategies, at times convoluted, aimed at circumventing their opponents. In April, the Ridges and their associates issued an invitation for a tribal assembly at the John Ridge home at Running Waters in Floyd County, Georgia. The purpose centered on a discussion of the proposed treaty. Georgia authorities allowed the meeting only because it involved removal. Yet Ross again attempted to block any action and encouraged treaty opponents to remain at home. As a result, only a few Cherokees bothered to attend. Realizing he needed a larger representation, Ridge called for another assembly to convene on Monday, 4 May. Yet sparse attendance again prevented action. The meeting adjourned but reconvened at Running Waters on the following 19 July. On this occasion, Ridge attracted a larger crowd. Focusing on the unpaid annuity, he had disclosed that the main business would concern the distribution of these funds.[32] The delivery of annuity payments was part of the leverage that Jackson continued to exercise. Because Georgia effectively had abolished tribal government, Jackson reasoned that the Cherokee national treasury no longer existed. Thus, the United States

[31] Ehle, *Trail of Tears*, 273–74; Remini, *Andrew Jackson and His Indian Wars*, 264–66.

[32] Ehle, *Trail of Tears*, 280–81.

held $6,666.66 of tribal funds in escrow until a general assembly of tribal members decided on a means of disbursement.[33] Under these circumstances, Ross feared the possible actions of a rump assembly. What if attendees decided to distribute the annuity to individual Cherokees rather than the Ross-controlled treasury? Ross therefore urged attendance.

This time, over 2,000 Cherokees assembled. Also present were federal agents who hoped to influence the results. One was the Reverend John Freeman Schermerhorn, a Dutch Reformed minister from New York. Schermerhorn, appointed official commissioner by the Jackson administration, had entered negotiations with the Ridge faction in March. Around 10 A.M., Bushyhead opened the meeting with prayer.[34] After preliminary remarks by Ross and John Ridge, Schermerhorn offered to address the crowd. But the Ross party refused. Instead, they protested that the agenda did not provide for a discussion of the treaty. Yet Schermerhorn quickly countered. He graciously promised to feed the crowd. Of course, his generosity hinged on being allowed the privilege to speak on behalf of the treaty the following morning. Ross reluctantly consented. Seizing this opportunity, some of the Treaty party maneuvered to weaken the position of Ross in the eyes of tribal members. Wishing to deprive Ross of the needed financial means to continue resistance, Archilla Smith shrewdly motioned for a distribution of annuity funds to individual Cherokees. Because approval required a vote of the sitting assembly, the Ridges and Smith moved to have the votes recorded. Through this maneuver, Ridge intended to spotlight and politically embarrass Ross supporters, for why would benevolent leaders oppose attempts to alleviate destitution? In reality, the Ridges and Smith hoped to curry favor with impoverished Cherokees and wear down the Ross opposition.

[33] McLoughlin, *Cherokees and Missionaries*, 253.

[34] Whitmire, *Noland's Cherokee Diary*, 15.

Edward Gunter, a Ross supporter, responded to these developments. He moved to prevent any such action. Instead, he motioned that John Martin, treasurer of the Cherokee Nation, receive the entire annuity. Although Ridge and his allies mounted a stiff resistance, they nevertheless experienced a humiliating defeat. The polling lasted three days and concluded on 22 July. Of approximately 2,200 ballots cast, only 111 favored Smith's motion. Yet the lopsided decision revealed a difference of opinion among the Bushyheads. Jacob Bushyhead, a younger brother of Jesse, favored the distribution of funds to the needy, but Jesse, Isaac, and their father sided with Ross.[35] Results for federal agents also proved frustrating. Schermerhorn did get an opportunity to explain the treaty to the crowd. But his words fell on deaf ears, for the majority of the crowd remained obdurate.

Preparations for removal nevertheless quickened. Even before the July assembly, United States authorities had initiated a census of the Cherokee Nation. The purpose was twofold. First, a fair distribution of the tribal annuity between Eastern and Western Cherokees required a determination of the population of the Eastern Cherokees. Second, an enumeration of warriors and headmen was necessary to ascertain the number needed for a majority vote on any future removal treaty.[36] But when census-takers began visits, they encountered opposition. Some Cherokees flatly refused to divulge information. Nathaniel Smith encountered such resistance when he attempted to enumerate the John Christie family. Christie, a full-blood head of a ten-member family, resided on the Hiwassee River in North Carolina. Christie refused cooperation unless "a Cherokee on the part of his tribe" accompanied Smith.[37] Responding to this potential impasse,

[35] Sharron Standifer Ashton, comp., *Indians and Intruders* (Norman OK: Ashton Books, 1997) 2:1–51.

[36] Congress, *Memorial of the Cherokee Representatives*, 49–50.

[37] Nathaniel Smith to John Ross, 16 June 1835, Congress, *Memorial of the Cherokee Representatives*, 48; James W. Tyner, ed., *Those Who Cried: The 16,000* (n.p.: Chi-ga-u Inc., 1974) 148.

Smith notified the Cherokee council then in session. Smith requested the assistance of a Cherokee in whom the council had placed confidence. The council appointed council member John Timson, still a ministerial associate of Bushyhead, to accompany Smith. When Tennessee governor William Carroll and Schermerhorn learned of these developments, they accused Ross of engineering resistance. This prompted an indignant reply from Ross. Still serving as principal chief, Ross claimed ignorance of the census. Furthermore, he argued that Cherokee citizens had every right to withhold information. Ross wrote,

> Being entirely ignorant of the intention of the Government on this subject, I had not information to give the Cherokees who called upon me to know what were the objects of certain gentlemen who, they stated, were travelling about and inquiring after their names and the numbers of their families, and stated, also, that those men were accompanied by certain Cherokee interpreters, who had previously been in the service of the enrolling and migrating agents....[38]

As tensions increased, it remained in the best interest of Ross to keep the peace. On 22 July 1835, a few days after the Running Waters council, Ross notified Schermerhorn of a solution. Ross appointed Bushyhead and four other respected Cherokees to accompany an equal number of United States census-takers.[39] Bushyhead accompanied Daniel Henderson and recorded Cherokee households in much of southeastern Tennessee. The enumeration provided population totals as well as other significant information about individual households. It revealed genders and ages, economic activities, property values, numbers of slaves, and literacy rates. In total, the census enumerated 2,528 Tennessee Cherokees.

By 15 October, the Cherokee national legislature convened in annual session at Red Clay. Schermerhorn, also at Red Clay, anxious-

[38] Moulton, *The Papers of Chief John Ross*, 1:342–43.

[39] Ibid., 1:344.

ly lobbied for the conclusion of a treaty. Weary of the impasse, Schermerhorn longed to return home. The previous month, he had notified his daughter that he expected to complete his duties in November, if not sooner.[40] Wishing to expedite matters, Schermerhorn pressed the Cherokee council to conclude a definitive treaty. If necessary, Schermerhorn meant to circumvent the Ross faction and opened with a salvo of threats. The clergyman threatened to convene a different "council of the nation, at such a time and place as they [federal commissioners] think best, to submit the propositions as they now stand."[41] And to reinforce his position, Schermerhorn disclosed that the Jackson administration and the governments of Georgia, North Carolina, Tennessee, and Alabama had ceased to recognize the legal status of the Cherokee national government. Any such action, of course, threatened to deprive the Ross government of funds.

In justifying his disclosure, Schermerhorn claimed that some of the National Council held United States citizenship. Because a number of Cherokee national leaders had signed the 1817 and 1819 treaties, they personally had received acreage and United States citizenship. Schermerhorn argued that national citizenship negated the right to hold office in other governments, including the Cherokee Nation. Because Ross held United States citizenship, this was a direct attack on him. Schermerhorn allowed some additional discussion. But he insisted that only the Cherokee people "assembled in general council" had the authority to conclude a treaty. Thus, he maneuvered to deprive the Ross-controlled national legislature of a voice.[42] Furthermore, Schermerhorn warned against the visit of another delegation to Washington while the treaty was being discussed. And if such emis-

[40] J. F. Schermerhorn to Caty [Schermerhorn], 17 September 1838, Schermerhorn Papers, 1830–1835, folder 4, Western Historical Manuscript Collection, Ellis Library, University of Missouri.

[41] Congress, *Memorial of the Cherokee Representatives*, 63.

[42] Ibid., 66.

saries made the journey, Jackson offered no guarantees of an interview.

Under this scenario, it became necessary for any government-recognized negotiations to take place within the Cherokee Nation. Ross quickly countered with another delaying tactic. He urged the present Cherokees voters to accept or reject the proposed treaty "upon the basis of five millions."[43] By using this figure, he intended to thwart the Ridge treaty signed the previous March, which had agreed to a $4,500,000 buyout. In accordance to this request, the people "in open assembly" promptly rejected the treaty.[44]

Calling Schermerhorn's bluff, the general council acted to remove the national legislature from negotiations and return deliberations to a special delegation. On 24 October, 1,076 assembled Cherokees signed a document. It authorized a twenty-man delegation, appointed by the Cherokee national legislature, to travel to Washington and negotiate another treaty. The signatories also proscribed any other delegation from negotiating with the United States government. Both John Ridge and Ross recommended delegates, but the majority of the delegates were Ross supporters.[45] Besides Ross, the delegation included two ministers, Bushyhead and Congregationalist John Huss.

While these sensitive negotiations developed, Bushyhead had remained engaged with congregational and denominational affairs. The organization of the Amohee church had occurred only weeks before. And before the Red Clay council convened, Bushyhead re-

[43] Ibid., 78.

[44] Ibid., 80.

[45] The delegates were John Ross, Richard Taylor, Lewis Ross, John Martin, James Brown, James Daniel, Thomas Foreman, Richard Fields, Sleeping Rabbit, Joseph Vann, John Benge, Oolenowa, Elijah Hicks, John Huss, John F. Baldridge, Peter of Aquohee, Jesse Bushyhead, John Ridge, Elias Boudinot, and Charles Vann. Before the delegation left for Washington, Boudinot resigned. Stand Watie then became the alternate.

cently had finished a preaching tour of Valley Towns. This visit had enhanced his credibility as a delegate among the mountain Cherokees. Before official selection, Ross notified the committee and council that "the people of the Valley towns seem desirous that Jesse Bushyhead should be appointed one of the delegates...."[46] Ross had good reason to recommend Bushyhead, for a sense of anxiety prevailed among the mountain Cherokees. During the recent visit to Valley Towns, Evan Jones reported good attendance at preaching services and described the response at the end of Bushyhead's closing sermon. Jones recorded that "a very general concern seemed to pervade the congregation, and a great number with weeping & mourning came forward to occupy the anxious seats...."[47] Some of this anxiety came from the emotional nature of the camp meeting environment. Yet some hearers likely were apprehensive over the forthcoming decisions at the Red Clay council later in October.

Also present at the Valley Towns camp meeting was Lieutenant Charles Fenten Mercer Noland, recently assigned as disbursing agent for Cherokee removal. Noland, accompanied by Schermerhorn and Currey, was on a tour of the Cherokee country in North Carolina. Noland reported scenic travels over rugged roads. On 26 September, Noland attended a Cherokee camp meeting and heard three sermons "in the Cherokee language" near the "Missionary Establishment" of Jones.[48] Noland noted that the Cherokees in the region were "very wild and much opposed to emigration."[49] Furthermore, the missionaries had a great deal of influence over them. Under these circumstances, it is plausible that the selection of Bushyhead had been proposed in order to defuse any smoldering violence.

[46] Congress, *Memorial of the Cherokee Representatives*, 83.
[47] Evan Jones to "Revd Dear Sir," 7 October 1835, ABHS.
[48] Whitmire, *Noland's Cherokee Diary*, 17–18.
[49] Ibid., 19.

The delegates selected at Red Clay bore the responsibility of negotiating a definitive treaty. They agreed to depart from the Cherokee agency on 1 December. Not to be outmaneuvered, on Friday, 30 October, Schermerhorn notified Ross of another called assembly set to convene at New Echota on Monday, 21 December 1835. The next day, eighteen of the Washington-bound delegates signed a letter to Schermerhorn and requested that he stay out of Cherokee affairs. Bushyhead was one of the two missing signatories. It is likely that he already had departed Red Clay in order to be at Amohee for the monthly first-Sunday service.[50] On 30 November, one day before the delegation planned to leave, Currey made a final attempt to deter their mission. Writing from the agency, Currey again stressed the futility of their mission—that is, Jackson's likely refusal to receive them. Moreover, Currey informed them that their absence would not invalidate additional negotiations, for while they were away, Schermerhorn and Carroll intended to meet with a rival delegation at New Echota.[51]

True to Currey's disclosure, an ad hoc assembly convened at the New Echota council house on Tuesday, 22 December. Calling themselves the general council, the body appointed a committee to conduct negotiations. The twenty-member committee consisted of Major Ridge, William Rogers, Robert Rogers, Elias Boudinot, John Gunter, Teasteskee, Charles Foreman, Charles Moore, John Adair Bell, George Chambers, Tayeskee, Archilla Smith, James Starr, Katihee, James Foster, Jesse Half-Breed, George Washington Adair, Andrew Ross, William Lassley, and Tekaheskee. Near midnight on 29 December, the committee signed a removal agreement known as the New Echota Treaty. Of course, the news alarmed most Cherokees. James J. Trott, an observer, wrote to Ross that the attendance at the proceedings was low. According to Trott, only about 100 warriors

[50] Congress, *Memorial of the Cherokee Representatives*, 99–100.
[51] Ibid., 103.

were in attendance who favored the treaty. With the permission of Currey and Schermerhorn, a three-member committee then nominated thirteen delegates to serve as delegates to accompany Schermerhorn and the treaty to Washington. Two of the nominees, John Timson and Roman Nose, received approval in absentia. By nominating these two, the committee meant to dilute the influence of Jones, for both had ties to Jones. Thus, the choice of Jones men hopefully served to reduce the objections of other Jones allies. Timson was a former interpreter, and the venerable Roman Nose was a North Carolina chief. But neither served. Knowing that Roman Nose stood against removal, the committee approved all of the nominees except him.[52] And although the committee approved Timson, a few days later he repudiated his selection.

In response, the Ross faction rushed to prevent ratification of the New Echota Treaty. Meeting at Red Clay, the rival anti-removal council drew up another document. It specified that only the commissioners chosen at Red Clay in October had official authorization to negotiate a treaty. The council emphasized that "we will never submit to any arrangement or treaty unless it is made by the proper authorized delegation of the nation, who were duly empowered and authorized at Red Clay general council, in October last...."[53] Signers of this protest included Hair Conrad, James Spears, Situakee, and Timson. All of these were friends or associates of Bushyhead.

While the New Echota proceedings had been taking place, Bushyhead was en route to Washington in company with the Ross delegation. The majority of the delegates hoped to lobby the Senate for a more favorable treaty. Yet internal dissension divided the delegation. Although the majority sided with Ross, John Ridge and Stand Watie continued to argue for removal. Even before the delegation departed, John Ridge and Ross had clashed. In a letter to Ross, Ridge

[52] Ibid., 113, 121.
[53] Ibid., 114.

protested the "diametrically opposite" views of Ross.[54] By early January, the delegates had arrived in Washington. On 2 January 1836, Bushyhead and sixteen others, including Watie and Ridge, requested an interview with Jackson through a letter addressed to Cass, still serving as secretary of war.[55] Five days later, Jackson obliged the Cass letter and met with the delegation. The chief executive made no promises other than pledging that "the Government would act with candor towards the delegation."[56] He also instructed them to put any treaty proposals in writing. But before meeting with the delegation, Jackson received a letter from Boudinot written at New Echota on the first day of the previous month. Boudinot informed the administration of the approaching New Echota assembly. He also warned the government against making overtures to the Ross delegation until a signed copy of the New Echota Treaty arrived in Washington.[57]

On 8 January, the delegates visited Elbert Herring, the commissioner of Indian affairs. Herring read a copy of Boudinot's letter to them. But wishing to withhold sensitive information, Herring prevented the delegates from viewing the letter. When the Antitreaty faction delegates learned that Ridge had concealed knowledge of the Boudinot communiqué, they became particularly annoyed with Ridge. On 29 February, Bushyhead and twenty other Ross men, including three recently arrived delegates, signed a document protesting the manner in which their mission had been undermined. Watie and Ridge did not sign.[58] But by that time, Schermerhorn had reached Washington with the New Echota Treaty.

[54] Ibid., 102.

[55] Ibid., 104–105.

[56] Ibid., 27.

[57] Ibid.

[58] By this time, the delegation numbered twenty-three. On 1 February 1836, three opponents to removal, Archibald Campbell, Daniel McCoy, and The Bark, had been selected as messengers by a Red Clay council. Their assignment was to join the twenty already in Washington and protest the New Echota ac-

Unfortunately for Bushyhead and his fellow delegates, the Senate ratified the Treaty of New Echota on 18 May 1836. Yet the anti-removal delegates almost prevailed, for the Senate narrowly approved the treaty by a single vote over the required two-thirds majority. Within a week, Jackson signed the document.[59] Sensing defeat, Bushyhead and the other delegates left for home, likely arriving near the first week in June. Once home, Bushyhead broke the sad news about ratification. He attributed the passage of the treaty to "our country being sold by a few unauthorized individuals."[60] Although some still hoped to ameliorate its terms and conditions, developments did not appear favorable. Federal agents soon commenced Cherokee property appraisals. In southeastern Tennessee, the process lasted from late August through October. On 13 October, the Jesse Bushyhead farm appraised for $1,614. Improvements included a log house with a "good floor and doors," a log kitchen separate from the main dwelling, a smokehouse, a large floored barn, two corn cribs, seventy-five acres of fenced land, and orchards with 122 apple trees and 120 peach trees.[61] This exceeded the average evaluation, making evident that Bushyhead was among the more prosperous Cherokees in the area. And the possession of substantial property made removal even more disturbing.

tions. The newly arrived delegates carried a protest supposedly "signed by upwards of twelve thousand people." See ibid., 29, 115–17.

[59] Remini, *Andrew Jackson and His Indian Wars*, 268.

[60] *Baptist Missionary Magazine* 17 (February 1837): 45.

[61] Hoskins, *Cherokee Property Valuations in Tennessee, 1836*, no pagination.

CHAPTER 4

The Seminole Mission

While the Senate debated the New Echota Treaty, events among Creeks and Seminoles rippled across the Cherokee Nation. According to the Treaty of Cusseta, ratified in 1832, Creeks had agreed to relinquish tribal ownership of all tribal lands east of the Mississippi in favor of individual allotments. White squatters quickly moved onto Creek lands, and other allotment holders sold their claims. After spending funds on property, white purchasers grew alarmed over continued Creek occupancy. Violence ensued as white settlers entered former Creek lands. In May 1836, conflict erupted in western Georgia between state militia and Creek warriors. The disturbance lasted throughout the summer. As a result, federal agents rounded up Creeks and forced them to move to Indian Territory, some handcuffed and chained. As Creeks trudged westward, Seminole warriors under Osceola also waged war in Florida.

In 1832, Seminole leaders had signed the Treaty of Payne's Landing. Pending the location of a suitable home in Indian Territory, the agreement permitted the Seminoles three years to complete removal.[1] Yet tribal leaders later repudiated the settlement. Moreover, Osceola, a charismatic Seminole chief, promised to kill any chief who dared to cooperate with federal officials. In December 1835, open warfare erupted after Seminoles ambushed an army detachment. The resulting conflict, known as the Second Seminole War, lasted until

[1] Gibson, *The American Indian,* 328.

1842. As the struggle continued, it proved extremely costly for the United States in lives and treasure.[2]

Aware of Creek and Seminole resistance, some whites in the Cherokee Nation likewise began to view Cherokees as genuine threats. In December 1834, even before the Creek and Seminole uprisings, whites living near the Cherokee agency began to "adopt measures of defense."[3] In light of the recent uprisings, General Wool determined to collect weapons from Cherokees in North Carolina. The general estimated that 5,000 mountain Cherokees remained staunchly opposed to removal. Once forced removal began, he feared that uprooted Cherokees from North Carolina, Georgia, and Alabama posed the possibility of violence as they assembled at disembarkation sites. In July 1836, Wool led an expedition to the Valley River in North Carolina. In order to facilitate the collection of arms, the general resorted to intimidation. He forced chiefs and headmen to remain under guard overnight. One of the chiefs was Roman Nose. The next day, Wool allowed his prisoners to return home but ordered all Cherokees to bring in their arms. Most complied, even though without weapons they were virtually defenseless.[4]

As 1836 rolled into 1837, a national economic downturn delayed forced removal. The Panic of 1837 provided Whigs in Congress, some of whom opposed Indian removal, more political leverage. Against this backdrop, the Antitreaty party discussed means to renegotiate the New Echota Treaty. Throughout August 1837, several thousand Cherokees once more assembled at Red Clay. Reaching a decision, they offered to cede Cherokee lands in Georgia but retain lands in Alabama, Tennessee, and North Carolina. Acting on this

[2] Remini, *Andrew Jackson and His Indian Wars*, 272–74.

[3] Whitmire, *Noland's Cherokee Diary*, 4.

[4] Brigadier General John E. Wool to Secretary of War Lewis Cass, 5 July 1836; Wool to Brigadier General R. Jones, 8 August 1836; and Wool to Major General A. Macomb, 12 October 1836; all from Letter Books, Special Collections, McFarlin Library.

initiative, Ross left for Washington to present the compromise to the Van Buren administration. But new developments presented Ross partisans with even more hope. One of the bargaining chips related to the government's attempt to end the Seminole conflict.

In July 1837, Colonel John H. Sherburne, a Georgian and special agent of Secretary of War Joel Roberts Poinsett, had approached Ross in Washington. Sherburne raised the possibility of Cherokee involvement in a peace mission to the Seminoles.[5] He rehearsed the matter with Ross at the Cherokee agency the following September and made an attractive offer. Should a Cherokee delegation serve as emissaries, a renegotiation of the New Echota Treaty seemed hopeful. Sherburne initially wanted Ross to lead the mission. But feeling obligated to attend to tribal affairs in Washington, Ross declined personal participation as a mediator. But before leaving Tennessee, Ross appointed Bushyhead as one of four emissaries. Bushyhead's integrity and language skills made him a key member of the delegation. The other mediators were Richard Fields, Hair Conrad, and Thomas Woodward. Major Polecat, a Seminole kinsman of Osceola, accompanied the emissaries as a Seminole interpreter.[6] Major Polecat understood Cherokee but not English. Bushyhead's principal responsibility was to translate messages from government agents into Cherokee for the benefit of Major Polecat. In turn, Major Polecat would communicate the contents in Seminole. Hopefully, the emissaries would garner cooperation from the Seminoles and laurels from

[5] Gary E. Moulton, "Cherokees and the Second Seminole War," *The Florida Historical Quarterly* (January 1975): 296; Jacqueline Fiorato, "The Cherokee Mediation in Florida," *Journal of Cherokee Studies* (Spring 1978): 112.

[6] Major Polecat has been identified as Osceola's cousin. Yet it is more likely that he was a member of the same clan rather than an actual cousin according to the English definition. See Mark F. Boyd, "Asi-Yaholo or Osceola," *Florida Historical Quarterly* 33 (January–April 1955): 260–61.

the Van Buren administration.[7] Upon his return to Washington, Ross discussed the mission with Poinsett.

It may seem strange that Cherokee opponents of removal, including Bushyhead, should willingly cooperate with the United States in efforts to coax another tribe into removal. According to Evan Jones, Bushyhead accepted the mission solely to stop bloodshed. But there were political aspects besides the explanation of Jones. The pacification of Seminoles promised to save lives and substantial sums of War Department funds. This was especially important as the Panic of 1837 stalled the national economy. The potential savings stood to confirm Ross and Cherokees as useful instruments of the national government. Besides diplomatic gains, Sherburne had also suggested the possibility of payment to the mediators. Sherburne suggested $5 to $8 per diem coupled with "a very liberal compliment" from Congress following the completion of successful mission.[8]

Still in Washington on 18 October 1837, Ross penned a personal message to the Seminole chiefs. Ross carefully crafted his letter in order to establish a positive environment for negotiations. He introduced the Cherokee messengers and forwarded the letter to the Charleston, South Carolina, post office. Referring to the message as his "talk," he established several conditions. First, any negotiation of a peace treaty was contingent on the surrender of the Seminoles. Second, pledges of respect and protection for war leaders such as Osceola depended on the cessation of hostilities. Third, the terms guaranteed government compensation to Seminoles for any losses incurred at the hands of whites. And after peace had been restored, Sherburne and the Cherokee mediators promised to accompany a Seminole delegation to Washington for a meeting with Van Buren.[9]

[7] McLoughlin, *Champions of the Cherokees,* 158; *Baptist Missionary Magazine* 18 (February 1838): 41.

[8] Congress, *Memorial of the Cherokee Mediators*, 2.

[9] Remini, *Andrew Jackson and His Indian Wars*, 273; Congress, *Memorial of the Cherokee Mediators,* 7.

Ross instructed the messengers to pick up the correspondence at Charleston while en route to Florida. He also gave additional personal instructions to the emissaries. Ross required them to keep General Thomas Sidney Jesup, the commander of United States troops in Florida, fully informed. He also instructed them to purchase plenty of tobacco and pipes in Charleston for use as gifts at the parleys. Moreover, Ross prohibited the mediators to discuss Cherokee affairs with the Seminoles. Instead, he defined their roles strictly as peace emissaries. It was the sole responsibility of the government rather than the mediators to discuss treaty terms. There were several reasons for this demand. Any perceived Cherokee support for Seminole emigration threatened to weaken arguments for allowing the Cherokees to remain in the Southeast. And once the Florida tribe had arrived in Indian Territory, there was the possibility of Seminole retaliation against Cherokees already living in Indian Territory. Above all, he warned the emissaries against provoking the Seminoles to further hostility, for more Seminole recalcitrance only fueled the use of force against perceived Cherokee resistance to the Treaty of New Echota. And any such suspicion potentially doomed the renegotiation of the New Echota Treaty.[10] Finally, the instructions plainly informed the mediators concerning their responsibilities after the conclusion of their assignment. Ross wrote, "[s]hould you succeed in your mission of peace, the Secretary of War is willing for you to come on here [Washington] with Colonel Sherburne, and also a delegation from the Seminoles, if they desire to send one...."[11] If the mission failed, they were to return to their homes via Charleston.

In spite of the best hopes of Ross, internal problems beset the mission from the beginning. Resentment first developed concerning the conduct of Richard Fields. On 19 October, Fields had met the

[10] Jesse Bushyhead to John Ross, 3 February 1838, Payne Papers, 2:21; Fiorato, "The Cherokee Mediation in Florida," 112–17.

[11] Congress, *Memorial of the Cherokee Mediators*, 5.

deputation at the Cherokee agency. The members decided to proceed from there as a group to Augusta, Georgia, and wait for further instructions. Following their discussion, they dispersed for the evening. But the next day, another letter arrived from Ross. After reading the contents, Fields immediately left for Augusta without consulting the other mediators. Rather than immediately follow, Conrad, Woodward, and Bushyhead decided to wait at the agency for further instructions from Ross. While the remaining mediators tarried, Major Polecat departed for Chattooga, Alabama, a settlement just across the northwestern Georgia border, on personal business. Woodward and Conrad took to the road on 28 October. And two days later, Bushyhead left home on horseback for Coosawatie, Georgia, approximately forty-five miles from Mouse Creek. Notified by express mail to wait for the delegation at Coosawatie, Major Polecat met Bushyhead there on Wednesday, 1 November. The following day, the two caught the stage and rendezvoused with Conrad and Woodward in Gainesville, Georgia. On Friday, the four team members departed for Augusta where they encountered Sherburne the next day. Remaining in Augusta over Sunday, the mediators caught the stage for Charleston on Monday. The five arrived in Charleston that evening and sought out Fields. However, Fields already had departed for St. Augustine, Florida, having picked up the Ross message at the Charleston post office.[12]

Before boarding a vessel on the morning of 8 November, Bushyhead hastily penned a message to Ross. The letter revealed a sense of frustration over the presumptive actions of Fields. Apparently, Bushyhead held reservations that Fields intended to assume leadership of the delegation and possibly weaken the position of the other

[12] Ibid., 1–21; Hair Conrad, Jesse Bushyhead, Thomas Woodward, and Major Polecat to John Ross, 3 February 1838, Payne Papers, 2:18; Moulton, *The Papers of Chief John Ross*, 1:520–46. For location of Chattooga, see Theda Perdue and Michael D. Green, *The Cherokee Nation and the Trail of Tears* (New York: Viking, 2007) 96.

mediators. Ross answered Bushyhead within the week and attempted to allay his concerns. Ross faulted Fields for failing to keep Bushyhead informed. Yet he claimed that Fields merely had acted in concert with Sherburne's instructions. Ross assured Bushyhead that his message to the Seminoles named Bushyhead and Conrad as "the Head of the deputation."[13] But as Bushyhead suspected, Fields indeed was maneuvering to assume leadership. While in Charleston, Fields had justified his presumptuous departure in a letter to Ross. Fields claimed "that his object for repairing immediately to St. Augustine...was to announce himself as one of the deputation, should circumstances make it necessary, & then to await your [Ross] arrival and cooperation previous to any definite steps."[14] But Fields did not wait on Ross or any of the other emissaries. On 9 November, Bushyhead, Conrad, Woodward, Major Polecat, and Sherburne reached Gary's Ferry, Florida, on the St. John's River and boarded the steamboat *Camden* for Picolata, Florida. They steamed south the next day and met with Jesup at Picolata. At the meeting, they learned that Fields already had met with Jesup. Moreover, Fields "had given a certified copy" of the Ross message to certain imprisoned Seminole chiefs and the general.[15] This was not a promising beginning, for it soured the general against the mission and portended a dangerous and delicate assignment.

By the time Fields and the other emissaries encountered Jesup, the general was in no mood to listen. As commander of United States forces in Florida for almost a year, his assignment had proven frustrating and challenging. Native resistance had not been subdued, for Seminoles had been wily and brave in combat. Moreover, the Florida terrain and climate posed supply and logistical problems for troops.

[13] Fiorato, "The Cherokee Mediation in Florida," 112; Moulton, *The Papers of Chief John Ross*, 1:546.

[14] Moulton, *The Papers of Chief John Ross*, 545–46.

[15] Jesse Bushyhead et al. to John Ross, 3 February 1838, in Payne Papers, 13:18.

Insects proved annoying and vectors for pathogens. Sawgrass and spongy soil destroyed shoe wear in short order. Moreover, some in Congress were critical of the operations. In December 1837, Jesup's forces numbered almost 9,000. Of these, there were 4,636 regular army plus volunteer units from Florida, Louisiana, Georgia, Alabama, Tennessee, Pennsylvania, New York, Missouri, and the District of Columbia. Indeed, over half of the enlisted men in the regular army were in Florida, meaning that few troops were available for service elsewhere. And the passing weeks had yielded little success as casualties and expenses rose. Against this backdrop, it is little wonder that Jesup objected to any interference from visiting Cherokees. On the other hand, the emissaries viewed Jesup as cool and obstinate.[16]

For almost the next six weeks, the messengers faced physical and mental challenges. This was especially true for Bushyhead and Major Polecat. More than the other emissaries, they endured hazardous travel in the Florida wilds. In the process, the two were often in genuine peril from hostile Seminoles as they engaged in tedious negotiations. Moreover, much of the discussions required the approval of Jesup. And from the beginning, the general mistrusted Ross and the emissaries. After reading the "talk" of Ross, Jesup felt that the Cherokee mediators meant to forge a new treaty. In this respect, he remained convinced that Ross was up to no good; that is, Ross simply intended to encourage the Seminoles to dawdle. And as long as the Seminoles thwarted relocation, it bought Ross time to delay Cherokee removal. Moreover, Jesup only wanted to enforce the existing Treaty of Payne's Landing. In order to prevent any alteration of the present agreement, he insisted that any communications with the Seminoles conform to his orders.[17] Furthermore, the general flatly

[16] John K. Mahon, *History of the Second Seminole War, 1835–1842*, rev. ed. (Gainesville: University of Florida, 1985) 190, 222–26.

[17] Charles L. Kieffer, *Maligned General: A Biography of Thomas S. Jesup* (San Rafael CA: Presidio, 1979) 192.

scorned the entire peace process as wasted effort and an endangerment of lives. Regarding the Seminole chiefs as liars, he feared for the safety of soldiers and settlers as long as Seminole hostility endured.

Jesup acted upon his fears. By the time the full delegation had arrived, troops were being positioned for offensive moves. Jesup thus hoped to "soon put an end to the War."[18] Nevertheless, possibly to satisfy Poinsett, Jesup allowed the emissaries to visit Seminole leaders Osceola, Coahajo, and Wild Cat, then imprisoned in Fort Marion at St. Augustine. Taking the road to St. Augustine, the mediators arrived later that evening where they reunited with Fields. The next day, 11 November, the mediators and Sherburne interviewed the chiefs.[19] Bushyhead reported meeting Osceola and described him as "a very mild, friendly and interesting man."[20]

It may have seemed odd that Osceola gave this benign impression, for previously he had demonstrated treachery toward United States authorities. After capture in 1835, Osceola had beguiled his keepers and gained freedom. Upon release, he had waged a bloody war. Wishing to curtail further attacks, the military acted to recapture the chief. Shortly before the mediators arrived, the government had seized Osceola and 100 other Seminoles under a flag of truce. This time, his captors did not intend to free Osceola and deemed any peaceful demeanor as another ploy designed to effect release. Accordingly, they did not slacken, and he did not regain his freedom. Yet Osceola shortly ceased to be a threat. When Bushyhead met Osceola, the chief had only a few weeks to live, for he died in captivity at Fort Marion on 31 January 1838.[21]

From the beginning of the talks, several developments complicated matters. Jesup persisted that any talks strictly adhere to the pro-

[18] Payne Papers, 2:19.

[19] Ibid.

[20] Jones to Corresponding Secretary, 22 December 1837, ABHS.

[21] Remini, *Andrew Jackson and His Indian Wars*, 274–76.

visions of the Treaty of Payne's Landing. So when preliminary talks began, the emissaries operated under constraints. In the first meetings, Major Polecat acted as spokesman. But the presence of two army officers seemed to cool open discussion. Sensing Seminole reluctance, Sherburne suggested the possibility of more direct communication with Seminoles still at large. Sherburne therefore questioned the chiefs concerning a visit to their council grounds. He wanted assurance regarding his personal safety and the security of the mediators. Wild Cat pledged that the mediators had nothing to fear. However, the guarantee carried stipulations. The army had to free some of the chiefs. This action would allow them to precede the emissaries and inform tribal leaders of their visit in advance. Yet, singling out Sherburne, Wild Cat stressed "very warmly" that the personal safety of the white emissary depended on the arrangement.[22] Taking Wild Cat's advice seriously, Bushyhead and Sherburne journeyed to Picolata to confer with Jesup. After a long meeting, Jesup still remained staunchly opposed to any negotiations outside the unconditional removal of the Seminoles.

Jesup, followed by Sherburne and Bushyhead, departed Picolata on 13 November and arrived back in St. Augustine later that day. That night, all of the mediators continued to pry at Jesup. Yet the general still appeared unmoved. Furthermore, Jesup warned the mediators that an unprotected visit to Seminole camps harbored danger. And should he free some of the prisoners, any Seminole appearing to act in concert with the government risked falling victim to hostile tribal members. Jesup had good reason to fear Seminole reprisals, for Seminoles regarded some of his acts as treacherous and insulting. Besides seizing Osceola and the other chiefs under a flag of truce, Jesup earlier had uttered humiliating remarks about Sam Jones, a respected chief. Jesup had called Jones a liar and refused to recognize him as

[22] Hair Conrad, Jesse Bushyhead, Thomas Woodward, and Major Polecat to John Ross, 3 February 1838, Payne Papers, 13:20.

chief. And in the event of capture, Jesup even threatened to have the warrior dressed in petticoats.[23]

Although Jesup remained unconvinced, there was a small breakthrough. The general responded after the emissaries once again urged reconsideration. The following day, Jesup allowed the mediators another interview with the prisoners. Although he kept Osceola under lock, the general liberated two others to serve as heralds. On 15 November, the two freed Seminoles left Fort Marion. They had ten days to contact the Seminole camps and report back to the mediators. The rendezvous was to occur at Fort Mellon, about ninety miles south of Fort Marion. Before the couriers left, Sherburne and the mediators provided the messengers with pipes and tobacco for the chiefs. In the meantime, the deputies planned to travel to Fort Mellon by boat.

On Saturday, 18 November, the mediators left St. Augustine and reached Picolata that evening. The following Tuesday, they departed for Fort Mellon on the steamboat *Poinsett*. Churning southward on the St. John's River, the voyage into the Florida wilds posed several dangers. Steamboat travel was hazardous and potentially deadly. Boiler explosions could scald passengers and crew. Submerged snags and low water often grounded vessels or penetrated hulls. And besides travel, there were other uncertainties. Soldiers remained in the field, and hostile Seminoles lurked in hiding. These circumstances threatened to spark hostilities and doom any negotiations. Before the day ended, the *Poinsett* ran aground. Passengers embarked on the *Cincinnati* the next day. The vessel reached the army camp at Volusia, where the mediators overtook Jesup. But while they remained there, the general took to the field in the company of troops. On Thursday, the mediators embarked on the *Forrester*. The vessel reached Fort Mellon the next day, six days after leaving St. Augustine.[24]

[23] Ibid., 13:21.
[24] Ibid., 13:22–23.

The team did not have to wait long to receive the two Seminole messengers. They arrived on the night of 25 November. The messengers brought word that Sam Jones and Mikanopy, the principal chief, intended to meet the emissaries at Foul Creek in four days. But the convening of any meeting hinged upon the lack of troops. Jesup arrived at Fort Mellon the following day and consulted with the mediators. The general remained adamant that talks served little purpose. He even threatened to refuse any order from the secretary of war if it meant negotiating another treaty. But he did furnish horses for the journey and released Coahajo, a confined Seminole, to serve as guide.[25]

On Tuesday, 28 November, the mediators and Coahajo rode out of the fort and turned their mounts toward the Seminole camps. As the riders continued, they realized the crucial value of time for Jesup had allowed six days for their return. And the deadline neared. Two days later, they reached the camp of Sam Jones after a ride of fifty miles. Mikanopy and Jones welcomed them and smoked the pipe of peace. For the next two days, Bushyhead and the others met several times with Seminole headmen and explained the "talk" of Ross. Mikanopy received the message favorably. In a gesture of goodwill, he offered to journey to Fort Mellon and discuss peace with Jesup. But on the day of anticipated departure, Jones balked, for by that time, Coahajo had related Jesup's "petticoats" slur to Jones. At this development, Mikanopy feigned illness and refused to travel. Because of his sullen attitude, the success of the entire peace process remained in the balance. It took all the diplomatic skills of the mediators to nudge Mikanopy into compliance. Finally, Mikanopy agreed. On Sunday night, 3 December, the delegation reached Fort Mellon, accompanied by a party of Seminoles. They included Mikanopy, twelve other

[25] Ibid., 13:23.

chiefs, several warriors, and some women.[26] Yet Jones was not among them.

Jesup immediately interviewed the mediators, more to gain military intelligence than for diplomatic progress. The following day, Bushyhead met with Jesup in private. Bushyhead counseled Jesup to tone down his vituperations against Jones. He reminded the general that it was in the best interest of the government for Jones to surrender and enter the fort. After all, chiefs and warriors still loyal to Jones remained at large. And without the cooperation of Jones, these combatants had no intention of surrender. On 5 December, Mikanopy requested another reading of the Ross message to the chiefs at the fort. After the reading, Mikanopy made a cunning proposal. As soon as the other chiefs and Jones entered the fort, the chiefs would select a Seminole delegation to journey to Washington. Following the confirmation of agreements there, they promised to return to Florida and prepare to lead their people west. Jesup regarded the offer as another attempt at delay. He nevertheless offered to negotiate with the chiefs, but demanded a sign of good faith. He ordered Jones, the warriors, chiefs, and families of the incarcerated Seminole chiefs to report at Fort Mellon. The terms required that they bring in their families and surrender weapons and white property. Of course, the plunder included fugitive African slaves, who had been accepted as tribal members. Furthermore, these conditions had to be met within seven to ten days. In order to expedite matters, Tarskeekee and another Seminole messenger set out from the fort to contact Jones and other outlying camps.[27]

The delicate negotiations pivoted on the cooperation of Jones. Realizing this, Sherburne reminded the Cherokee emissaries that,

[26] Ibid., 13:26; Frank L. White, Jr., "The Journals of Lieutenant John Pickell, 1836–1837," *The Florida Historical Quarterly* 38 (October 1959): 162.

[27] Hair Conrad, Jesse Bushyhead, Thomas Woodward, and Major Polecat to John Ross, 3 February 1838, Payne Papers, 13:27–28.

without Jones, the mission remained incomplete. Likewise, Jesup also pressed them to contact Jones a second time. Yet this was too much. The mediators refused, explaining that they had fulfilled their obligation. But feeling pressured, the delegation relented. Yet they did so under certain conditions. Jesup had to treat Jones respectfully and recognize him as a chief. If so, they offered to send Bushyhead and Major Polecat after Jones. Their selection of Bushyhead and Major Polecat revealed their confidence in the two. In such delicate negotiations, Bushyhead and Major Polecat possessed the credibility and linguistic skills necessary for success. In return, Jesup pledged his cooperation.

Bushyhead did not indicate a personal reluctance to return after Jones. But on the other hand, the trip posed risks. Jones no doubt had spent time brooding over Jesup's insults. Under these circumstances, a military guarantee of safety was not possible. In addition, another complication had developed. During the course of events, Wild Cat and seventeen Seminole warriors had escaped from Fort Marion. By the time Bushyhead and Major Polecat left Fort Mellon, Wild Cat already had reached Jones and sabotaged the mission of the two mediators. Wild Cat insisted that the Cherokees were part of a ruse. The real purpose of the talks had been to capture Jones, take him to Washington, and hang him. Clearly, the lives of Bushyhead and Major Polecat rested on the whims of Jones.

On 6 December, Bushyhead and Major Polecat set out for the camp of Jones. The next day, they arrived at the old council grounds, but Jones was not there. Fearing capture, Jones had retreated another eight or ten miles further into the wilds. When Bushyhead and Major Polecat finally reached the camp of Jones, they found a hostile environment. The chief, apparently unpleased, was under the watchful protection of armed warriors. When the two emissaries sat down to parley, Jones asked why they had bothered to come. He saw no purpose for additional meetings and scorned the demands of Jesup. Jones felt that it was unreasonable for warriors and chiefs to transport their families and property to a fort for talks. Bushyhead quickly countered. He assured Jones that Jesup had promised to receive Jones with respect. Furthermore, Bushyhead defended his second trip. He insisted that some other messenger from Jesup may have failed to tell all the truth. For this reason, Bushyhead had deemed it necessary to come in person. At this response, the son of Jones reacted. He stood ominously behind Bushyhead with gun in hand. Speaking directly to Bushyhead, the young warrior accused Bushyhead of deception. At that point, Tarskeekee interceded. He denied any duplicitous designs on the part of the Cherokees. Instead, he insisted that the mediators always had been truthful. After Tarskeekee spoke, Bushyhead and Major Polecat felt it best to leave the Seminoles to their deliberations. Alive but still in jeopardy, they returned to the old council grounds.[28]

Throughout 8 and 9 December, Bushyhead and Major Polecat remained at the old council grounds. While there, they consulted with visiting Seminoles and sent messages back to Jones. Bushyhead kept urging Jones and any other holdouts to report to Fort Mellon. Bushyhead furthermore offered to wait and accompany the Seminoles on their way to the fort. But the followers of Jones were little inclined to cooperate, even though stragglers continued to arrive at the camp. This made Bushyhead anxious. The deadline for Jones and his party to enter Fort Mellon had been set for 12 December, and Jesup surely grew impatient. As the hours passed, a peaceful solution seemed more unlikely, for if the Seminoles did not comply soon, they risked becoming targets of Jesup's renewed offensive. Under the circumstances, Bushyhead and Major Polecat had no choice but to depart. Before parting, Bushyhead gave a plaintive farewell to Jones. He implored the chief to cooperate; otherwise, responsibility for any bloodshed would rest with Jones. Bushyhead and Major Polecat then hastened in order to arrive at the fort on time. Riding for the fort on 11 December, Bushyhead encouraged Seminoles en route to enter the fort

[28] Ibid., 13:28–30.

as early as possible the next morning. Hopefully, their cooperation would influence Jesup to extend the deadline. Although some Seminoles did continue to trek toward the fort, most remained at large.[29]

On 12 December, a courier from Tarskeekee overtook Bushyhead and Major Polecat. The Seminole relayed word from Tarskeekee. The chief was still in the camp of Jones and wanted Jesup to know that he was not able to come in on the appointed day. He claimed illness and requested a horse. Otherwise, he was unable to travel afoot. If Jesup met these conditions, he promised to surrender as soon as possible. Bushyhead, Major Polecat, and the courier continued toward the fort and entered after sunset. Bushyhead promptly informed Jesup about the developments. Bushyhead urged Jesup to allow the Seminoles three more days to comply. Jesup consented. Knowing that the next seventy-two hours meant life or death for many Seminoles and soldiers, Bushyhead volunteered to return to the field that night in search of holdouts. Bushyhead, accompanied by Fields, Major Polecat, and the Seminole messenger, mounted their horses and galloped thirty miles before stopping to camp. The next morning, they continued their journey. By noon, they were within a mile or two of Tarskeekee. Bushyhead then learned disappointing news. The courier informed him that Jones had authorized him to mislead Jesup. Furthermore, Jones never had intended to surrender but only regarded Jesup's invitation as a ploy to imprison his people. The holdouts simply had been buying time. At this disclosure, Bushyhead, Major Polecat, and Fields turned back for Fort Mellon. They arrived on Thursday morning, 14 December.[30]

After reaching the fort, Bushyhead informed Jesup of the latest circumstances. This time Jesup did not wait. He immediately seized

[29] Ibid., 13:32; White, Jr., "The Journals of Lieutenant John Pickell, 1836–1837," 167.

[30] Payne Papers, 13:32; White, Jr., "The Journals of Lieutenant John Pickell, 1836–1837," 168.

the weapons of Seminoles at the fort and ordered their confinement. This included Mikanopy and over seventy men, women, and children. After securing his prisoners, Jesup began steps to renew offensive actions. Unfortunately, his undue haste toward cooperative Seminoles doomed any remaining hopes for mediation and nullified the promises of Bushyhead. In so doing, he also had imperiled future tribal relations between Cherokees and Seminoles. Wishing to save face, the mediators requested permission to visit the captives and distance themselves from any hint of treachery. Jesup refused. They then asked Jesup to convey their sentiments to the prisoners. Again, the general withheld permission. He only agreed to allow the delegation to visit the prisoners after the captives had been transported to St. Augustine.[31]

The frustrated mediators boarded the steamship *Camden* and reached St. Augustine on 17 December. They arrived in time to see Mikanopy and the other prisoners marched into the fort. The next day, the delegation met with the confined Seminoles and stressed their innocence from any collusion with Jesup. Moreover, the mediators promised to report the whole sorry affair to Ross. Hopefully, Ross would influence Poinsett to bring about some remedy for the prisoners. The incarcerated Seminoles accepted the apologies and promised to hold the Cherokees guiltless. Instead, they placed full blame on Jesup.[32]

The mediators and Sherburne left St. Augustine on 19 December. Their mission had not yielded the results for which Ross had hoped. So according to their instructions, the members prepared to return home. But before departing, Sherburne once again approached the Seminole chiefs. He enticed them with hopes of remaining in Florida. Yet the offer centered on three conditions: a cessation of hostilities, the surrender of runaway slaves to their American owners, and

[31] Payne Papers, 13:33.
[32] Ibid., 13:34.

agreement to defend southern Florida from foreign invaders. If they consented, the United States would grant them the southern half of Florida, essentially "from Tampa Bay to the eastern shore." The chiefs reacted in astonishment. After all, the right to remain had been their aim all along. For icing on the cake, Sherburne made an additional promise. Should Washington accept these conditions and offer a new treaty, Sherburne pledged to return to Florida and accompany them to Washington for the signing. In response, Osceola and each chief gave some form of assent.

When the mediators reached Savannah, Sherburne requested that they render additional services, for he still needed them to cement any forthcoming treaty. Moreover, the mediators had incurred considerable expenses, most chargeable to the government. In order to prevent the frowns of auditors, it remained in the best interest of Sherburne to redeem the failed mission. Sherburne therefore induced the delegates to travel directly to Washington instead of taking the road for home. At first, the mediators turned a deaf ear, for pressing personal concerns claimed their attention.[33] Spring planting approached, and their families needed them. And if a Cherokee exodus did occur, there was much to do in preparation. But Sherburne was persistent. Bushyhead later recorded that Sherburne "finally prevailed on us" with hints of additional pay.[34] Unfortunately, Sherburne did not specify an amount or present a contract concerning payment or expenses. This proved to be a costly mistake for the mediators. Accepting Sherburne at his word, they decided to accompany him to the capital. Instead of reuniting with their families for Christmas, the season caught them en route to Washington, where they arrived on 30 December.

After reaching the capital, they informed Ross about their failed mission. Indeed, the negotiations had garnered more harm than good

[33] Congress, *Memorial of the Cherokee Mediators*, 17.
[34] Payne Papers, 2:34.

for the Cherokee Nation. Although the mediators had been instrumental in the capture of Mikanopy, some government officials blamed them for treacherously stoking the fire of Seminole resistance. Disappointed at the results of the Ross emissaries, Washington tossed aside any Cherokee hopes for an adjustment of the New Echota Treaty. And instead of ending hostilities, the Seminole quagmire lasted for approximately five more years. Yet Ross defended the integrity of the mediators. He especially mentioned Bushyhead as a Cherokee preacher of "unblemished character," with "his bible in his pocket for his shield."[35] But some authorities at the Cherokee agency in Tennessee seemed not to hold that opinion. Rather, they distrusted the motives of Bushyhead. While in Washington, Bushyhead had written a letter to Stephen Foreman in Tennessee and informed him of developments.[36] But soldiers intercepted the message and delivered it to the commanding officer at the agency. Violating personal privacy, the commander "handed it round for all to read."[37]

The party remained in Washington for over three months, all along anticipating reimbursement. As they waited, their expenses mounted. Frustrated that the government took little interest in a new Seminole treaty, they appealed to Poinsett concerning remuneration. To their amazement, Poinsett denied any responsibility for expenses incurred in Washington. Before leaving Washington for home, each mediator submitted a request for reimbursement. Each one requested funds to defray the entire costs of the mission, including their time in Washington and their return to the Cherokee Nation. On 20 March 1838, Poinsett issued a statement of refusal. The secretary totally rejected any expenses of the delegates from Florida to Washington and back to the Cherokee Nation. Rather, he considered their visit to

[35] Moulton, *The Papers of Chief John Ross*, 1:587.

[36] Ibid., 1:588; Fiorato, "The Cherokee Mediation in Florida," 112–17.

[37] Jane Bushyhead to Martha Thompson, 10 March 1838, Cleveland Public Library, Cleveland, Tennessee, photocopy.

Washington as "unauthorized" and "unnecessary."[38] Poinsett even refused to consider Sherburne's suggested $5 per diem for the time in Florida. Bushyhead's request totaled $1,079.69 for 157 days of service. This figure included a per diem while in transit to Florida and during the time there. Other expenses included the stay in Washington and an estimate of the charges incurred in returning to the Cherokee Nation. The mediators reminded Poinsett of Sherburne's promises. But Sherburne remained silent, and Poinsett refused to reconsider. In a mood of frustration, the team directed a message to Congress. The communique recalled their services in Florida and Sherburne's enticements. They concluded with an angry accusation, charging that Sherburne had "exceeded his authority" and "ought to meet the consequences."[39] In the end, Poinsett only approved a pittance for the entire delegation. Bushyhead received a scant $13 reimbursement. This amount included only horse hire and stage tickets from Bushyhead's home to Augusta and additional charges for medicine and barber bills.[40]

Running short on funds, the emissaries had little choice but to set out for Tennessee. It was not an easy trip. By the time they reached Campbell's Station near Knoxville, they no longer possessed stage fare. Afoot, they trod between fifteen to twenty miles to Blair's Ferry, a steamboat landing on the Little Tennessee River. From there, they obtained mounts and rode to the agency. After being in the saddle for at least forty miles, they arrived on the night of 4 April 1838. In spite of the tumultuous events, Bushyhead's sojourn in Washington yielded one positive result. At some point, either in 1836 or 1838, he had sat for a portrait. This is the only existing likeness of Bushyhead. But he almost failed to return to Tennessee with the painting. While traveling through Virginia, the portrait bounced off

[38] Congress, *Memorial of the Cherokee Mediators*, 14.
[39] Ibid., 4.
[40] Ibid., 21.

the stage. Fortunately, Lewis Hildebrand, a brother-in-law of Bushyhead, also was returning from Washington on a separate stage. Hildebrand retrieved the painting and delivered it to Bushyhead in Tennessee.[41]

The Seminole mission had been costly for Bushyhead. It had exposed him to personal peril and removed him from family for over five months. Yet he had remained in contact with family and close friends through mail. He had sent at least three letters to Tennessee, one to Evan Jones, another to Stephen Foreman, and one to his daughter.[42] But the condition of Eliza and the household must have been of particular interest. Shortly before or after his departure, his youngest son had fallen into a fire and received fatal burns. The child agonized until his death in January 1838. Away in Florida, Jesse was not at home to console Eliza. But even after his return, Bushyhead had little time to grieve. Under the terms of the New Echota Treaty, the United States Senate had allowed Cherokees two years to prepare for emigration. Accordingly, departures were to begin the latter part of May 1838.[43] This gave Bushyhead only weeks before the initial deadline. Although events temporarily delayed the exodus, much preparation remained. In October 1838, within seven months of his return, Bushyhead and his family said goodbye to home and the graves of loved ones. They turned to new challenges beyond the Mississippi. The last four years had been critical for Bushyhead. His linguistic skills and esteem among Cherokees and some whites had rendered him crucial to negotiations and tribal leadership. It also burdened him with the responsibility of conducting approximately 1,000 emigrants on an arduous journey west.

[41] Moulton, *The Papers of Chief John Ross*, 1:625.

[42] Jane Bushyhead to Martha Thompson, 10 March 1838; *Baptist Missionary Magazine* 18 (February 1838): 41; Fiorato, "The Cherokee Mediation in Florida," 112–17.

[43] Perdue and Green, *The Cherokee Nation and the Trail of Tears*, 113.

CHAPTER 5

The Trail West

During April 1838, removal seemed more unavoidable even though the Van Buren administration briefly considered delaying departure until May 1840. This possibility briefly offered Cherokees hope for more favorable terms. But Georgia governor George Gilmer refused to agree with the proposed postponement. Instead, Gilmer threatened to use force if United States troops interfered with attempts of Georgia citizens to seize Cherokee lands.[1] Furthermore, Gilmer sent militia to expel Cherokees from the state. Challenged with this development, Van Buren reconsidered and proceeded with an 1838 target date.

On 17 May, Major General Winfield Scott published Order 25. Headquartered at the Cherokee agency, Scott was the overall commander in charge of removal. The directive ordered troops to bring in Cherokees in preparation for final removal. Wishing to defuse resistance, Scott urged humane treatment and discouraged violence. The instructions directed soldiers to escort Cherokee families and their slaves to assembly camps. Families could remain together, but the able-bodied had to walk. Some Cherokees used their horses and wagons to transport possessions as well as the aged and infirm. But poorer families, lacking means of transport, took very little property, usually only bedding and light cooking vessels. From assembly camps, emigrants traveled to three river port embarkation sites. The ports

[1] Charles C. Royce, *The Cherokee Nation of Indians* (Chicago: Aldine Publishing, 1975) 168.

were Ross's Landing, Gunter's Landing in Alabama, and the Cherokee agency. Sometime around the latter part of May 1838, Bushyhead and his family assembled at Camp Hetzel, only a short distance from his home. Living near the camps and having some degree of wealth, emigrants such as the Bushyheads came in on their own. These families usually owned wagons and had a few days to gather possessions. Yet the government had initiated procedures for property left behind. Scott charged government claims agents with the task of inventorying abandoned property. Agents bore responsibility for collecting movable possessions and delivering them to owners before the final departure. Recompense for any unmovable property was to occur at an undetermined future date. Bushyhead served as one of the claims agents.

A week after publishing Order 25, Scott issued Order 34. This command scheduled the roundup process to being on 26 May in Georgia and ten days later in North Carolina, Tennessee, and Alabama. After Cherokees assembled at the embarkation points, Scott planned to have them transported virtually the entire distance via steamboat. The anticipated river routes wound up the Tennessee to the confluence of the Ohio, and then downstream to the Mississippi. From the junction with the Mississippi, the course continued south to where the Mississippi met the Arkansas. The final leg of the route was northwest on the Arkansas until reaching disembarkation sites.[2]

Scott planned for removal to occur in a timely and orderly manner. Yet weather, Cherokee resistance, and in some cases an overzealous military proved otherwise. By summer, militia and regular troops, with twelve to fourteen pieces of artillery, had moved against holdouts

[2] Orders. No. 25 Headquarters, Eastern Division. Cherokee Agency, Ten. May 17, 1838, Correspondence of the Eastern Division Pertaining to Cherokee Removal April–December 1838, National Archives, M1475, roll 2; *Baptist Missionary Magazine* 19 (July 1839): 178; Controversy over Horse, 4 September 1838, correspondence of the Eastern Division pertaining to Cherokee Removal April–December 1838, National Archives, M1475, roll 2.

in northern Georgia.[3] Soldiers surrounded homes without warning. Residents had little time to gather belongings and entered holding camps with little more than the clothes on their backs. And once they arrived in camps, an overly warm summer and close confinement compounded their misery. By 16 June, Evan Jones reported that Bushyhead and his family, Stephen Foreman, "and several men of character and respectability, with their families" remained in close quarters at Camp Hetzel.[4] Moreover, a lack of rainfall had made river and overland travel difficult. Scott later testified that the levels of water in the Hiwassee and Tennessee Rivers had made them virtually impassable. The Arkansas River also was low. And the dry weather posed difficulties for overland travel. In an official report, Scott recorded that "the land routes, in great part, had become sickly, with a scarcity of good drinking water."[5]

In light of these challenges, plans for removal soon changed. On 9 and 11 June, prominent Cherokees, including Bushyhead, presented Scott with two requests. They sought to delay roundups and reschedule departure until autumn. On 19 June, Scott agreed to a conditional postponement until 1 September but refused to suspend the forced assemblage of Cherokees. In a letter to tribal leaders, including Bushyhead, he mandated that postponement had to meet certain requirements. First, leaders must not foster hopes of delay beyond 1 September. Second, any detainee leaving camp for personal business had to have special permission from a military commander or the su-

[3] William Thompson to Elias Boudinot, 14 July 1838, E. C. Boudinot Papers, box 1, OHSL.

[4] *Baptist Missionary Magazine* 18 (September 1838): 237.

[5] Congress, Committee on Indian Affairs, House Report 1098, *Removal of the Cherokees West of the Mississippi*, report prepared by William Alexander Harris, 27th Cong., 2nd sess., 27 (LexisNexis Academic, 2006) Serial Set ID: 411 H.rp. 1098; Also see Ehle, *Trail of Tears*, 324–28, 339–42; Thurman Wilkins, *Cherokee Tragedy: The Ridge Family and the Decimation of a People,* 2nd ed., rev. (Norman: University of Oklahoma, 1986) 319–20.

perintendent of Cherokee emigration. Also, Cherokee authorities had to keep good order in the camps and prevent drunkenness. Finally, their cooperation was mandatory in obtaining an "exact list" of "names, families, ages, and sexes" of emigrants.[6] The same day, twenty-five prominent Cherokees, including Bushyhead and Thomas and Stephen Foreman, signed a letter to Scott. They acknowledged, "We have, Sir, the honor to be your friends." Moreover, they agreed to "respectfully accept those conditions."[7]

On 23 July, John Ross and seven other Cherokee leaders presented another request to Scott. In keeping with the War Department's instructions to Ross, they asked "that the Cherokee nation will undertake the whole business of removing their people to the west of the river Mississippi."[8] On 13 July, Ross had returned from Washington. In his negotiations with the War Department, Ross had gained the right, subject to approval by Scott, to serve as superintendent for removal.[9] In this capacity, Ross and the Cherokee leadership assumed responsibility for leasing wagons, draft animals, teamsters, and supplies. This development proved mutually beneficial, for it removed much of the burden from military and government authorities. It also allowed Cherokees to receive payment for services and the use of personal animals and wagons. On 25 July, Scott agreed but with certain stipulations. First, chiefs and leaders pledged to honor the promises made to Scott on 19 June. Second, Cherokee "functionaries shall send intelligent Indian runners" to encourage recalcitrant Cherokees to report to holding camps. And finally, departure of all Cherokees and

[6] George Lowrey and others to Major General Scott, 9 June 1838, Correspondence of the Eastern Division Pertaining to Cherokee Removal April–December 1838, National Archives, M1475, roll 1; Congress, *Removal of the Cherokees West of the Mississippi*, 5–6.

[7] Cherokee Leaders to General Scott, 19 June 1838, Letters Received by the Office of Indian Affairs, 1824–1881, National Archives, M234, roll 115.

[8] Congress, *Removal of the Cherokees West of the Mississippi*, 4.

[9] Ehle, *Trail of Tears*, 345–48.

fugitive Creeks among them had to begin in "convenient" detachments at three-day intervals on 1 September.[10] This being done, plans called for all detachments to be en route by an unspecified time in October.[11]

On 26 July, the Cherokee National Committee and Council met at the Aquohee camp and agreed to Scott's provisions. As clerk of the council, Bushyhead recorded the proceedings. The Cherokee legislature empowered a committee composed of John Ross, Richard Taylor, Samuel Gunter, Edward Gunter, James Brown, Elijah Hicks, Situakee, and White Path to appoint persons "as they may deem necessary to aid and assist in the said removal."[12] Under this arrangement, virtually every committee-appointed detachment leader had held a position in the legislature or the committee responsible for appointments. The Ross brothers, John and Lewis, stood to profit greatly as administrators. John was the principal supervisor and Lewis served as overall contracting agent.[13] Assistant detachment leaders and support personnel were Cherokees or respected whites. Detachment leaders officially assumed their duties at different dates, extending from 28 August through September.[14]

Yet postponement did little to improve conditions in the camps. On 1 July, Captain John Page, principal distributing agent for Cherokee removals, reported that 11, 674 detainees had entered holding camps.[15] The logistics of providing clothing, rations, and medical care

[10] Congress, *Removal of the Cherokees West of the Mississippi*, 5.

[11] *Arkansas Intelligencer*, 17 June 1843.

[12] Winfield Scott to Joel R. Poinsett, 10 July 1838, transcribed copy dated 28 July 1838, Letters Received by the Office of Indian Affairs, 1824–1881, National Archives, M234, roll 115.

[13] Perdue and Green, *The Cherokee Nation and the Trail of Tears*, 130.

[14] Removal Account Book, folder 913, Gilcrease Museum; *Baptist Missionary Magazine* 19 (June 1839): 129.

[15] John Page to Lt. R. Andersen, 1 July 1838, Correspondence of the Eastern Division Pertaining to Cherokee Removal April–December 1838, National Archives, M1475, roll 1.

for the population of the camps grew increasingly problematic. However, evidence indicates that efforts to ameliorate the trauma of dislocation did occur. Although he continued vociferously to oppose removal, Evan Jones credited camp military commanders with treating detainees "with great respect and indulgence."[16] General Nathaniel Smith, the federal superintendent of removal, allowed some detainees to return to their homes in order to dispose of property. And on occasions, Smith acted to investigate when unlawful seizures of property occurred.[17] But soon poor sanitation and close quarters resulted in disease, disorder, and deaths. Elizur Butler had remained among the Cherokees and described the sickness at the Red Clay camp: "The dysentery prevailed at the council ground to an alarming degree. Of about two thousand Cherokees encamped there, seventeen died in one week. The complaint was of a very putrid character. In one instance a corpse became very offensive in eleven hours after death."[18] Moreover, white whiskey peddlers added to the potential for degradation, violence, murder, gambling, and debauchery. On the evening of 4 October, missionary Butrick, visiting from Candy's Creek, recalled the "constant yell of drunkards" going to and from a whiskey shop "set up by a white man."[19]

In the midst of these difficulties, Bushyhead and white missionaries continued evangelism and provided spiritual solace. At some point before 16 May, Bushyhead had baptized forty-seven converts on a preaching tour. On Sunday, 10 June, Bushyhead interpreted while Butler preached to a large crowd at Red Clay. Aware of the numerous listeners, Butler chose his text from Matthew 25:32: "And before him shall be gathered all nations." The message provoked a tearful emotional release as Butler admonished the faithful to minister

[16] *Baptist Missionary Magazine* 18 (September 1838): 237.

[17] Chase, "Cherokee Removal Records," *Cherokee Tracer* 10 (Summer 2000): 71–72.

[18] Elizur Butler to David Greene, 12 July 1838, ABCFM 18.3.1, vol. 10.

[19] Daniel S. Butrick Journal, 4 October 1838, ABCFM 18.3.3, vol. 4.

to the hungry, sick, and suffering.[20] As the summer progressed, Evan Jones reported on the ministry of Bushyhead in the midst of the upheavals. Jones mentioned that a "glorious revival" occurred throughout the camps and resulted in 170 baptisms.[21]

For the next several weeks, Bushyhead combined ministerial and official duties. On 21 June, Scott requested that Bushyhead travel to North Carolina in order to induce holdouts to comply with removal. Scott placed great faith in Bushyhead, whom he regarded as "a Cherokee of great influence."[22] The General specifically wanted Bushyhead to persuade Hog, a leader of a Cherokee band, to bring in his followers. Scott reported that Bushyhead firmly believed "it is best, under all the circumstances, for the remaining Cherokees in the mountains and other hiding places to come in at once."[23] Scott instructed Bushyhead to report to Brigadier Abraham Eustis at Fort Butler, near the confluence of the Hiwassee and Valley Rivers. And Scott even allowed Jones, still under military interdiction, to accompany Bushyhead. After reaching the fort, their instructions ordered them to inform Eustis of their mission. Knowing that further resistance was futile, the two accepted the assignment.

On their journey, they encountered a detachment of several hundred Cherokees under military escort. The column was on the way to assembly camps. Jones and Bushyhead recognized a number of converts from Valley Towns. In passing, the two ministers took the opportunity to console the uprooted. Arriving at Fort Butler, Bushyhead successfully induced Hog to bring in his people. Yet, in doing so, Bushyhead risked his personal reputation and the standing

[20] *Baptist Missionary Magazine* 19 (June 1839): 128; Elizur Butler to David Greene, 15 June 1838, ABCFM 18.3.1, vol. 10.

[21] *The Baptist* (4 November 1838): 358.

[22] Winfield Scott to Brigadier General [Abraham] Eustis, 21 June 1838, Letters Received by the Office of Indian Affairs, 1824–1881, National Archives, M234, roll 115.

[23] Ibid.

of Hog in the eyes of his band. For approximately four months later on the trail west, Hog brought Bushyhead woe when conditions became intolerable. While near the fort, Jones and Bushyhead held services and supervised the baptism of three Cherokee females. Yet, while at Camp Hetzel, some remained aware of Bushyhead's absence and grew anxious concerning his return. His many duties threatened to separate him from his family should the detachments begin moving in his absence. Fearing this possibility, fifty detainees petitioned Scott to delay their removal until Bushyhead returned. The signatories included Going Snake, speaker of the National Council, and Bushyhead's father.[24]

After returning in July, Bushyhead's days became more harried. Bushyhead and Roman Nose had been selected respectively as chief and assistant conductors. The two had garnered the respect of the mountain Cherokees, which composed some of their detachment. Yet the illiterate Roman Nose was not able to transact documents. So J. Powell, the detachment's white physician, acted as Bushyhead's unofficial assistant.[25] The official duties of Bushyhead as conductor began on 3 September. His responsibilities included the enrollment of detachment members and procurement of wagons, oxen, and supplies. Moreover, he continued to assess property claims. Because Cherokees hoped to receive payment before departure, the settlement of claims remained pressing. Yet Bushyhead continued to reserve time for ministry. On Sunday, 26 August, Bushyhead and Jones baptized fifty-six believers, including one white woman.[26] The next day, Bushyhead approved the claim of Sam Smith for a mare and colt stolen from

[24] Ibid. *The Baptist Missionary Magazine* 18 (September 1838): 238; Memorial of Camp Hetzel Cherokees to Commanding General [Scott], 5 July 1838, Correspondence of the Eastern Division Pertaining to Cherokee Removal April–December 1838, National Archives, M1475, roll 1.

[25] Records do not fully identify Powell and only refer to him as "J. Powell."

[26] *Baptist Missionary Magazine* 18 (November 1838): 292.

Smith about ten years before. And eight days later, Bushyhead helped adjudicate the contested ownership of a horse won in a card game.[27]

As August waned, Scott's deadline neared. On 1 September, Bushyhead notified John Ross that his detachment would "receive Wagons" on Monday, 3 September.[28] But circumstances did not unfold smoothly. The oppressive drought endured. And as September progressed, most detachments still had not taken to the road. Scott became frustrated over the lack of progress. He anticipated that each detachment would contain an average of 1,000 emigrants. Yet detachments had been slow in forming. By mid-September, emigrants were still entering camps. Butrick reported a tragedy concerning a traumatized member of Bushyhead's detachment. On the way to join the party, the emigrant was not able to continue. Reclining at the foot of a tree, he placed the muzzle of his musket to his head and took his own life.[29]

Yet, as September grew to an end, all detachments still remained in camp. Scott assumed that cooler weather and fall rains would facilitate departures. At least 4,000 emigrants had enrolled in detachments, and they only waited for the order to begin the exodus. In light of these developments, Scott grew impatient with Ross and his continued excuses. Ross assured Scott that "the great anxiety" of the emigrants coupled with "the many embarrassments arising from sickness and other intermeddling influences" had slowed departure.[30] Then, there were the concerns of emigrants related to the ordeal of

[27] Marybelle W. Chase, trans., "1838 Cherokee Claims," *Cherokee Tracer* 9 (Spring 1999): 40; Controversy over Horse, 4 September 1838, Correspondence of the Eastern Division Pertaining to Cherokee Removal April–December 1838, National Archives, M1475, roll 2.

[28] Moulton, *The Papers of Chief John Ross*, 1:667; Cherokee Contingents, Sequoyah Center, box 1, file 21, doc. 1.

[29] Butrick Journal, 21 September 1838.

[30] John Ross to Winfield Scott, 2 October 1838, Sequoyah Center, box 276, file 32.

relocation and lack of payment for outstanding property claims. But this did not placate Scott. On 3 October, he penned a critical letter to Ross. Justifying his growing impatience, Scott pointed to Bushyhead as an example for readiness. The general mentioned that "Mr. Bushyhead is anxious to march."[31]

On Friday, 5 October, two days after Scott wrote to Ross, the Bushyhead train lumbered out of camp. It was the third of twelve overland-bound detachments to depart.[32] Approximately 900 emigrants, 150 loose horses, draft animals for each wagon, and 46 wagons composed the party. The official muster roll listed fifteen in the Bushyhead household: Bushyhead, his wife, four males, four females, and five slaves. Bushyhead's wife was approximately six months pregnant at the time of departure. Other family members included Isaac and the elder Bushyhead. Isaac, having returned from Indian Territory, furnished a wagon and drove a team. Some close neighbors of Bushyhead from Mouse Creek also traveled with the train. Bushyhead also recorded "sixty-six members of the church in the Baptist connection in the detachment," including ministerial associates Beaver Carrier and Oganaya. Others such as Hair Conrad and Major Polecat would help establish the future Cherokee Nation in the West.[33] The detachment also included three of Bushyhead's personal wagons. Only seven other emigrants in the train owned wagons. Twenty wagons, the largest number in the wagon train, belonged to

[31] Moulton, *The Papers of Chief John Ross*, 1:676–77.

[32] The thirteenth detachment under John Drew traveled via steamboat.

[33] Moulton, *The Papers of Chief John Ross*, 1:683; Muster Roll of Cherokee Indians to Emigrate West of the Mississippi, National Archives, Microfilm A-42. Detachment members included Doublehead, Roman Nose, James Hair, Beaver Toter (also listed as Beaver Carrier), James Bigby, Jr., Thomas Foreman, Foster, and Oganaya. See Removal Account Book; *The Baptist* 4 (November 1838): 358; *Baptist Missionary Magazine* 19 (July 1839): 178.

Jesse Mayfield. Those without wagons either had sold them to provide funds for the trip or were too poor to own one.[34]

From the Cherokee agency, detachments headed west to Blythe's Ferry on the east side of the Tennessee River. Based on the course taken by the detachment under B. B. Cannon in 1837, the route lay across the mountains and northwest to Nashville. From Nashville, the road cut to Hopkinsville, Kentucky, and on to Golconda, Illinois. From Golconda, it turned west across the tip of Illinois to Jonesboro, just across the Mississippi River from Cape Girardeau, Missouri. Crossing the Mississippi, the route continued west to Springfield, Missouri, where it angled to the southwest and into northwestern Arkansas. The last settlement on the journey was the small Arkansas settlement of Cane Hill, approximately twelve miles from the eastern boundary of the Cherokee Nation West.[35] Filled with Cherokees and their possessions, wagons creaked, whips cracked, and oxen bellowed and strained under loads. No doubt infants and small children wailed, and the elderly and infirmed pondered when death would overtake them.

In many ways, each detachment resembled a mobile community. Small units of United States dragoon accompanied the detachments, but they mostly served to discourage straggling and preserve order.[36] The leadership of each detachment was responsible for self-

[34] The official report of John Ross at the end of the journey indicated a total of forty-eight wagons instead of forty-six in the train. But Bushyhead acquired one of the extra two shortly after departure. The remaining wagon may have been supplied by the government or also acquired along the route. And it is possible that Ross made a mistake in tallying the numbers. John Ross Papers, folder 485, Gilcrease Museum; Removal Account Book.

[35] B. B. Cannon Journal, 1837, Western Historical Manuscript Collection, Ellis Library, University of Missouri-Columbia; Muster Roll of Cherokee Indians to Emigrate West of the Mississippi, National Archives, Microfilm A-42.

[36] Henry William Perrin, ed., *County of Christian, Kentucky* (Chicago and Louisville: F. A. Battey Publishing, 1884; rep., Easley SC: Southern Historical Press, 1979) 37 (page reference is to reprint edition).

governance, security, route planning, and conveyance. Because arms often had been surrendered, there were only a few rifles in each detachment, perhaps a dozen or less. But each detachment contained an official Cherokee security force known as regulators. Most likely, the regulators possessed these weapons. When the detachment left, at least twenty-four men served in paid positions. Besides the regulators, other paid personnel included conductors, assistant conductors, physicians, assistant physicians, wagon masters, assistant wagon masters, commissary agents, teamsters, and interpreters.[37] Situakee, a mountain headman and close friend of Evan Jones, conducted the fourth detachment, composed of residents from the Valley Towns vicinity. Because Situakee was illiterate, Evan Jones served as assistant conductor. This placed much of the planning and paperwork on Jones.[38] Approximately 2,200 emigrants traveled in the third and fourth detachments. In addition to Baptists, the detachments included members of Congregationalist-Presbyterian missions.[39]

Although the Bushyhead detachment was among the first to get on the road, morale and logistical problems soon appeared. The train did not go far before it halted. Sometime before Thursday, 11 October, the column camped for several days about six miles east of Blythe's Ferry. Uncertainty about government funding concerned them, for John Ross still had not received the $264,960 requisitioned from Scott nine days before. Emigrants remained in camp until the arrival of Lewis Ross, the general contracting agent, and Captain

[37] H. S. Scott to Winfield Scott, 11 October 1838, Letters Received by the Office of Indian Affairs, 1824–1881, National Archives, M234, roll 115.

[38] McLoughlin, *Champions of the Cherokees*, 181.

[39] *Baptist Missionary Magazine* 19 (July 1839): 179. Evan Jones wrote that about "500 members of the churches were embodied in two of the detachments." See *Baptist Missionary Magazine* 19 (June 1839): 127. A Nashville paper reported 500 Baptists in the two detachments. In light of the total numbers of Baptists in the Bushyhead detachment, this figure seems exaggerated. *The Baptist* 4 (November 1838): 357; S. A. Worchester to David Greene, 19 March 1839, ABCFM 18.3.1, vol. 10.

Page with news about rations. On 15 October, Scott approved the request, making funds available for rations and supplies.[40] And early on Monday, 15 October, the detachment rumbled into Blythe's Ferry. Emigrants drew their first rations the next day.[41] But because local citizens imposed hindrances, progress again slowed. Powell blamed townsmen for purposely wanting to keep the detachments near town as long as possible. If this occurred, merchants and whiskey runners stood to reap more profits. Also, ferry owners proved uncooperative. By 10 A.M. on Tuesday, only twenty wagons had been ferried across the river. A frustrated Powell estimated that the remaining wagons would not cross until sometime the following day. Convinced of the necessity of another personal transport, on 18 October, Bushyhead acquired his fourth wagon and spent the rest of the journey driving its team.[42]

Leaving Blythe's Ferry, the detachment passed near modern Dayton and almost immediately began the arduous ascent of Walden's Ridge. The terrain and problems with morale posed serious challenges to Bushyhead over the next several days. The climb was some of the most difficult terrain of the entire trip. According to Butrick, the ridge was "a steep mountain about one mile & half from the bottom to the top."[43] This seemed to be an estimate of the actual altitude, but the distance of the linear incline was more. The route of the modern highway stretches nearly ten miles. Descending the ridge, the wagons jostled for ten miles until they reached the Sequatchie Valley at the foot of the Cumberland Mountains. The crossing challenged oxen and emigrants, for the rugged ground required double-

[40] John Ross Receipt of Funds, 16 October 1838, National Archives Document copy at Sequoyah Center, box 276, file 32.

[41] Abstract of Provisions issued to a detachment of Cherokee Emigrants, Jesse Bushyhead, Conductor, John Ross Papers, folder 518, Gilcrease Museum.

[42] Removal Account Book.

[43] Butrick Journal, 5 November 1838. The linear distance along modern Tennessee State Highway 30 to the crest is close to ten miles.

teaming the wagons and slowed progress. This necessity reduced the number of wagons available for transport. Then, there were the aged and infirmed. On 21 October, the detachment rested in the Sequatchie Valley. While camped, wagon masters made repairs on their wagons. While in camp, Bushyhead took the opportunity to send a message to Ross. He requested permission to purchase an additional wagon for "the exclusive purpose of conveying the very old and infirm."[44]

Yet there were other problems. The detachment was moving farther from home, and concerns remained about the lack of payment for property. Moreover, the distribution of provisions proved difficult. Based on the journey of the Cannon party, detachments expected to draw rations at frequent intervals and at determined distribution points. Averaging approximately fifteen miles each day, the Cannon party had journeyed approximately ten weeks before reaching its final destination.[45] The government had solicited bids for soap, teams of oxen, packhorses and fodder, and rations in advance.[46] Rations consisted of "one pound of fresh beef or three fourths of a pound of salt pork, or bacon, & three fourths of a quart of corn or corn meal, or one pound of flour to each person, and four quarts of salt to every one hundred rations."[47] Furthermore, requirements ordered contractors to deliver "good and wholesome" supplies "at such times, and places, and in such quantities" as directed by the conductors.[48]

Yet plans for supply often proved impractical and delays frequently occurred. Instead of receiving rations almost daily, Bushyhead's column received rations only every three to five days, for

[44] Moulton, *The Papers of Chief John Ross*, 1:683, 685.

[45] B. B. Cannon Journal, 1837.

[46] Congress, House Committee on Indian Affairs, House Document 288, *Removal of Cherokees*, report prepared by James Cooper, 27th Cong., 3rd sess., 57–69 (LexisNexis Academic, 2006) Serial Set ID: 429 H.doc. 288.

[47] *Hamilton* (TN) *Gazette*, 26 July 1838.

[48] Ibid.

the slow pace interfered with more timely arrivals at supply points.[49] This forced conductors to send wagons ahead and haul supplies back to camps. In turn, this required some teamsters to unload personal possessions in order to free up space for supplies. The resultant unloading and loading of wagons became onerous and consumed valuable time. In his letter of 21 October requesting another wagon for the aged, Bushyhead also expressed his frustration with supply agents. The next supply point was McMinnville, at least a two-day journey away. In light of this difficulty, Bushyhead candidly confessed that "a difficulty has occurred between the Agent of the contractors and myself upon this subject."[50] Bushyhead did not mince words. He lamented that "the detachment cannot progress under such circumstances."[51] Instead, he proposed a more efficient means of distributing supplies; that is, contractors should transport rations to campsites and not necessarily depots. But his message also revealed even a more serious challenge concerning detachment morale. Hog and some of the mountain Cherokees were stirring discontent. Bushyhead felt that Ross needed to address the supply issue in order to prop up sagging morale among Hog's band.[52]

On Friday, 26 October, the Situakee detachment rumbled past the Bushyhead party. Jones, still an assistant conductor, found the Bushyhead party resting in camp by a small stream a short distance east of McMinnville. When Jones encountered Bushyhead, he quickly discovered that all was not well. Bushyhead faced serious problems with livestock and personnel. According to Bushyhead, some of the oxen had become unfit for yokes as a result of eating poison ivy. Bushyhead promised to renew his march the following Monday. At least Bushyhead offered that explanation. But bearing daily responsi-

[49] Abstract of Provisions issued to a detachment of Cherokee Emigrants, Jesse Bushyhead, Conductor.

[50] Moulton, *The Papers of Chief John Ross*, 1:683.

[51] Ibid.

[52] Ibid.

bility for the train had become a heavy weight. Even more serious concerns surrounded desertions. Some of the North Carolina Cherokees increasingly resisted going any further. Only three days before, about fifty persons under Chunalusky had abandoned the detachment. Chunalusky's band set out to return to North Carolina via Knoxville. Yet their effort was unsuccessful, for at some point they fell into the hands of the United States military. Instead of viewing the mountains of North Carolina, Chunalusky wound up staring at the inside of the agency guard house back at Charleston.[53] Although thwarted in the attempt, Chunalusky's actions prompted questions about the failure of Bushyhead to stop the deserters. At some time between Chunalusky's departure and the camp outside of McMinnville, Lieutenant H. S. Scott probed Bushyhead. But Bushyhead had little to say. He stoically replied that it was not his responsibility to coerce deserters into remaining.[54]

Also, Hog continued to burden Bushyhead. In view of the recent desertions and Hog's influence over the North Carolina Cherokees, more desertions, if not mutiny, seemed possible. As mentioned earlier, Bushyhead and Jones had been involved in encouraging mountain Cherokees to surrender. But Hog's band increasingly complained, for the government still had failed to provide promised recompense for lost property. On 26 October, Jones noted that Bushyhead "has had a distressing time with the dis tents [*sic*]. Old Hog is a dead weight on his hands."[55] On the same day, Powell and Bushyhead sent a letter of protest to Ross concerning the failure of the government to recompense Cherokees for lost property. According to the letter, most Cherokees in Bushyhead's column had not re-

[53] Muster Abstract of Rolls of Emigrating Cherokees, Correspondence of the Eastern Division Pertaining to Cherokee Removal April–December 1838, National Archives, M1475, roll 2.

[54] Lt. H. S. Scott to Winfield Scott, 26 October 1838, Letters Received by the Office of Indian Affairs, 1824–1881, National Archives, M234, roll 115.

[55] Moulton, *The Papers of Chief John Ross*, 1:686.

ceived payment or "guarantee for getting their just dues" from the government.[56] And even if claimants received some payment, the government afforded little guarantees for fair settlements. Being absent from their homes, Cherokees had no power to prevent whites from defrauding them out of property. And by this time, some of the detachment members had become destitute. A document in the John Ross Papers includes a list of thirty-two impoverished Valley River emigrants. Some of these had become so desperate that Ross authorities had to advance payment on their prospective claims.[57] Meeting in council, members of the detachment demanded that any ongoing actions by claims commissioners in their old homelands immediately halt. Instead, emigrants preferred to transfer the account books to the new Cherokee settlement in Indian Territory and settle affairs there.

Ten days after leaving McMinnville, the Bushyhead party reached Nashville. While the detachment encamped outside the city, a letter from Ross reached General Scott. Word of the desertions apparently had disturbed the general. In his response, Ross allayed any concerns and reported good order in the Bushyhead detachment. Bushyhead's protests over supply distributions also had prompted a positive response. William Shorey Coodey, a contractor and nephew of John Ross, reassured Bushyhead on 27 October. Coodey promised that blankets and shoes waited for the detachment in Nashville.[58] In light of this upturn, Ross informed Scott that Bushyhead expected to "proceed without delay."[59]

[56] Ibid., 1:685.

[57] The List of Names from Valley River N. Carolina, Hog's Party, John Ross Papers, folder 481, Gilcrease Museum.

[58] Evan Jones to John Ross, 27 October 1838: Moulton, *The Papers of Chief John Ross*, 1:686.

[59] John Ross to W[infield] Scott, 12 November 1838, Correspondence of the Eastern Division Pertaining to Cherokee Removal April–December 1838, M1475, roll 2.

Besides drawing supplies, the stay in Nashville also provided Bushyhead an opportunity to solicit financial support for Baptist missions in Indian Territory. Likely, Jones had contacted Baptist leaders in the city and prearranged a visit from a delegation of Cherokee Baptists. On 5 November, Jones, Bushyhead, and Ahtzthee paid a visit to an assembly of Baptists. The purpose of the meeting centered on missions. Ahtzthee preached in Cherokee while Bushyhead interpreted. The service was so moving that the audience contributed a spontaneous offering. Two nights later, on a rainy and cold Wednesday, Jones and Bushyhead again met with Nashville Baptists. Bushyhead related the traditional customs and religion of the Cherokee people, but also mentioned the success of the Christian message among them. One listener described the presentation:

> He told us he recollected most distinctly the first time he ever heard the name of the Saviour, he recounted to us some particulars of his conversion, and that of his Father and Mother, and gave us a short account of the effects of his own, and the preaching of Oganiah, and others, among his countrymen, and especially of the glorious revival that prevailed among them in their camps this summer.... He adverted to the opposition to missions waged by some Tennessee Baptists, and presented himself and hundreds of his brethren as living instances of the blessing of God upon missionary labours.[60]

After finishing, Bushyhead, moved to tears, stepped down from the podium and took his seat. Jones then addressed the group. He informed listeners about the Bible translation project in which he and Bushyhead had been engaged. Another passing of the plate followed, but receipts were modest. The total offerings during two services "for the salvation of the noble hearted Indian" amounted to $29.11.[61]

[60] *The Baptist* 4 (November 1838): 358.

[61] Ibid. This offering was not an excessively large sum, even in 1838. A fair price for a carriage and two horses in Nashville was $300. See Moulton, *The Papers of Chief John Ross*, 1:693.

Shortly after the above events, Bushyhead's detachment broke camp for the next segment of the journey. Mustering 926 members, the detachment drew rations and resumed their march in the cold and rain. Bushyhead chose to move out instead of remaining near Nashville until the weather improved. Several hundred miles lay ahead, but whiskey traders and unscrupulous merchants also posed a threat. So, he felt it better to resume the exodus.[62] Continued cold and rain made progress difficult as oxen and travelers slogged along rutted and mud-mired roads. Also, the lack of provisions further up the route added to the difficulty, for contractors had failed to supply what the emigrants desired. Elijah Hicks, the leader of the first detachment to enter Kentucky, had complained about meat rations between Hopkinsville and the Mississippi River. It seemed that the contractor for that segment had arranged only to supply beef. Hicks expressed disappointment at the lack of bacon or pork, part of the common diet of the emigrants. The oversight was especially frustrating because these items were readily available.[63]

Once emigrants entered Kentucky, it became more apparent that any return to their homelands was unlikely. Traveling through southwestern Kentucky, the detachments passed through Hopkinsville, Princeton, and Salem before reaching the Ohio River. At Hopkinsville, emigrants drew rations and camped less than a mile from town.

[62] Moulton, *The Papers of Chief John Ross*, 1:689, 694; Information about numbers comes from government muster records. The amount of rations drawn allowed depended on the numbers traveling with a detachment when emigrants received rations. Numbers in detachments changed as some emigrants from other detachments joined; still others drove their own teams and united along the way, others died, straggled, joined other detachments, or deserted. Still others did not draw provisions but furnished their own rations. The numbers in the Bushyhead detachment varied from 850 to 1,018 at different times. The author is indebted to Professor Daniel Littlefield of the University of Arkansas at Little Rock for these details and also information contained in Abstract of Provisions issued to a detachment of Cherokee Emigrants, Jesse Bushyhead, Conductor.

[63] Ibid., 1:684.

As in many settlements, their presence drew the curiosity of local whites. James F. Buckner, a local attorney, recorded that some citizens opened their homes to prominent Cherokee families. Also, town churches welcomed emigrants. While at Hopkinsville, two venerated chiefs died. Fly Smith had arrived with the Moses Daniel detachment. Stephen Foreman also traveled with the Daniel train. The journey and weather had been too much for Fly Smith. He was ill upon arrival. The following morning, the Daniel detachment renewed the journey, but Foreman and his wife chose to remain and minister to Fly Smith. Yet the old chief failed to rally, and died later in the day. The Bushyhead group arrived in Hopkinsville near the same time. White Path, the past champion of full-bloods, traveled with the Bushyhead detachment. Sick and exhausted, the seventy-five-year-old White Path neared death. The next morning, he drew his last breath. Later that day, a burial party interred both chiefs beneath a small grove of cedars near the camp. The somber occasion did not go unremembered. A crowd gathered in a Hopkinsville church, where Bushyhead and Stephen Foreman delivered eloquent funeral orations. [64] The ministers reminded the audience of significant events in the lives of the deceased. Occasionally, the speakers alluded "to the history and trials of the Cherokees."[65]

The latter part of November found the Bushyhead detachment within sixty to eighty miles east of the Ohio River. Illness associated with the rigors of travel and weather had resulted in sixty deaths. Sickness also had stricken Powell and no doubt affected his ability to aid Bushyhead. And several of Bushyhead's family suffered. His father, sister Susan, and Isaac had taken ill. The elder Bushyhead and Susan dropped out of the detachment. After recovering, they planned to join another detachment or catch up later. On Thursday, 6 December, Richard Taylor's detachment camped near to where Jesse

[64] Perrin, *County of Christian, Kentucky*, 37–38.
[65] Ibid., 38.

Bushyhead and his very pregnant wife had found temporary lodging in the home of a local family. Butrick, traveling with the Taylor party, visited the Bushyheads. Butrick had fond memories of the Bushyhead family and their involvement with the Candy's Creek mission. The elder Bushyhead had attended services, and Susan had served briefly as a teacher in the mission school. As Butrick prepared to return to camp, the elder Bushyhead requested prayer.[66] The old man may have feared death in a strange land or grown weary of hard traveling, for the recent deaths of Fly Smith and White Path surely remained in his thoughts. Moreover, inclement weather continued to compound suffering for the other infirmed. Three days earlier, Butrick had reported the ground covered with snow and sleet.[67]

Among many emigrants, the Kentucky experience only stoked a smoldering sense of outrage against the Treaty party. Even before the exodus, threats of assassinations proved genuine, as demonstrated by the murder of Jack Walker. Of course, vendettas were not a new development among prominent Cherokees. In his younger days, even Major Ridge, a signer of the New Echota Treaty, had helped to assassinate a negotiator of an unauthorized Cherokee treaty. And even among Butrick's congregation, there had been talk of ecclesiastical disciplinary action. On the eve of their departure, some of his church members vowed to deny "Christian fellowship with those who made, signed or executed the New Echota treaty" once emigrants reached the West.[68]

Bushyhead also expressed his sentiments concerning treaty signers. Yet his comments seemed to harbor a more sinister fate than excommunication. Word of Bushyhead's sentiments reached General Jesup, who was then visiting family in Kentucky.[69] According to

[66] Butrick Journal, 4 October 1838 to May 1839; William Holland to David Greene, 9 February 1837, ABCFM 18.3.1.

[67] Butrick Journal, [10 December 1838].

[68] Butrick Journal, 31 October 1838.

[69] Kieffer, *Maligned General*, 218.

Jesup, Bushyhead had divulged that "all signers of the Treaty of N[ew] Echota should be put to death upon the arrival of the Eastern Cherokees west of the Mississippi."[70] Perhaps Bushyhead's statement had been taken out of context, for his remarks did not reflect the character of a Christian minister. Knowing that the Cherokee blood law was still in force, Bushyhead simply may have referenced it in a funeral address. And he remained quite aware of the assassination of his brother-in-law a little over four years before. In view of the recent deaths, the heavy weight of justice surely loomed. But Jesup may have formed his opinion based on his mistrust of Cherokee motives related to the Seminole mission in Florida less than a year ago. Jesup certainly remembered the standing of Bushyhead among the Cherokee delegates. The general therefore took Bushyhead's words at face value. Yet, regardless of intent, a chilling and bloody fulfillment of Bushyhead's alleged threat echoed a few months later in Indian Territory.

The Bushyhead column spent December crossing the southern tip of Illinois before camping on the eastern bank of the Mississippi River. The distance across Illinois was less than sixty miles. Under normal circumstances, this was not a difficult journey. But frigid weather remained unabated and slowed the march. Travel had become especially difficult for Eliza Bushyhead. Heavy with child, her delivery date drew near. While camped near Jonesboro, Illinois, Winstead and Anna Davie sympathized with Eliza and Jesse and opened their home to them.[71] Leaving Jonesboro, the Bushyhead party pulled up and camped beside the Situakee detachment. Under normal conditions, the local ferry required little time to transport wagons. But thick ice floes had clogged the river and prevented ferry traffic. For a month, the Bushyhead party and other detachments huddled at

[70] Poinsett Papers, [no date] Pennsylvania Historical Society, Philadelphia.

[71] Joan Gilbert, *The Trail of Tears across Missouri* (Columbia: University of Missouri, 1996) 51.

Willard Landing until the river cleared.[72] In late December or early January, the Bushyhead column crossed the Mississippi and reached Moccasin Springs on the Missouri side. While there on 3 January 1839, in the midst of sorrow and challenges, Jesse and Eliza celebrated the birth of Eliza Missouri, their seventh surviving child.[73]

From Moccasin Springs, the trail turned northwest through the lead mining district of Farmington and on to Rolla. A shorter road to their destination lay through southeastern Missouri and northwestern Arkansas, but this route was not as desirable as the northwestern track. Southeastern Missouri had few settlements, and the terrain was boggy. Because towns afforded emigrants the opportunity to obtain supplies and repair wagons, detachments avoided more sparsely settled routes.[74] After reaching Rolla, the detachment turned to the southwest. By Sunday, 3 February, it had stopped at the Gasconade River approximately fifty miles east of Springfield. As was their practice throughout the journey, the Bushyhead party remained in camp on Sundays and, circumstances permitting, held preaching services. On this occasion, the sermons proved effectual. Before leaving the Gasconade River, Bushyhead baptized three females in the icy waters.[75] According to Jones, a week later Bushyhead's congregants "en-

[72] *Baptist Missionary Magazine* 19 (April 1839): 89, and 19 (July 1839): 178.

[73] The death of one of Jesse's sisters may also have occurred near Moccasin Springs. A small knoll above Moccasin Springs marks the possible grave of Nancy Bushyhead Walker Hildebrand, the widow of John Walker, Jr. and wife of Lewis Hildebrand. As early as 1875, a story circulated that the grave contained the remains of one of Jesse's daughters. But the tradition is incorrect. If the grave is connected to Jesse Bushyhead, it is more likely a sister of Bushyhead. See Gilbert, *The Trail of Tears across Missouri*, 58–59; A. E. Schroeder, Rebecca B. Schroeder, Donald M. Lance, comps., *Remembering Eliza Missouri Bushyhead* (n.p.: Missouri Chapter of the Trail of Tears Association, 2001) 16.

[74] Gilbert, *The Trail of Tears across Missouri*, 60.

[75] *Baptist Missionary Magazine* 19 (October 1839): 255.

joyed the presence of God" as they "collected together, in the midst of our camps, and surrounded the Lord's table."[76]

Leaving Missouri, the wagons jostled through northwestern Arkansas along the road leading to Fayetteville. On 23 February, after 142 days en route, the detachment arrived in the Western Cherokee Nation. The next day, members drew their final rations as a detachment.[77] Thereafter, families and not detachments received rations. The Situakee detachment had arrived twenty-one days earlier. The last detachment, the Hildebrand party, arrived on 25 March. The time on the road for the twelve overland detachments varied from 93 to 143 days.[78]

The official duties of Bushyhead as conductor ended on 27 February. On Tuesday, 19 March, Bushyhead penned a letter to the Baptist Board. Realizing the need for continued funding, he wanted to remain in touch with his benefactors. In so doing, he painted as positive a picture as possible about the spiritual strengths of his traveling congregation:

> We were detained one month on the road at the Mississippi, by the ice. There were eighty-two deaths in the detachment while on the road. There were sixty-six members of the church in the Baptist connection in the detachment. Out of this number we selected two brethren to keep up regular worship during our travel; to wit, Tsusuwala...and Foster who has lately joined the Baptist church, quite an active and useful man. These two brethren performed the duty enjoined on them by the brethren, faithfully. They frequently held prayer-meetings, and exhorted the brethren on evenings during the week, and on every Lord's-day, except when the weather would not

[76] Ibid., (July 1839): 178.

[77] Abstract of Provisions issued to a detachment of Cherokee Emigrants, Jesse Bushyhead, Conductor.

[78] Names of People Who Rendered Services During Removal, John Ross Papers, folder 912, Gilcrease.

> admit of it; for we rested every Lord's-day, except that one time we traveled five miles, to get to the forage for our teams.[79]

The journey for the Bushyhead detachment had been expensive, arduous, and in many cases deadly. The numbers in the column who completed the journey differed according to reports. The handwritten muster roster of Captain Page totaled 864, while the John Ross account reported 950 emigrants, including desertions and additions along the way. Expenses submitted by Ross for the detachment totaled $105,923.12 ½ cent. This included payment to the owners of 48 wagons and 430 riding and draft animals used in transportation.[80] The journey had been personally stressful for Bushyhead as well. But the financial outcome could have been worse. As in the Seminole mission, Bushyhead could have gone unpaid. But at least he received recompense for his services as conductor, wagon leaser, and wagon driver. Although not fully recompensed until 29 December 1841, his payment totaled $3,665.[81]

Removal had proved devastating for the Eastern Cherokees. Fatalities in the holding camps and en route, combined with the deadly effects of the journey on the aged and infirmed after arrival, claimed thousands. In 1835, the Cherokee population in the East had numbered approximately 16,500. By 1840, that total had been reduced by 4,000. This is the estimated mortality figure often accepted by modern scholars. Of course, the precise number of deaths is impossible to determine, for exact records do not exist. Butrick estimated 5,000 deaths, while Elizur Butler approximated that over 4,000 had perished.[82] But estimates alone do not indicate the total picture. Besides

[79] *Baptist Missionary Magazine* (July 1839): 178.

[80] Muster Abstract of Rolls of Emigrating Cherokees, Correspondence of Eastern Division Pertaining to Cherokee Removal April–December 1838, National Archives, M1475, roll 2; Moulton, *The Papers of Chief John Ross*, 2:45; Congress, *Removal of the Cherokees West of the Mississippi*, 9–10.

[81] Removal Account Book.

[82] Butrick Journal, 23 May 1839.

deaths on the journey, fatalities from poor rations and inadequate shelter occurred in the first year after arrival. Furthermore, the figures do not project losses based on interruptions in pre-removal population trends. These include declining fertility rates, which resulted from the trauma associated with economic uncertainty and demographic upheaval. Considering population trends before and after removal, a theoretical overall population reduction of 8,000 may have resulted.[83]

But other challenges lay in store. Besides dealing with physical and emotional trauma, a new government had to be formed. Very soon three political factions emerged: Western Cherokees, the Ross faction, and the Treaty party. Western Cherokees, also known as Old Settlers, were those living in Arkansas Territory before removal. These included the descendants of Cherokees who had been arriving in Arkansas since the 1790s. Some of the Western Cherokees had left the East voluntarily and without inducements from the government. Others had accepted offers of compensation and had arrived in the twenty-year period before the signing of the New Echota Treaty. Of course, the opponents of the treaty in the East composed the Ross faction, also known as the Antitreaty party. Finally, the Watie-Ridge-Boudinot nucleus continued to compose the Treaty party. Augmented by the arrival of Treaty party emigrants, by the late 1830s, the Western Cherokees and Treaty party numbered around 5,000, or about 25 percent of the entire tribal population. But the sudden arrival of over 10,000 of their kinsmen, most of whom supported John Ross, posed serious economic and political problems. Having established farms and homes on some of the best land, Western Cherokees considered the newcomers an economic threat. And there was the question of government annuities. Which faction would the United

[83] Russell Thornton, "Cherokee Population Losses during the Trail of Tears: A New Perspective and a New Estimate," *Ethnohistory* 31 (Autumn 1984): 289–300.

States recognize as the legitimate Cherokee Nation? Although they did not possess a written constitution, Western Cherokees had established a political framework and drew government annuities. Wishing to preserve their government and maintain some influence, they looked to John Rogers and John Brown for leadership. Further complicating this mix was the Treaty party. Aware of assassination threats, Treaty party supporters remained reluctant to cooperate with the Ross faction, for assassination and other forms of retribution seemed likely. Aware of this Damoclean sword, they certainly did not wish Ross supporters to gain a majority in the legislature, courts, and law enforcement entities. Thus, for the Treaty party, an alliance with the Western Cherokees therefore became even more important, for it allowed the Treaty party the opportunity to mitigate the influence of John Ross.

Yet Ross partisans did not favor subjugation to a minority faction. They did not wish to live under what they considered as an inferior government without a written constitution. Moreover, the majority of emigrants wanted a voice in the distribution of their share of treaty-promised annuities. And if smoldering tensions went unresolved, civil war remained a possibility. In this event, the United States would have an excuse to withhold annuities and dissolve the political structures of all Cherokee factions.[84] The challenges associated with removal certainly had proven traumatic. Yet, in many ways, the real test had just begun.

[84] Gerard Alexander Reed, "The Ross-Watie Conflict: Cherokee Factionalism in the Cherokee Nation, 1839–1865" (Ph.D. diss., University of Oklahoma, 1967) 90–92.

CHAPTER 6

Establishing a New Life in the West

Bushyhead settled near the Arkansas border and four miles north of present Westville, Oklahoma. The residence was not far from a tributary of the Illinois River. The nearest settlement of significant size was Cane Hill, Arkansas, which had a post office, stores, and churches. The location of Bushyhead's new home offered several advantages. Fort Wayne, a small military post seven miles to the north, provided security.[1] It also was accessible to the Arkansas commercial centers of Fayetteville, about twenty-five miles to the northeast, and Van Buren, fifty miles south on the Arkansas River. Evan Jones also settled nearby. By May 1839, Jones had acquired a cabin "about two miles south" of Bushyhead's residence.[2] Locating so close to Bushyhead, Jones planned to collaborate with him in translating the Bible. Over time, the Bushyhead settlement became known by several names. Because the recent emigrants first received government rations there, the location became known as "Breadtown." But as early as April 1839, some documents listed the site as "Bushyhead." In 1842, the United States postal service officially listed the post office as "Cherokee." And because a Baptist mission eventually opened at the site, in later years, the settlement also became known as "Baptist."[3]

[1] Margaret Sixkiller Bagby, Interview by J. W. Tyner, 31 March 1970, History Materials of Northeast Adair County, Oklahoma, vol. 10, transcript ID: T-559-3, Western History Collections, University of Oklahoma, Norman.

[2] *Baptist Missionary Magazine* 19 (October 1839): 255.

[3] Thomas Foreman et al. to S. G. Simmons, 16 April 1839, Letters Received by the Office of Indian Affairs, 1824–1881, Cherokee Agency West 1839,

The Treaty of New Echota had obligated the government to furnish rations to emigrants for one year after arrival. In keeping with these terms, on 27 September 1838, the Little Rock mercantile firm of Glasgow and Harrison received a government contract for rations. The merchants agreed to supply three months of rations for up to 8,000 Cherokees "in their new country west."[4] In a subsequent contract with the same company, on 15 January 1839, the government set aside five distribution sites, one of which was the Bushyhead settlement. Beginning on 1 March 1839 and continuing at monthly intervals until 1 March 1840, recipients remained eligible for rations. But after the rationing period had passed, emigrants still needed provisions. Subsequently, Brigadier General Matthew Arbuckle at the Western Cherokee agency at Fort Gibson authorized a five-month extension of rations.[5]

Yet rations were insufficient, and serious problems involving shelter and sustenance remained unsolved. Hundreds of recently arrived emigrants went hungry. Moreover, the newcomers continued to live in tents or crude shelters. And irregularities regarding the distribution of rations became evident. Personnel at each site consisted of a United States agent, contractors for Glasgow and Harrison, and an interpreter. Contractors were responsible for purchasing rations and delivering them to depots. Cherokee recipients then exchanged government-issued tickets for supplies. Bushyhead assisted as an interpreter from 1 April 1839 to sometime in July 1840. For his services, he received $2.50 per day. But his task was not easy. Some of the

National Archives, M234, roll 83; Evan Jones to Lucius Bolles and Heman Lincoln, 23 June 1842, American Baptist Foreign Mission Society, 1817–1959; E. C. Routh, "Early Missionaries to the Cherokees," *Chronicles of Oklahoma* 15 (December 1937): 456.

[4] Congress, House Committee on Indian Affairs, House Report 271, *Frauds upon Indians*, report prepared by James Cooper, 27th Cong., 3rd sess., 88 (LexisNexis Academic, 2006) Serial Set-ID: 428 H.rp. 271.

[5] Ibid., 98.

agents were discharged soldiers. As such, they were not always paragons of integrity. The agent at the Bushyhead settlement was Castillion Lyon, a brother-in-law of Bushyhead.[6] Benjamin F. Thompson described Lyon as "a great drunkard."[7] Living at Beattie's Prairie, twenty-five miles north of the Bushyhead settlement, the brothers Benjamin and James Allen Thompson had mercantile interests. Their business links made them aware of fraudulent agents and contractors. James related how unscrupulous whites paid cash to Cherokees for their ration tickets at far below the actual value of intended merchandise. The defrauders, in turn, exchanged the coupons for supplies, which they sold for a considerable profit. In a statement to Congress, James detailed the practices of the contractors and the poor quality of beef. On one occasion, the agents even "drove an old blind ox...to the place of issue, and compelled the Cherokees to receive."[8] And because some cattle were unfit for slaughter, emigrants often preferred to use the better quality animals as stock rather than meat. The testimony also mentioned another means of deception. Cherokees often arrived at the depots and camped overnight until rationing began the following morning. At first light, agents and contractors chose to deal with the poor and ignorant, for the morning shadows made it easier to obscure faulty rations.[9]

Cherokees soon perceived the sleight of hand and raised objections. When Bushyhead voiced protests on site, he risked the ire of contractors. By 16 April 1839, the chicanery had become so flagrant that other Cherokee leaders became alarmed at the poor quality and paltry amount of rations. And because the weather had warmed, additional problems developed with the preservation of beef. Noted

[6] Grant Foreman, ed., *A Traveler in Indian Territory: The Journal of Ethan Allen Hitchcock, Late Major-General in the United States Army* (Cedar Rapids IA: Torch Press, 1930) 81.

[7] Congress, *Frauds upon Indians*, 98.

[8] Ibid., 97.

[9] Ibid.

Cherokees Hair Conrad, Stop, William Proctor, Samuel Foreman, and Stephen Foreman joined Bushyhead in petitioning governmental authorities on behalf of all the detachments. Instead of beef, the six recommended the issuance of bacon. Seasoned with salt, pork was less likely to spoil. In a sense of urgency, they urged that "something be done without delay."[10] Three days later, John Ross also protested. Wishing to alleviate suffering, Ross petitioned the "General Government" to deliver funds to agents of the Cherokee Nation who would oversee distributions.[11] At least ninety-six Cherokees signed the petition. One was Beaver Carrier, who continued to serve as one of Bushyhead's ministerial associates. The protests apparently had some effect. On 28 April 1840, Arbuckle entered an agreement with John Martin, still treasurer of the Cherokee Nation. According to the terms, Martin received an appointment as contractor and the responsibility of overseeing a more equitable delivery of rations at several sites. The Bushyhead settlement remained as a distribution point. Other sites were the Martin residence, James Allen Thompson's store at Beattie's Prairie, Walter Scott Adair's residence in the Flint District, and Daniel McCoy's residence on the Illinois River.[12]

Distribution problems did not go unnoticed by Congress. Several months later, Major Ethan Allen Hitchcock, an officer assigned to investigate the supply abuses, had the opportunity to discuss the issues with Bushyhead. Hitchcock toured the "Indian country west of the State of Arkansas" from the first part of December 1841 through February 1842.[13] In doing so, he conducted extensive interviews with numerous individuals and, in 1843, submitted 100 reports to the House of Representatives. In one of his reports, the major attested to

[10] Thomas Foreman et al. to John Ross, 16 April 1839, John Ross Papers, folder 532, Gilcrease Museum.

[11] Congress, *Frauds upon Indians*, 149.

[12] Articles of Agreement, 28 April 1840, between John Martin and General M[atthew] Arbuckle, box 374, file 80, doc. 1, Sequoyah Center.

[13] Congress, *Frauds upon Indians*, 31.

Bushyhead's character. He described him as "a most interesting and respectable man; of great intelligence; and one whose veracity no man will question who has the pleasure of his acquaintance."[14]

But if rations went wanting, there was no shortage of animosity and faction. By spring and early summer 1839, division among Cherokees compounded with white hostility had resulted in a volatile mixture. The recent arrival of thousands of Cherokees instilled a sense of insecurity among whites along the Arkansas border. It was only a matter of time before outbreaks of violence occurred. On or about 1 April 1839, a brawl occurred between a small number of Cherokees and Isaac Wallace, a white citizen of Benton County, Arkansas. The Cherokee assailants then retreated into the Cherokee Nation. The attack had left Wallace near death. Moreover, his wounds seemed to confirm the fears of Arkansans concerning Cherokee hostility.[15] One of the accused assailants was John R. Nicholson, a resident of the Cherokee Nation. Five days later, Archibald Yell, a popular and ambitious politician from Fayetteville, notified Arbuckle of the quarrel. Yell had recently resigned his seat in the United States House of Representatives and returned to Arkansas in March. Intent on winning the governor's office, he curried political favor by stoking fears of Cherokee atrocities.[16]

Although negative rumors about Nicholson quickly spread, the potential for other crimes also claimed the attention of authorities. About 20 April, John Moseley, a white married to a Cherokee, went

[14] Ibid., Congress, House Committee on Indian Affairs, House Document 219, *The Report of Lieutenant Colonel Hitchcock, Respecting the Affairs of the Cherokee Indians*, 27th Cong., 3rd sess., 34 (LexisNexis Academic, 2006) Serial Set ID: 425 H.doc. 219.

[15] A[rchibald] Yell to M[atthew] Arbuckle, 5 April 1839, Letters received by Army of the Southwestern Frontier, 1838–1840, Arkansas History Commission, ML0604, roll 3.

[16] William W. Hughes, *Archibald Yell* (Fayetteville: University of Arkansas, 1988) 60, 62, 64.

to Lieutenant C. M. Hammond, the commander of troops at Camp Illinois. The camp was in the vicinity of Bushyhead's cabin and near the homes of many of the North Carolina Cherokees. Moseley warned the lieutenant that Nicholson had been inciting the mountain Cherokees to attack Camp Illinois in retaliation for suffering endured during removal. The alleged attack was to occur on the night of 26 April. Furthermore, Moseley implicated Situakee in the plot. On 25 April, Hammond requested that Arbuckle rush two or three companies of dragoons as reinforcements. With a sense of alarm, Hammond urged that the troops arrive by 3 P.M. at the latest. The general promptly ordered two companies to proceed from Fort Gibson to Camp Illinois. The next day, Arbuckle notified Ross of Hammond's fears and urged Ross to get any disorderly Cherokees under control.[17]

Arbuckle also quickly dispatched Captain George A. McCall from Fort Gibson to investigate the disturbances. McCall rode to the home of Ross at Park Hill, about five miles south of Tahlequah, and requested the aid of Ross. Ross was not able to accompany McCall but recommended the services of Stephen Foreman and Cherokee leader Walter Scott Adair. McCall enlisted Adair and Foreman, and the trio set out for Camp Illinois. They called at Bushyhead's cabin on Tuesday, 30 April, but Bushyhead had gone to Cane Hill. After questioning Moseley and Hammond, the investigators concluded that all was peaceful and the accusations untrue. McCall stated that the story had originated with Moseley and another unscrupulous white man. McCall hinted that the rumor bearers were whiskey runners. Because the Cherokee Nation remained off limits to the whiskey

[17] McLoughlin, *Champions of the Cherokees*, 188–89; Moulton, *The Papers of Chief John Ross*, 1:709–10; Lt. C. M. Hammond to General [Matthew]Arbuckle, 25 April 1839, John Ross Papers, folder 534, Gilcrease Museum; Matthew Arbuckle to John Ross, 26 April 1839, John Ross Papers, folder 536, Gilcrease Museum.

trade, the duo supposedly had circulated the hearsay as a means of revenge.[18]

Yet the events unsettled Evan Jones. Jones considered the allegations against his old friend Situakee serious enough to intervene. Moreover, it was likely that Jones previously had ministered to several of the mountain Cherokee families implicated in the story. Jones and the respected Old Fields visited Bushyhead's cabin on the day of the supposed attack and sought to enlist his aid in quelling the emergency. Bushyhead still was not at home. Fortunately, the rumor of attack proved false. But in seeking to avert violence, prominent Cherokees, Jones, and military authorities had sought the aid of Bushyhead. This confirmed the continuing influence that Bushyhead exercised in his community.[19]

But Arkansans remained uneasy and made preparations for defense. Yell already had warned Arbuckle concerning white vigilantes. In order to prevent a border war, Yell urged the general to deliver Nicholson to Arkansas authorities for trial in a state court. Also, Yell requested that regular army troops police the border. And he appealed to Arbuckle for weapons, including artillery, for the Arkansas militia in Fayetteville. As the crisis festered, Ross feared Nicholson might fall victim to vigilantes. At the request of Nicholson, Ross requested that Arbuckle place Nicholson under the protection of United States troops. Yet Arbuckle denied any knowledge of vigilantes actually entering the Cherokee Nation. But on 15 May, he promised to station one or more companies along the Benton County line to intercept vigilantes.[20]

[18] Congress, House Committee on Indian Affairs, House Document 129, *Memorial of the Delegation of the Cherokee Nation*, report prepared by George Hicks, 26th Cong., 1st sess., 40–47 (LexisNexis Academic, 2006) Serial Set ID: 365 H.doc. 129.

[19] McLoughlin, *Champions of the Cherokees*, 189.

[20] A[rchibald] Yell to Matthew Arbuckle, 5 April 1839; Report of Matthew Arbuckle, 15 May 1839, Letters sent by Army of the Southwestern Frontier,

Cherokee fears of white intervention were valid, for at Cane Hill, a case of white-on-white vigilantism shortly occurred. The circumstances involved the murders of a white family at Cane Hill in June. One of the suspects was Nicholson. On Monday, 29 July, a mob had lynched three of the accused.[21] The next day, the Reverend Andrew Buchanan, a Cumberland Presbyterian minister and head of the Cane Hill Independent Regulators, sent a letter to Ross through the hands of George Bushyhead. Buchanan demanded that Ross deliver Nicholson, whom the Regulators considered to be a "Ross man." Strengthening the demand, the letter justified the recent vigilante justice.

In light of increasing tensions, Cherokees realized that tribal unity was necessary to counter aggression. Also, there remained the question of annuity funds. Leaders of both Eastern and Western Cherokee factions wanted separate control of annuity distributions. Realizing the urgency of a resolution, Eastern Cherokees, mostly Ross supporters, and Western Cherokees agreed to a meeting. Several thousand Cherokees assembled four miles north of Tahlequah at the Takatokah campgrounds, also known as Double Springs, during the first week of June. On 14 June, John Ridge, Elias Boudinot, Major Ridge, John A. Bell, and Stand Watie arrived. All of the five had either signed or supported the New Echota Treaty. Acting only as observers and having no official capacity, the Ridges, Boudinot, and Watie did not long remain. They likely remembered the Jack Walker,

1834–1854, National Archives M1302. Accessed at Arkansas History Commission, ML0602, roll 1; Moulton, *The Papers of Chief John Ross*, 1:709–10; Report of Matthew Arbuckle, 15 May 1839.

[21] *History of Benton, Washington, Carroll, Madison, Crawford, Franklin, and Sebastian Counties, Arkansas* (Chicago: Goodspeed Publishing, 1889; rep., Greenville SC: Southern Historical Press, 2002) 157 (page reference is to reprint edition); Andrew Buchahanan to George Bushyhead, 30 July 1839, John Ross Papers, folder 611, Gilcrease Museum.

Jr. murder almost five years earlier and departed the same day.[22] Unfortunately, their absence deprived the Treaty party of a voice in the proceedings. Ross attempted to carry the meeting by proposing a nine-member committee to organize a plan for government. Yet Western Cherokee chiefs rejected his proposal. First, they felt that their existing government was quite legitimate and inclusive of the newcomers. Second, the plan of Ross allowed Western Cherokees only three of nine seats on the committee. This was too much for the Old Settler chiefs. They feared a Ross-dominated government. But Ross posed another reason for their reluctance. Ross accused Western Cherokee chiefs of requiring "the unconditional submission of the whole body of the people who have lately arrived."[23] The lack of cooperation on the part of Western Cherokee leaders particularly irked Ross and his supporters, for before departing their homelands, the Eastern Cherokee National Council had designated a definitive arrangement concerning any future government. The agreement stipulated the reestablishment of the former government, which surely included leadership, in the West.[24] In response, Western Cherokees abruptly broke off the proceedings on 19 July. Ross later described those remaining at the council grounds as "astonished and dissatisfied" at these developments.[25]

Realizing the impasse but also the necessity of establishing a working government, some Eastern and Western Cherokees took a crucial step and assembled an ad hoc meeting. After deliberations, both factions selected one of their esteemed members to jointly preside over the proceedings. Western Cherokees selected George Guess, still known as Sequoyah. Both Eastern and Western Cherokees respected Guess. Before migrating from Alabama to Arkansas

[22] McLoughlin, *Champions of the Cherokees*, 192; Ehle, *Trail of Tears*, 372.
[23] Moulton, *The Papers of Chief John Ross*, 1:716.
[24] Denson, *Demanding the Cherokee Nation*, 41.
[25] Ibid., 2:20.

Territory in the early 1820s, Guess had developed the Cherokee syllabary. The Ross faction chose Jesse Bushyhead, still identified from his position as a detachment leader as "Captain Bushyhead."[26] On 20 June, the two sides agreed to call another general convention to assemble at Illinois Camp Ground the following month on Monday, 1 July. The participants selected a meeting site south of Fort Gibson and near the mouth of the Illinois River.[27] After Guess and Bushyhead had signed the document, Ross supporters lost little time in producing an official endorsement of the proceedings. In so doing, the remnants of the Eastern Cherokee legislature, composed of the National Committee and the National Council, formally approved the resolution. Some of the signatories included Principal Chief John Ross, Bushyhead, Stephen Foreman, Richard Taylor, George Lowrey, and Edward Gunter. Bushyhead signed as clerk of the National Council, the same position he had held when the legislature last had convened in 1838.[28]

Some historians have painted the responses of Bushyhead and Guess as magnanimous—that is, heroic actions at a time of crisis.[29] In

[26] Stan Hoig, *Sequoyah: The Cherokee Genius* (Oklahoma City: Oklahoma Historical Society, 1995) 41–43.

[27] Reed, "The Ross-Watie Conflict," 95; Congress, Department of War, Senate Document 140, *Report of the Secretary of War, communicating (in compliance with a resolution of the Senate) the report and correspondence of the board of inquiry, to prosecute an examination into the causes and extent of the discontents and difficulties among the Cherokee Indians*, report prepared by William Wilkins, 28th Cong., 2nd sess., 47 (LexisNexis Academic, 2006) Serial Set ID: 457 S.doc. 140; Resolution of General Council of the Eastern and Western Cherokees, 20 June 1839, John Ross Papers, folder 562, Gilcrease Museum.

[28] All signers had held positions of leadership in the Cherokee national legislature in 1838. It is interesting to note that one, Edward Gunter, served in 1838 as a member of the Executive Committee. Two days later Gunter became a suspect in the murder of Elias Boudinot. See Congress, *Removal of Cherokees*, 7–8.

[29] Grant Foreman, *Sequoyah* (Norman: University of Oklahoma, 1938) 33; Morris L. Wardell, *A Political History of the Cherokee Nation, 1838–1907* (Norman: University of Oklahoma, 1938; second printing) 16 (page reference is to

reality, the move for the Illinois Campground meeting played into the hands of Ross, for absent the cooperation of their chiefs, Western Cherokees had little reason to participate in the ad hoc assembly. Also, an interim of almost three weeks allowed Ross time to organize his forces. Ross nevertheless described the resolution as a spontaneous product of "the People" who formed "a branch of the Genl. Council."[30] Yet, with the exception of Guess, all the signers had been in the Ross circle.[31] And while Guess was an "Old Settler," by this time, he had become willing to cooperate with the Ross faction.

News of the forthcoming council promised a resolution of the crisis, but some Ross supporters expressed concerns. They blamed the Treaty party for delaying the formation of a unified government and thus jeopardizing annuity payments. But above all, Ross partisans distrusted their political influence in the coming government. By supporting the New Echota Treaty, the Treaty party already had forfeited any degree of trust in the present or future. And this time, Ross supporters intended to refuse the Treaty party any such opportunity. Accordingly, some Ross men took matters into their own hands. After the meeting officially dismissed on 20 June, three hundred Ross partisans remained behind. The rump assembly covertly selected assassins to carry out the Cherokee custom of blood revenge for the unauthorized sale of tribal lands, for under Eastern Cherokee law, execution for such offensives still remained legal. The attendees drew lots, and the chosen assassins made plans to carry out their assignments. There is no evidence that Bushyhead had direct knowledge of the coming crimes. In fact, it seems that Guess and Bushyhead may have proposed the coming Illinois Campground meeting in order to

second printing); Grace Steele Woodward, *The Cherokees* (Norman: University of Oklahoma, 1963) 224.

[30] Moulton, *The Papers of Chief John Ross*, 1:716.

[31] Jesse Bushyhead, Richard Taylor, Stephen Foreman, George Lowrey, Going Snake, and John Ross signed the document. See John Ross Papers, folder 562, Gilcrease Museum.

prevent bloodshed. Both had bitter memories of recriminations, for assassination had touched both of their families. Likewise, Ross later claimed to have had no knowledge of the plans. However, his son, Allen Ross, was at the meeting and witnessed the drawing of lots. Rather than tarnish Ross with blame, the ringleaders instructed Allen to return home and keep his father well out of the way.[32] But if Ross was not a participant, he hardly could have been surprised when he learned of the killings. Likewise, Bushyhead must have remembered his words of retribution spoken in Kentucky the previous November.

The assassins acted with quick precision. In the early morning hours of Saturday, 22 June, twenty-five intended assassins rode to the home of John Ridge at Honey Creek, less than a mile inside the Cherokee Nation and near the extreme southwestern corner of Missouri. Members of the party included John Vann and brothers Archibald, James, and Joseph Spears. Daniel Colston, another participant, had served as a detachment leader the previous year. Colston also had served as the namesake for Bushyhead's third child. Hunter, a full-blood Cherokee and half-brother to Spears and Colston, also accompanied the group. Colston and the Spears trio entered the Ridge home and muscled him into the yard. Knives flashed, and Ridge fell from twenty-five stab wounds. The final slash severed his jugular. Members of the group then rode south to Beattie's Prairie, east of modern Jay, Oklahoma, where they bragged about their bloody deed.

About forty-five miles to the southwest, a second group assembled in a wooded spot at Park Hill. The location was near the construction site of the Boudinot house and less than two miles south of the John Ross home. Members of this party included Johnston, Soft-Shelled Turtle, Money Taker, Car-soo-taw-dy, Duck-wa, and Joseph Beanstick, also known as Beanstalk. Edward Gunter and a man named Sanders also may have participated. Around 9 A.M., Boudinot arrived at the site. Pretending to want medicines, four assassins lured

[32] Reed, "The Ross-Watie Conflict," 97.

Boudinot away from the workmen. Quickly seizing their opportunity, the killers delivered fatal knife and tomahawk wounds. After the bloody assault, the attackers fled. In minutes, Boudinot lay dead.

An hour later, Major Ridge was riding along the Van Buren Road, which paralleled the east side of the Arkansas border. The assassins waited with primed muskets at a concealed location a mile within the Arkansas line and not too far from Bushyhead's settlement. The murderers had been trailing Ridge since the previous day. When Ridge came within range, they fired a volley. Ridge died on the spot. James Foreman, Bird Doublehead, Jefferson and James Hair, and two Springstons, presumably Isaac and Anderson, received blame.[33] Virtually all of the participants in the triple murders had been acquaintances of Bushyhead. They had known him either from his days at Candy's Creek or from his leadership roles in the Eastern Cherokee Nation. At least one, James Hair, had been a member of his detachment.[34] And others would soon participate with him in the writing of a constitution.

In the interim, Ross supporters proceeded with plans to write a constitution and implement a government. But all was not well, for Watie men vowed vengeance. With civil war looming, a united government became even more paramount as a semblance of civility. On 1 July, nearly 2,000 Cherokees, corporately known as the national convention, assembled at the Illinois Camp Ground. However, the proceedings only stoked existing tensions along the frontier. While the Nicholson affair smoldered, Arkansans along the western border also took notice of the assassinations. They feared an all-out war. After all, Major Ridge had been waylaid within Arkansas. And the possibility seemed genuine for more violence to spill over into Arkansas.

[33] Wilkins, *Cherokee Tragedy*, 335–38; Names of Cherokees charged with the Murder of the Ridges and Boudinot, 27 November 1839, Papers of Cherokee Agency West, 1840, National Archives, M234, roll 84.

[34] Bushyhead Detachment Employees.

Moreover, the forthcoming mass meeting of Cherokees at the Illinois Camp Ground did little to calm fears. Army Captain William Armstrong, acting superintendent of Indian affairs of the Western Territory posted at Fort Gibson, took seriously the potential for violence. Armstrong warned Ross that further bloodshed could result in "serious consequences."[35] Armstrong furthermore warned that Arbuckle might request militia support from the governors of Arkansas and Missouri. Indeed, Arbuckle disclosed his concerns to Ross in a letter on 8 July, stressing the importance of adopting "such measures that will restore peace to your nation."[36] In light of possible military intervention, some of the encamped Cherokees at the Illinois council grounds quickly responded to Arbuckle. The following day, Bushyhead, Ross, and twenty-eight others sought to allay the concerns of the general. They promised that whites had nothing to fear from Cherokees.[37]

As these developments unfolded, the turbulence drew national attention. Eastern newspapers sensationalized the recent assassinations. The Philadelphia *National Gazette* forecasted imminent civil war because "Ross had waylaid and shot Ridge."[38] According to the same source, Arbuckle had expressed concern that a united force of 20,000 Indians threatened to invade Arkansas. The *Atkinson's Evening Post*, also a Philadelphia paper, warned that Cherokees had encamped near the Sabine River in Nacogdoches County, Texas, and threatened to attack Texas troops.[39] Three weeks later, the same pa-

[35] William Armstrong to John Ross, 8 July 1839, John Ross Papers, folder 579, Gilcrease Museum.

[36] Congress, Office of Indian Affairs, Senate Document 1/6, *Report of the Commissioner of Indian Affairs*, report prepared by Thomas Hartley Crawford, 26th Cong., 1st sess., 373 (LexisNexis Academic, 2006) Serial Set ID: 354 S.doc. 1/6.

[37] Ibid., 373.

[38] *National Gazette*, 20 July 1839.

[39] *Atkinson's Evening Post*, 6 July 1839.

per also erroneously disclosed the assassination of John Ross. Yet the article offered a ray of hope; that is, it predicted that Bushyhead, "a pacific chief[,] will succeed in effecting a reconciliation between the parties."[40]

Indeed, the national press exaggerated rumors. Yet the lack of preparation of United States forces along the frontier added to concerns, for few troops garrisoned the scattered frontier forts. Aware of the tinderbox, Major-General Edmund Pendleton Gaines, commanding the Western Division of the United States Army, sent an ominous message to the commanding officers of Forts Towson and Jesup, in present southeastern Oklahoma and western Louisiana, respectively. On 15 July, Gaines warned them about Cherokee unrest. And since the past year, unconfirmed reports had disclosed the presence of numerous Cherokees encamped along the Sabine River in East Texas.[41] Such reports disturbed Texas authorities. Only three years before, the Republic of Texas had proclaimed independence from Mexico. The government of the fledging republic feared a Cherokee linkup with Mexican forces in an attempt to recapture Texas for Mexico. Putting their concerns into action, the Texas militia struck. On 16 July 1839, Texas forces defeated a band of Texas Cherokees in present Van Zandt County, Texas. Some of the surviving Cherokees fled to Indian Territory. Others sought refuge in the United States and Mexico. Alluding to the recent dispersal of Texas Cherokees, Gaines was uneasy. He feared even more violence should any Cherokees choose to retaliate. And if war occurred, settlements in western Arkansas and northwestern Louisiana remained vulnerable.[42]

[40] Ibid., 27 July 1839.

[41] A. S. Wright to Mr. [Josiah H.] Doak, 21 August 1838, Grant Foreman Papers, vol. 75, box 36, 18, Gilcrease Museum [typewritten copy].

[42] Major-General Edmund P. Gaines to Commanding Officers of Forts Towson and Jessup, 15 July 1839, Letters Received by Office of Indian Affairs, 1824–1881, Cherokee Agency West, 1839, National Archives, M234, roll 83.

The unsettled state also troubled other Native peoples in Indian Territory. On 1 July, John Ross wrote to Creek Chief Roley McIntosh and other headmen. Ross was careful to notify them of the "false rumours" that might circulate concerning difficulties among the Cherokees. As a result, Creek leaders lost little time in communicating with Arbuckle. Opothleyoholo, principal Creek chief, wrote Arbuckle and inquired about Cherokee unrest. Having recently been driven from Alabama at bayonet point, Creeks did not relish another intervention by United States soldiers.[43]

Against this backdrop, representatives from the Eastern Cherokees and a minority of Western Cherokees finally assembled at the Illinois Camp Ground. The delegates realized the explosive nature of recent events and took action.[44] On 12 July, Guess and Bushyhead, along with twenty-five other delegates, signed a letter to Arbuckle. The document assured the general that "past grievances" had been buried "in oblivion," provided that all parties agreed to maintain peace in the future.[45] And on 7 August, twenty-seven delegates, again including Guess and Bushyhead, attempted to defuse the pending Nicholson affair. They petitioned Montfort Stokes, Cherokee agent at Fort Gibson, concerning the possible unlawful extradition of Nicholson to Arkansas authorities.[46] Signing the letter as "Your friends & Brothers," the appellants stressed the innocence of Nicholson. They furthermore warned that the extradition of Nicholson or any other Cherokee "may lead to the disturbance of the peace and tranquility of

[43] Moulton, *The Papers of Chief John Ross*, 1:725; Matthew Arbuckle to Opothleyoholo, 4 July 1839, Letters sent by Army of the Southwestern Frontier, 1834–1854, ML0602, roll 1.

[44] Congress, Senate Document 140, *Report of the Secretary of War*, 6.

[45] George Lowrey et al. to M[atthew] Arbuckle, 12 July 1839, Letters of Cherokee Agency West, National Archives, M234, roll 84.

[46] Almost all of the signatories had signed the letter of 12 July.

the Country."[47] Two of the petitioners, Bird Doublehead and Edward Gunter had a particular interest in preventing extraditions. Less than seven weeks before, they had been accused as assassins in the murders of the Ridges and Boudinot.

Meanwhile, the convention addressed the ticklish issue of unity. Fearful of reprisals and careful to maintain political control, Ross supporters meant to deprive certain Treaty party supporters from future political influence. They particularly had Watie in mind. By this time, Watie had emerged as a primary leader of the Treaty party. One of the first decrees, approved 7 July, offered amnesty to "some of the friends" of the Ridges and Boudinot. This proposal mainly applied to Watie, his supporters, and signers of the New Echota Treaty.

Superficially, this action offered to protect the Treaty party from retribution. Yet the Ross faction required certain stipulations. Signers of the New Echota Treaty, or those who had vowed revenge against the killers of the Ridges and Boudinot, had to appear before the national convention and disavow past threats and aggressive acts. If they refused, their safety remained in jeopardy. But a particularly vexing requirement concerned their exclusion from government. All who accepted amnesty became ineligible for "any office of profit, trust, or honor" for a stated period of at least five years.[48] And even after this time, their full restoration of political status was at the discretion of future national legislatures.

Of course, these moves virtually stripped Watie and his close associates of any present or future tribal offices. And in order to discourage Watie forces from retaliation, the convention resolved the

[47] John Ross et al. to Matthew Stokes, 7 August 1839, Letters of Cherokee Agency West, 1839, Letters Received by the Office of Indian Affairs, 1824–1881, National Archives, M234, roll 83.

[48] Congress, Senate Committee on Indian Affairs, Senate Document 298, *Message of the President of the United States, relative to the internal feuds among the Cherokees*, report prepared by James Knox Polk, 29th Cong., 1st sess., 108–109 (LexisNexis Academic, 2006) Serial Set ID: 474 S.doc. 298.

same day to organize eight auxiliary police companies. A captain, lieutenant, and other subordinate officers supervised the units. The convention placed the eight companies under the overall command of Bushyhead and Looney Price, a Western Cherokee who served as second in command.[49] Although respected, the appointment of Bushyhead to a prominent position merely provided a facade of legitimacy.[50] In essence, his appointment more clearly identified him as an instrument of the Ross faction. In addition, the soon-to-be-organized national legislature received the authority to "control, modify, suspend, or discontinue" the companies. Seemingly temporary in tenure, the units provided Ross with an official personal security force. When Arbuckle learned that the policy targeted Watie and his supporters, he strongly protested. He felt that amnesty was nothing more than a fiat to deny the Treaty party its rightful place in the new government, for if Treaty party supporters refused to submit to Ross, Arbuckle feared for their lives. In fact, he thought them vulnerable to legally sanctioned murder.[51] And if this occurred, civil war became more likely. Arbuckle thus implored the Ross delegates to temper their terms. Yet they flatly refused and continued to form their government.

But unification remained elusive. On 12 July, the convention passed the Act of Union. This instrument formally implemented the political unification of the Western and Eastern Cherokees. Signatory delegates included Bushyhead, fourteen other Eastern Cherokees, and seventeen Western Cherokees.[52] Following this breakthrough, the

[49] Looney Price was part of the Western Cherokee minority who backed the John Ross government.

[50] Polk, *Message of the President*, 110; Reed, "The Ross-Watie Conflict," 104.

[51] Congress, *Memorial of the Delegation*, 26th Cong., 1st sess., 74–76; Congress, *Removal of the Cherokees West of the Mississippi*, 74-75.

[52] Congress, *Removal of the Cherokees West of the Mississippi*, 74; Congress, Committee on Territories, Senate Report 744, [Untitled], report prepared by

next step focused on the writing of a constitution and the election of national officers. However, some Western Cherokee chiefs refused to participate in a Ross-dominated convention. Armstrong also remained skeptical of the actual degree of support among Western Cherokees and blamed Ross for proceeding with only a few Western Cherokees.[53] Western Cherokee leaders John Brown, John Looney, John Rogers, and John Smith likewise considered any Ross-called convention "altogether irregular."[54] In an effort to undermine Ross, Rogers and Brown took steps to write their own constitution. In early August, they invited a fifteen-member committee of Eastern Cherokees to meet with a committee of the same number of Western Cherokees at Fort Smith, Arkansas. The purpose of the meeting was the preparation of a document "to be laid before the national council and chiefs" then in session.[55] Yet Ross supporters refused. After all, Ross partisans had the numerical advantage.

Faced with this challenge, Ross supporters sought to blunt the Rogers and Brown opposition. On 27 August, a select group of Ross men, including Bushyhead, warned Armstrong concerning moves by certain Western Cherokees. The messengers were aware of efforts of Ross' enemies to undermine the constitutional convention. They reported that Rogers and Brown had encouraged Cherokees to boycott the Ross assembly. Moreover, on 9 August, Rogers, Brown, and Looney had sent a letter to Armstrong. They accused Ross partisans of political usurpation and the murders of the Ridges and Boudinot. In the face of such serious allegations, Ross supporters dared not al-

George Washington Patterson, 45th Cong., 3d sess., 68 (LexisNexis Academic, 2006) Serial Set ID: 1839 S.rp. 744; John Ross et al. to M[atthew] Stokes, 21 June 1839, Letters Received by the Office of Indian Affairs, 1824–1881, National Archives, M234, roll 83; Congress, Senate Document 140, *Report of the Secretary of War*, 6.

[53] Ibid., *Report of the Commissioner*, 375–76.

[54] Ibid., *Memorial of the Delegation of the Cherokee Nation*, 59.

[55] *Report of the Commissioner of Indian Affairs*, 380.

low the accusations to stand uncontested. On 23 August, Isaac and George Bushyhead, early emigrants to the West, joined with over 261 "people of the Western Cherokee nation" to call for the deposition of Rogers and Brown.[56] Of course, the document may not have been a true representation of Western Cherokee support, for like George and Isaac, some of the signers may have been more linked to the Ross faction; that is, they may have arrived a short time before the main detachments. Yet Ross partisans temporarily had countered Rogers and Brown.

A few days later, delegates assembled at Tahlequah in national convention and drew up a constitution. The document became official on 6 September 1839 when Guess, Jesse Bushyhead, and forty-six others signed. The new government clearly had a majority of Ross supporters, and five of the signatories had been implicated in the Ridge-Boudinot assassinations.[57] The document created the executive, legislative, and judicial branches. It also divided the nation into eight districts for electoral and administrative purposes. Similar to the constitutional arrangement in the East, a principal chief and an assistant principal chief filled executive roles. But unlike the arrangement in the East, the executives received election through popular vote rather than being selected by the legislature. The National Committee and the council composed the bicameral National Council, the term that identified the new legislative branch. Members of both houses served two-year terms. Two delegates from each district served in the National Committee, and three members from each district sat in the council. A chief justice headed the Supreme Court. Associate justices also served as circuit court judges in the eight districts. The high court justices served four-year terms and received their positions by vote of

[56] Congress, Senate Document 140, *Report of the Secretary of War*, 115–19.

[57] James Spears, John Spears, Edward Gunter, Soft-Shelled Turtle, and Daniel Colston signed. See *Cherokee Laws, 1840* [title page torn, publisher and place of publication unknown], Rare Book Collection, Gilcrease Museum.

the National Council.[58] Beginning in 1843, electors in each district would choose the principal and assistant principal chiefs as well as members of the National Council. But for the present, the convention elected the first national officers.

The convention voted on 9 September. The positions of principal chief and assistant chief went to John Ross and Joseph Vann, respectively. Although formally listed as an Old Settler, Vann had emigrated not long before the detachments arrived. Moreover, he had been in the Ross camp in the old nation. The Bushyheads also were among the officeholders. Jesse Bushyhead, Walter Scott Adair, Looney Price, and George Hicks received appointments as Supreme Court associate justices. With the exception of Price, all of the justices had aligned with Ross in the East. And by this time, Price, the lone Western Cherokee justice, had been drawn into the Ross orbit. The legislature named John Martin as chief justice and established the first Monday in October as the beginning of the annual session of the court. For their services, each justice received $5 per day while the court remained in session. The elder Bushyhead along with twenty-four others won two-year terms in the council. Thirteen of the council listed themselves as "Old Settlers," but only two of the total forty seats in the national legislature went to Treaty party allies.[59]

Although the United States Constitution served as a model for the Cherokee government, several notable differences existed. One concerned a religious test oath for officeholders. The United States Constitution banned religious oaths as a requirement for officeholders. Yet the Cherokee ordinance required a religious affirmation. Article VI, Section 1 of the Cherokee Constitution prescribed, "No person who denies the being of God, or a future state of reward and

[58] *Constitution and Laws of the Cherokee Nation* (St. Louis: R. & T. A. Ennis, 1875) 9–19.

[59] W. Coodey to John Ross, 4 October 1839, John Ross Papers, folder 658, Gilcrease Museum; John Ross Papers, folder 662, Gilcrease Museum; Congress, Senate Document 140, *Report of the Secretary of War,* 42.

punishment, shall hold any office in the civil department of this Nation."[60] In a similar vein, some states had banned ordained ministers from holding state offices. But the Cherokee Constitution omitted this restriction. This omission allowed Stephen Foreman and Bushyhead to hold prominent positions in government.

Yet, in spite of the best hopes, genuine union proved superficial. The summer's proceedings had given Ross political control of the nation and, potentially, its finances. As a result, the opponents of Ross quickly moved to discredit the new government. Underscoring alleged financial malfeasance and the illegitimacy of the summer's proceedings, they repudiated the Ross government at a meeting at Price's Prairie on 20 August. Moreover, Watie men resolved to send John A. Bell and Watie to Washington to meet with Poinsett. And because of disorder and the perceived exclusion of Western Cherokees and the Treaty party, United States authorities refused to recognize the Ross regime. Once again, the Ross government felt impelled to defend its legitimacy. They moreover determined to petition Washington concerning several unresolved issues. These concerns revolved around interest on investments, annuity payments, and unsettled individual property claims. On 12 October, the national legislature adjourned after selecting John Ross and eight delegates, including Jesse Bushyhead, to journey to Washington "as early as practicable."[61] In case any of the appointees were unable to make the trip, the council authorized Ross to name replacements.

About 15 November, Ross and eight others left for Washington. For some unknown reason, Bushyhead and two other chosen representatives did not join the delegation. On 31 December 1839, shortly after arriving in Washington, the delegation requested a meeting with President Van Buren and Secretary of War Poinsett. Yet anticipated hopes of a speedy resolution of Cherokee claims evaporated. Van Bu-

[60] *Constitution and Laws of the Cherokee Nation*, 14.

[61] Congress, *Memorial of the Delegation of the Cherokee Nation*, 26.

ren and Poinsett felt that Ross had blood on his hands. They took seriously the accusations that seemed to implicate the chief in the Ridge-Boudinot assassinations. Although Van Buren and Poinsett agreed to communicate with the delegates, they refused a face-to-face with Ross, pending the outcome of further investigations.[62] Moreover, other troubling reports from Arbuckle soon reached Poinsett. In November 1839, Western Cherokees had met at Takatoka in another attempt to reorganize their rival government. Considering the Ross government illegal, they had sought the aid of Arbuckle in bringing about tribal union more on their terms. Communications from the general to Poinsett also indicated Arbuckle's personal mistrust of Ross. Without mincing words, Arbuckle wanted Ross removed from office. Poinsett therefore recommended a reduced political role for Ross. In doing so, Arbuckle and Poinsett favored the deposition of Ross and the election of one-third of officeholders from the Western Cherokees.[63]

Realizing this renewed challenge, Ross partisans called for another national assembly to convene on 15 January 1840. In response to the Ross appeal, almost 2,000 Cherokees again met at Tahlequah to hammer out differences. Of this number, only a small number of Western Cherokees attended. Yet the meeting yielded some positive results. The delegates cancelled the amnesty decree that had been so distasteful to the Treaty party. They also formally ratified the Act of Union and the Ross-sponsored constitution issued the past fall. Yet Arbuckle decided to use this development as an opportunity to remove Ross. Arbuckle informed John Rogers of his plan for power sharing. He proposed a triumvirate in which Rogers and emigrant

[62] Ibid, 27.

[63] Reed, "The Ross-Watie Conflict," 151; Moulton, *John Ross, Cherokee Chief*, 116–22.

leaders George Lowrey and John Martin would serve as chiefs of a unified nation.[64]

The next step of Arbuckle was to coerce the two factions into cooperation. On 21 April, the general spoke to an assembly of Cherokees at Fort Gibson. Arbuckle informed them about his desire to exclude Ross from office. But Ross partisans refused to accept Arbuckle's meddling. On 22 April, twenty-two Ross supporters, including Jesse and Isaac Bushyhead, signed a letter to Arbuckle. In a diplomatic tone, the letter strongly protested the encroachment of Arbuckle and Poinsett on tribal sovereignty. The message furthermore stressed the necessity of free elections, for little hope existed for guarantees of basic rights without a truly elective government.[65] As a result, Arbuckle retreated from his moves to exclude Ross. After several delays, Arbuckle then persuaded the two factions to meet at Fort Gibson on 10 June 1840. If they refused to cooperate, Arbuckle threatened to play a trump card and divide the nation into two autonomous governments. Finally, on 26 June, both sides agreed to accept the existing constitution as it stood. Ross supporters also agreed to allocate part of the per capita payments from Cherokee lands in the East to the Western Cherokees. And Western Cherokees received assurances to "a just proportion" of government positions in the new constitutional term. [66] Known as the Fort Gibson "arrangement," the agreement meant that Treaty party and Western Cherokees shared legislative and judicial seats.[67] After United States authorities sanctioned the union, the newly organized Cherokee government in the West became known as the official Western Cherokee Nation.

[64] M[atthew] Arbuckle to John Rogers, 15 December 1839, Letters Cherokee Agency West, 1840, National Archives, microfilm 89; Moulton, *John Ross, Cherokee Chief*, 120.

[65] John Martin et al. to [Matthew] Arbuckle, 22 April 1840. Letters Cherokee Agency West, 1840, National Archives, microfilm 89.

[66] Reed, "The Ross-Watie Conflict," 153.

[67] Congress, *Report of the Secretary of War*, 42.

Yet official union did not end unrest. Some Watie supporters still had no intention of cooperating with a Ross government, even if it included them. As proof, death threats against leading Ross partisans appeared. In a letter dated 9 February 1841, Lewis Ross informed his son, John McDonald Ross, of an aborted conspiracy. The assassins originally had planned to strike on 12 January. According to the details, leaders of the Treaty party had targeted John Ross, Lewis Ross, Jesse Bushyhead, and others in the Ross inner circle. Fortunately, Watie partisans John A. Bell and George W. Adair had disclosed the plot. This gave Lewis hope that future murders would not materialize. Having been forewarned, Lewis gave assurance that he had sufficient protection. He bolstered his claim by asserting that plenty of "defenders" had pledged to lay down their lives for him.[68] And fortunately, John Ross already had left for Washington on a diplomatic mission. The tocsin having been sounded, there were no assassinations. Possibly, Watie supporters realized the futility of violence, for additional assassinations held the potential for bloody retaliation. And at a time of delicate negotiations with Washington, attacks against the Ross faction would strengthen the position of Ross backers before Poinsett.

Perhaps the recent involvement of Bushyhead as chief justice in the case of Archilla Smith may have had something to do with the death threats. On 17 October 1840, Chief Justice Martin had died. Less than a month later, the National Council selected Bushyhead to succeed Martin. Bushyhead had no formal legal education, but neither was there any educational requirement for judges, even high court justices. And because justices only received pay on a daily basis during court sessions, the work was not that lucrative.[69] Thus, legal professionals were either unavailable or, for political reasons, did not

[68] Lewis Ross to John [McDonald Ross], 9 February 1841, John Ross Papers, folder 758, Gilcrease Museum.

[69] Strickland, *Fire and the Spirits*, 156.

seek appointments. Justices nevertheless held high-profile positions, for they adjudicated a number of different types of cases, both criminal and civil. For example, Bushyhead's judicial responsibilities ranged from "complete criminal jurisdiction" to witnessing depositions for property claims.[70]

Bushyhead soon experienced the negative aspects of a magistrate's position. As the new chief justice, Bushyhead stepped into the politically charged case of Archilla Smith. Son of the respected chief Cabbin Smith, Archilla had been politically prominent in the East. In March 1835, Archilla had been in Washington and helped negotiate the removal treaty. And back in Georgia by the following December, he had signed the New Echota Treaty. In March 1837, Archilla and family were members of a pro-treaty detachment that had emigrated following the New Echota proceedings. The 466 passengers boarded vessels at Ross's Landing on the Tennessee River. The boats, with Major Ridge in the group, reached Fort Smith before the end of the month.[71] Although in a position of prominence, the young and illiterate Smith had also acquired a reputation for violence. John Howard Payne, a white poet and Ross supporter, described Archilla Smith as "a violent & dissipated Cherokee."[72]

In late 1839, Smith had killed John MacIntosh. The slaying occurred in the Cherokee Nation at an encampment of Creek refugees. The free flow of liquor from a nearby whiskey seller had contributed to a volatile environment. MacIntosh, boasting his bravado, was in a belligerent mood. Feeling threatened, Smith angrily produced a knife. In response, MacIntosh lunged at Smith. In the ensuing scuffle, Smith slashed at MacIntosh several times. MacIntosh then swung and struck Smith with his fist. The struggle continued after MacIn-

[70] *Constitution and Laws of the Cherokee Nation*, 19; "Deposition of Eight Killer," John Ross Papers, folder 809, Gilcrease Museum.

[71] Grant Foreman, "Notes and Documents," *Mississippi Valley Historical Review* 18 (September 1931): 232–45.

[72] Payne Papers, 1:134.

tosh had mounted his horse. Attempting to prevent escape, Smith grabbed the bridle and plunged a knife into MacIntosh. Breaking free, MacIntosh rode eighty-to-ninety yards before falling to the ground. The unfortunate MacIntosh quickly died there. But authorities were slow to arrest Smith, for he was popular among the Treaty party and political unrest was rife. He remained at large for about a year before being apprehended and sent to trial in December 1840.

But before Smith's arrest, he also had been implicated in a threat to assassinate Bushyhead. Around noon on 20 August 1840, an unidentified Cherokee had visited Bushyhead's cabin and delivered a sober warning. He advised Bushyhead against sleeping at home that night. According to the messenger, "certain men would probably be there that night to take him."[73] True to the warning, nightriders arrived and milled around Bushyhead's cabin. Constant barking from guard dogs alerted those inside that something was amiss. Daniel Butrick was a guest in the home of Bushyhead that night. The next day, Butrick received information from unnamed sources concerning the details of the frightful night. Butrick made a chilling entry in his journal: "Archilles [*sic*] Smith, his half-brother and son and three of Watie's sons, and Mr. Fields" were in company "to kill a number of men among whom Mr. Bushyhead is one."[74] Although Butrick's accusation may have been based partially on hearsay, surely Bushyhead took the threats seriously, for a prudent man dared not ignore Smith's past hostile behavior.

Because Smith was Cherokee, the case fell under the jurisdiction of the Cherokee judicial system. The trial was historic, for it was the first case argued before the Supreme Court under the new government.[75] In a larger sense, the integrity of the Ross government was on the line. Associate Justice Looney Price first heard the case in a circuit

[73] Butrick Journal, 20 August 1840.
[74] Butrick Journal, 21 August 1840.
[75] Moulton, *The Papers of Chief John Ross*, 2:78.

court venue. The trial opened on the council grounds at Tahlequah on 15 December 1840. The courthouse was a small log structure with a dirt floor. Benches or rough boards provided seating for the jury, witnesses, and interpreters. A twelve-man jury heard the trial. Stand Watie and William Holt served as defense attorneys. Isaac Bushyhead, as a district judge, was the prosecutor. Because two jurors were not able to agree on a guilty verdict, the jury became hopelessly deadlocked. The jury then asked Price to discharge them from the case. Price did so. But before the impanelment of a new jury, Price suddenly fell ill. Feeling unable to continue, Price asked permission to resign his seat. Rather than delay the trial for the appointment of Price's successor, the sheriff requested that Bushyhead preside over a special court.[76]

The case opened before Bushyhead on Tuesday, 22 December. Aiming to prevent a new trial, Holt opened with a plea of double jeopardy. He argued that Smith deserved his freedom, for one jury had already failed to convict Smith. Thus, a second trial violated the Cherokee constitutional prohibition against double jeopardy. Isaac Bushyhead disagreed. He countered that the proceedings merely extended the initial trial. Jesse Bushyhead likewise did not accept the double jeopardy argument. Rather, he proceeded with the selection of a new jury. After a new jury had been formed, the trial continued. Watie then pointed to discrepancies in the testimonies of witnesses. Watie reasoned that Smith had acted in self-defense. According to Watie, the murders of Boudinot and the Ridges only a short time before the MacIntosh affair had made Smith mindful of his own safety. Feeling threatened, Smith had acted to prevent his own death. Finally, Watie even proposed that Smith had killed MacIntosh accidentally. Again, Isaac Bushyhead disagreed. He argued that Smith

[76] John Howard Payne, *Indian Justice: A Cherokee Murder Trial at Tahlequah in 1840* (Norman: University of Oklahoma; rep., Harlow Publishing, 1933; rep. 7–15, 49–51 (page references are to reprint edition).

had killed MacIntosh with malice. The prosecutor pointed to the sworn testimonies of witnesses as proof. And although witnesses differed on minor details, their versions did not discredit the savage attack on MacIntosh. The trial lasted five days. On Saturday, 26 December, after deliberating past dark, the jury rendered a guilty verdict. Bushyhead pronounced the sentence that same night. Although the punishment was in accordance to Cherokee law, it was severe. The chief justice sentenced Smith to death by hanging.

If tried in a modern American court, numerous irregularities would invalidate the conviction. Certainly, several aspects were questionable. Because of the recent political turbulence, a fair trial may not have been possible for such a well-known supporter of the New Echota Treaty. Moreover, Smith did not receive adequate counsel. With limited education, Watie was certainly not a qualified attorney. And there was a potential conflict of interest on the part of the chief justice and prosecutor. Allegedly having been threatened four months earlier by Smith, the chief justice had good reason for prejudice. Finally, language became a barrier for some of the jury did not understand English. After a new jury had been selected, the chief justice instructed the jury foreman to translate from English to Cherokee for non-English-speaking jurymen. But the foreman was incapable of the task. Because of his linguistic skills, Jesse Bushyhead had to assume the responsibility of translating. Although the prosecuting and defending counsels apparently did not object, as translator, Bushyhead compromised his role as presiding justice.

Although sentenced to death, Smith maintained hope for an executive pardon. The newly adopted constitution provided the opportunity for clemency in capital crimes.[77] Following sentencing, Smith immediately appealed to the chief justice for permission to petition Ross. Bushyhead promised to investigate the legal parameters and immediately consulted Methodist preacher Young Wolf, the jury

[77] *Constitution and Laws of the Cherokee Nation*, 1840.

foreman, and several jury members. During removal, Young Wolf had traveled with Evan Jones and likely was an earlier acquaintance of Bushyhead.[78] Yet, after discussing an appeal with the jury, Bushyhead denied Smith's request. Apparently, the chief justice and jurors considered the evidence damning enough to deny clemency.

But the refusal did not end efforts to free Smith. Without the court's sanction, Watie, Holt, and George Washington Adair personally delivered a petition to Ross two days later. The petition requested that Ross reprieve Smith. Adair reminded Ross that an executive pardon carried great potential for national healing. The 104 petitioners included those outside the Ross circle, such as Watie, his father, and two brothers. Four of the signatories had been among the jury pool. The petitioners justified their request in order that "peace and harmony may prevail."[79] Ross had a short time before the scheduled execution to decide Smith's fate. The principal chief reviewed the petition and spoke with Watie, Holt, and Adair. Yet he denied pardon or reprieve. Instead, Ross stressed that the petition lacked the approval of Bushyhead and the court, even though it included names of some in the jury pool. Also, he observed that the document did not "set forth one single reason why the criminal should not suffer."[80] The denial sealed the fate of Smith. Under Cherokee law, he had exhausted all possibilities of clemency. On 1 January 1842, ten days after the case opened before Bushyhead, the condemned man bravely died on a makeshift gallows.

The execution raised the possibility of a renewed vendetta, for Smith supporters had legitimate reasons to question the lack of a pardon. Yet, under the circumstances, it seemed that Bushyhead had

[78] Cherokee Removal, Oklahoma, OTOTA, Sequoyah Center, box 379.

[79] Moulton, *The Papers of Chief John Ross*, 2:78, and also 2:77; Petition of T. J. Pack et al., 28 December 1840, Gary Moulton Papers, box 5, folder 7, OHSL; Kenny A. Franks, *Stand Watie and the Agony of the Cherokee Nation* (Memphis: Memphis State University, 1979) 77.

[80] Payne, *Indian Justice*, 93.

done his best to oversee an equitable court. There were several examples of fair play. He had instructed the jury concerning related aspects of litigation. In so doing, he carefully defined and gave concrete examples of legal terminology. He explained the differences between circumstantial and non-circumstantial evidence and willful slaying and self-defense. Bushyhead also had provided the jury ample opportunity to question individual witnesses. And before the jurors deliberated the verdict, he cautioned them against the old Cherokee law of blood revenge. Rather, he urged them to base their decisions on written Cherokee law. Aware of the politically charged nature of the case, Bushyhead had stressed that neither Smith's politics nor his past character was on trial. Concerning a pardon, he reminded them that only the principal chief had the power to grant clemency. Finally, when pronouncing sentence, the chief justice revealed a sense of genuine remorse. Bushyhead lamented, "would to Heaven you [Smith] had been proven innocent instead of guilty, that I might have been spared the sad necessity or pronouncing upon a fellow-citizen, who has flung away such opportunities of being useful to his country."[81]

Following the Smith affair, Bushyhead once again traveled to Washington. In spring 1841, Ross had discussed delayed annuity payments with the newly elected President William Henry Harrison. But before the resolution of any issues, Harrison died, barely six weeks into his term. Vice President John Tyler succeeded Harrison. In discussions with the Tyler administration, Ross became optimistic. He hoped that the new Whig government would renegotiate the New Echota Treaty. And under any new arrangements, federal authorities would have to recognize the Ross government as the only lawful Cherokee government. Such recognition stood to negate the legitimacy and bargaining power of remnants from the Old Settler and

[81] Ibid., 67–70, 72–87.

Treaty party factions.[82] Eastern Cherokees also stood to gain a fairer price for their homeland and full reimbursement for pre-removal losses. Finally, the discussions raised hopes regarding federal guarantees of permanent ownership of their new lands. Having returned from Washington, Ross addressed the National Council on 1 December 1841.

With Bushyhead as interpreter, Ross informed the assembly of his anticipated visit to Washington. He summarized a letter from Tyler, which seemed to promise a new treaty and indemnity for losses. Ross stressed the importance of pursuing these positive developments. The legislature agreed. Before its adjournment in late 1841, the National Council selected Ross, Bushyhead, John Benge, David Vann, and William S. Coodey as delegates to Washington. Ross, Bushyhead, and Benge left for Washington the last week of March 1842. While en route, they visited Lawrenceville, New Jersey, where Bushyhead's oldest son, Dennis Wolfe Bushyhead, and the two eldest sons of Ross were students.[83]

After reaching Washington, the delegates presented several requests to John C. Spenser, the new secretary of war. They desired guarantees that would safeguard future tribal possession of existing lands and the removal of federal troops from the Cherokee Nation. They also wanted Cherokee courts to have sole jurisdiction over Cherokee citizens rather than surrounding state courts. Other issues concerned a limitation on the number of licensed traders in the Cherokee Nation and changes in the management of Cherokee public funds. Furthermore, they stressed the final resolution of removal and

[82] Denson, *Demanding the Cherokee Nation*, 43.

[83] McLoughlin, *Champions of the Cherokees*, 216; John Bartlett Meserve, "Chief Dennis Bushyhead," *Chronicles of Oklahoma* 14 (September 1936): 349–59. Because of illness, Vann was not able to go, and David Carter took his place in July. Moulton, *John Ross, Cherokee Chief*, 132–33; Grant Foreman, *The Five Civilized Tribes* (Norman: University of Oklahoma, 1934) 321–22; Moulton, *The Papers of Chief John Ross*, 2:123.

resettlement claims under the New Echota Treaty. After several months, Spencer proposed concessions. But the terms failed to fully address their demands, and the delegates rejected the proposal. Spencer then countered with a delaying tactic. He insisted that a new treaty hinged upon the invalidation of the New Echota Treaty by the Cherokee Nation. Although most Cherokees disdained the treaty, any nullification risked the interruption of annuity payments. At this crucial point, negotiations collapsed and the delegates left Washington. By 22 September, Bushyhead had reached home in time for the opening session of the Cherokee high court the first Monday in October.[84]

While the delegation was in Washington, unrest continued in the Cherokee Nation. Murder claimed the lives of several Cherokees and whites in 1842 and 1843. Part of the disturbances resulted from outlaw gangs and festering feuds between Ross and Watie supporters. In June 1842, Worcester described the recent murder of James Foreman by Watie at a Maysville, Arkansas store. Maysville, a short distance from the Honey Creek settlement, harbored mercantile interests, which profited from the sale of liquor to thirsty whites and Cherokees. Major Hitchcock had described Maysville as "a miserable place complained of universally as a grogery [*sic*], filled with what are called groceries."[85] The site of the crime lay only a few feet outside the Cherokee national border. Foreman and Watie happened to encounter each other in the store and exchanged harsh words. Watie accused Foreman of complicity in the murder of Major Ridge. A scuffle ensued, and Watie stabbed Foreman. Watie then finished Foreman off with a gunshot.[86] In turn, the friends of Foreman targeted Watie. In March 1843, an unidentified resident of Beattie's Prairie, only a few

[84] Moulton, *John Ross, Cherokee Chief*, 133; Evan Jones Journal, 22 September 1842, ABHS, FM-98.

[85] Grant Foreman, ed., *A Traveler in Indian Territory*, 78.

[86] S[amuel] A. Worcester to David Green, 22 June 1842, ABCFM 18.3.1, vol. 10, item 163; Moulton, *The Papers of Chief John Ross*, 2:124.

miles southwest of Maysville, released ominous news. He reported that armed patrols were active at night and sought to behead treaty men.[87]

The lawlessness was a precursor to disturbances that occurred during the national elections in August 1843. This was the first election for principal and assistant chiefs and the second election for the national legislature since the organization of a government four years earlier. During the summer, Ross and George Lowrey campaigned as Whigs for principal chief and assistant principal chief, respectively. Opponents Joseph Vann and Walter Scott Adair ran on the Locofoco ticket, a faction of the national Democratic party. Watie men feared the possible results. If victorious, Ross candidates stood to control national finances and annuity funds for another four years. Rather than endure Ross, Watie men favored the division of the nation into two separate governments, each with its distinct annuity.[88]

Yet the election was not entirely peaceful. On 7 August, the day of the election, a disturbance occurred about forty miles from Fort Gibson at a precinct polling station in the Saline District. Unfortunately, the incident proved fatal to Isaac Bushyhead. Because of the practice of *viva voce* voting, electoral results were easily available to anyone within earshot of the polls.[89] Serving as official precinct judges, David Vann and Isaac Bushyhead, both Ross men, supervised the voting at the David Vann settlement. Vann was the treasurer of the Cherokee Nation and a brother-in-law of local sheriff George West. When voting neared an end, the two polling judges scratched out the election results in a note to be delivered with the returns to Archibald Campbell and Jack Spears. Campbell and Spears were firmly in the Ross camp. Both had signed the Act of Union and the 1839 Consti-

[87] *Arkansas Intelligencer*, 18 March 1843.

[88] Reed, "The Ross-Watie Conflict," 186.

[89] Moulton, *John Ross, Cherokee Chief*, 135–36; *Arkansas Intelligencer*, 19 August 1843; *Constitution and Laws of the Cherokee Nation*, 12.

tution and also held national offices under the Ross government.[90] The message confidently asserted that "there is no doubt we have elected every one of our men"—by this, they meant Ross, Lowrey, and National Council candidates.[91] Indeed, the final tallies confirmed a one-sided victory for Ross and Lowrey. The two candidates won by almost a two-thirds margin. Ross also garnered a veto-proof majority in the National Council.

But some opponents of Ross in the Vann settlement grumbled over the results. Members of the local West family were among the opposition. Jacob West, a resident of the Cherokee Nation for over thirty years, had taken a Cherokee wife in the East. Jacob was the father of John, George, and Ellis.[92] At least two of his sons bore grudges against the Ross faction. John, an outspoken supporter of removal, had been a signatory of the New Echota Treaty. Because of this, he had felt personally singled out for retribution.[93] George had held the sheriff's office but was not returned to office. Instead, voters elected John Brown. Other disgruntled participants were John Work, a notorious white man lodging with John West, and Matthew Thompson, son of merchant James Allen Thompson.[94] Wishing to deprive Ross of votes, these malcontents had intimidated local Ross supporters and plotted to destroy ballots.

Following the polling, Isaac Bushyhead and Vann finished tabulating the official returns at the house of Samuel W. Bell, a brother of John A. Bell.[95] Unfortunately, the residence afforded Ross' enemies a

[90] Constitutional and Laws of the Cherokee Nation, 622. Congress, *Report of Secretary of War*, 42–44.

[91] David Vann and Isaac Bushyhead to A[rchibald] Campbell and Jack Spears, 7 August 1843, John Ross Papers, folder 889, Gilcrease Museum.

[92] Bell, *Genealogy*, 462.

[93] Congress, *Memorial of the Cherokee Representatives*, 113; Congress, *Report of the Commissioner of Indian Affairs*, 376.

[94] Moulton, *The Papers of Chief John Ross*, 2:176.

[95] Bell, *Genealogy*, 47.

location from which to intimidate Bushyhead and Vann. In the course of finalizing the returns, an argument erupted. In a heated exchange of words, Ross opponents hurled abuse at Vann. Vann then suggested that the tabulators adjourn to a private place more removed from disturbances. Yet Ross opponents evidently felt this was a ploy to skirt scrutiny. As Isaac and Vann began to walk away, attackers assaulted Isaac. Wrestling loose, he jumped a fence and raced 100 to 150 yards. George West and Work pursued Isaac. Overtaking him, Work fatally stabbed Isaac. Meanwhile, Vann had tried to mount his horse. But bystanders overpowered him and brutally beat him with clubs. The elder West encouraged the assailants with cries of "kill him."[96] During the melee, Thompson struck Vann on the head with a brick bat while another Ross supporter, Elijah Hicks, also suffered injury. The assailants then destroyed the election returns. However, more than the polling process may have contributed to the violence. There was a possible sense of betrayal over support for national removal. In the East, the names of Isaac Bushyhead, Vann, and Hicks had once appeared on a petition with John Walker, Jr.; Watie; Boudinot; the Ridges; and John West.[97] The document had urged cooperation with removal. But by 1843, the three victims had transferred their allegiance to the Ross camp.

The attacks disturbed the Ross faction and United States military authorities. Reports of unrest quickly reached Thomas Hartley Crawford, the commissioner of the Office of Indian Affairs. Crawford promptly informed Secretary of War James Madison Porter that Ross had not been harmed. Yet, in case the need arose, Crawford was careful to inform Porter about the numbers of available troops on the frontier. In Cherokee country, Ross supporters took precautions and

[96] P. M. Butler to T. Hartley Crawford, 12 August 1843, Letters Received by the Office of Indian Affairs, 1824–1881, National Archives, M234, roll 87.

[97] Petition to Committee and Council, 15 May 1833, Letters Received by the Office of Indian Affairs, 1824–1881, National Archives, M234, roll 75.

placed a heavy guard around their principal chief. Moreover, Cherokee vigilantes rounded up whites suspected in the slaying and delivered them to the commander at Fort Gibson. Yet Ross knew that some of the accused had escaped to Arkansas and remained out of Cherokee jurisdiction. Ross therefore appealed to United States authorities for assistance.[98] The same request sought to "break up such councils or assemblages" held on the Arkansas border by the enemies of Ross, namely John Rogers, James Starr, and John A. Bell.[99] Brevet Brigadier General Zachary Taylor, commander of the Southwest Frontier District headquartered at Fort Smith, considered Cherokee laws adequate to deal with the crisis. Yet Taylor ordered the commandant of Fort Gibson to assist Cherokees in providing "every facility in securing the murderers."[100]

While United States and Cherokee authorities took action, Jesse mourned the murder of his brother. For at least sixteen years, they had been involved in personal business and national issues. Four days after the murder, Jesse took personal responsibility for the apprehension of the killers. Jesse placed a detailed announcement in the Van Buren *Arkansas Intelligencer*. Published on 19 August, the article denounced the "atrocious murder" and offered up to $1,250 for the arrest of Work, George West, and Ellis West. Bushyhead gave full physical descriptions of the accused, including vocal characteristics of

[98] T. Hartley Crawford to J. M. Porter, 30 August 1843, Letters Received by the Office of Indian Affairs, 1824–1881, National Archives, M234, roll 87; W. Jones Howard to J. M. Porter, 12 September 1843, Letters Received by the Office of Indian Affairs, 1824–1881, National Archives, M234, roll 87; *Arkansas Intelligencer*, 19 August 1843; Moulton, *John Ross, Cherokee Chief*, 136; Moulton, *The Papers of Chief John Ross*, 2:166–67, 176; Congress, Senate Document 140, *Report of the Secretary of War*, 114.

[99] Moulton, *The Papers of Chief John Ross*, 2:177.

[100] Z[achary] Taylor to the Adjutant General of the Army, 15 August 1843, Letters sent by Army of the Southwestern Frontier, ML0602, roll 1.

the soft-spoken West brothers. The notice appeared in several subsequent editions of the paper.[101]

It did not take long for the legal process to work. Within days, authorities captured Work, Jacob and John West, and another suspect. Work rested in an Arkansas jail, where he awaited trial in a Little Rock federal court.[102] Yet two other suspects evaded arrest. Many believed that George West, one of the two fugitives, had absconded to Texas. After an Arkansas federal judge denied Jacob a writ of habeas corpus from Cherokee custody, he stood trial in a Cherokee court as a criminal accessory. As a longtime resident of the nation, Cherokee authorities considered Jacob to be a Cherokee citizen. The trial of Jacob West opened on 25 September 1843 in the Saline District. He was the first of the accused to stand trial. Charged with abetting the escape of Work and George in a capital offense, he became subject to the death penalty.[103]

David Carter, a member of the Western Cherokee faction, presided over the trial. Yet there were some legal concerns related to the imminent expiration of Carter's temporary judicial appointment. Originally issued to fill a vacancy as a district judge, his commission was due to expire on 2 October. The case of Jacob went to the jury either on 11 October or the following day. After the trial of Jacob, the case of John West was next on the docket. The Cherokee national legislature scrambled to appoint Carter as a permanent justice of the Cherokee Supreme Court, even while he presided over the trial of Jacob. Yet defense attorneys argued that doubts over the validity of his term nullified the trial of Jacob West. Fearing that Carter might not receive confirmation in time, Associate Justice Elijah Hicks summoned Bushyhead.[104] In a letter to Ross, William S. Coodey

[101] *Arkansas Intelligencer*, 19 August 1843.

[102] Moulton, *The Papers of Chief John Ross*, 2:176.

[103] Congress, Senate Document 140, *Report of the Secretary of War*, 121, 126–27.

[104] Moulton, *The Papers of Chief John Ross*, 2:153–54.

mentioned the imminent arrival of Bushyhead at the courthouse that evening.[105] However, authorities evidently empowered Carter to adjudicate in time, for there is no indication that Bushyhead officially participated in the trial. The jury found the defendants guilty, and Carter pronounced sentence on Jacob and John.

The enemies of Ross attempted to insert uncertainty into the legal process. Before the trial opened, they had vowed retribution.[106] The *Arkansas Intelligencer* reported a conspiracy to assassinate John Ross, Jesse Bushyhead, Coodey, John Benge, and Elijah Hicks. The rumored attacks coincided with the opening day of the trial. The rumors were not accidental, for the would-be assassins intended to cause fear among Ross backers and paralyze the court proceedings. Yet the hearsay proved false, and the trials finished in good order. Jacob received the death penalty, but John was more fortunate. There was support for a commutation of his sentence, for the physically towering John had served as councilor from the Saline District in 1841.[107] When pronouncing the sentence, Carter scheduled the execution of John for 21 October. But a petition submitted to Ross resulted in "executive clemency."[108] Yet John did not go unpunished. In 1844, Ezekiel West reported John had received 100 "lashes on his bare back."[109] The other wrongdoers likely received lashings as well.[110]

[105] Grant Foreman, *Five Civilized Tribes*, 327; Z[achary] Taylor to the Adjutant General of the Army, 15 August 1843, Records of Headquarters, Army of the Southwestern Frontier, and headquarters, second and seventh military departments, 1835–1853, National Archives, M1302, roll 1; Congress, Senate Document 140, *Report of the Secretary of War*, 113; Moulton, *The Papers of Chief John Ross*, 2:181–82.

[106] *Arkansas Intelligencer*, 30 September 1843.

[107] Grant Foreman, ed., *A Traveler in Indian Territory*, 59; Congress, Senate Document 140, *Report of the Secretary of War*, 43.

[108] Congress, Senate Document 140 *Report of the Secretary of War*, 114.

[109] Ibid., 95.

[110] *Arkansas Intelligencer*, 4 November 1843; Moulton, *John Ross, Cherokee Chief*, 136.

As stated, there is no evidence that Bushyhead filled a judicial role. But if he did, defense attorneys nevertheless had cause to raise issues over alleged trial irregularities. For questions concerning the official capacity of Carter already had been raised. In December 1844, United States authorities investigated the outbreaks of violence and questioned Carter about the case. In response, Carter testified that the Wests had "as fair and impartial a trial as any other citizen of the Cherokee nation could have had under similar charges."[111]

Bushyhead's political involvement often had placed him in jeopardy. By the time of the West trials, he had been a prominent public figure for five turbulent years. But before his death in 1844, Bushyhead became party to still another political controversy. In 1833, the Western Cherokee government had nationalized all salt works that processed brine from surface pools. Salt, essential to the preservation of meat, was a necessary commodity on the frontier. The government therefore meant to prevent the monopolization and sale of salt at exorbitant prices. Yet the act had allowed some existing private salines to continue for another five years. In 1841, the new Cherokee government also exempted artificial salt works, those using wells and mechanical means, from seizure. But if the Cherokee government found it necessary to take possession, it pledged to pay producers liberal reimbursements for improvements, for such operations had required substantial investments in large pots, kettles, pipes, furnaces, shelters for workers, sheds, and salt houses. Then, on 30 October 1843, the new legislature cancelled exemptions for artificial salt works.[112] Under the new law, operators had to abandon their works. This action upset some producers. Feeling targeted, they protested the imminent confiscation of their works at the hands of the Ross government. And by the end of 1843, some still occupied their leases.

[111] Congress, Senate Document 140, *Report of the Secretary of War*, 114.
[112] Ibid., 127–28.

Wishing to facilitate seizures, the legislature had arranged for reimbursements. The same 1843 law that had ended exemptions also provided a means to determine property values. Accordingly, the legislature created appointments for salt works assessors. James M. Payne, George Hicks, and Bushyhead received these posts. The agents evaluated at least two large salt works and possibly others. Beginning in early January 1844, the three agents worked together and likely finished evaluations early in the year. Either before the assessments or as a result, Payne and Hicks developed a deep respect for Bushyhead. Shortly after his death, Payne and Hicks lamented his passing and reflected "the deep reverence so mournfully expressed by our fellow-citizens."[113] Yet not all leaseholders held such sentiments.

John Rogers occupied the Grand Saline works. Rogers still resented his deposition as chief of the Western Cherokees by the Ross government. Moreover, his brother, Lovely Rogers, had been arrested as an accomplice in the murder of Isaac Bushyhead. Lovely had gained release only after agreeing to testify at the trial. In January 1844, the agents assessed the value of the John Rogers operation at over $3,024. Along with salt production equipment, his property included sixty-five acres, timberland, an orchard, slave quarters, family dwellings, and carriages. Slow to vacate the premises, Cherokee authorities removed Rogers and his family from the property two months later. But as late as January 1845, Rogers had not been reimbursed.[114] Bluford West, another son of Jacob West, operated a separate saline less than two miles from the Grand River. Bluford had not been a participant in the murder of Isaac Bushyhead. He had been part of the old Western Cherokee faction, but also had been elected as district judge for the Saline District under the Ross government.[115] Located near good land and with access to wood for fuel, West had

[113] Ibid., 104.
[114] Ibid., 95, 111.
[115] Ibid.

invested heavily in his operation. But Payne, Hicks, and Bushyhead failed to evaluate the property. In a statement to Cherokee authorities, Payne explained the oversight. Payne disclosed that a large part of the valuable property lay outside the works. He also noted that an accurate property assessment was problematic because the saltwater content was "very weak." Payne furthermore recommended that the national legislature delay action in order to determine a more exact settlement.[116] In the meantime, the agents had allowed West to remain on the property. Later, United States army inspectors evaluated the property at $19,425. Of course, Rogers complained bitterly to federal authorities about perceived discriminatory treatment. He felt that his eviction was another oppressive act of the Ross government. As such, its primary purpose served to deprive Rogers of the livelihood necessary to remain in the Cherokee Nation.

In response to Rogers and his supporters, Porter organized an investigatory commission. General Roger Jones, Lieutenant Colonel Richard Barnes Mason, and Pierce Mason Butler, the Cherokee agent who had replaced Stokes, composed the commission.[117] In 1844, the commission reported positive developments in the Cherokee Nation. Yet Captain Albemarle Cady, who had gathered some information for the commission, voiced some concerns. Cady of the Sixth United States Infantry generally lauded the Cherokees for their just laws and constitutional government. Although he failed to mention Bushyhead, his report to Congress voiced reservations about the inequities of the salt law.

> Whatever may have been the motive for such an enactment, it cannot be doubted that the tendency of it would be to the erection of a monopoly in the hands of the Government, and a consequent repression of individual industry and enterprise, or, at the best, a be-

[116] Ibid., 106.

[117] Carolyn Thomas Foreman, "General Richard Barnes Mason," *Chronicles of Oklahoma* 19 (March 1941): 28.

> stowal of favors and privileges upon particular individuals, to the ultimate disadvantage of the people.[118]

The salt works controversy ended the public service of Bushyhead, for he died during the approaching summer. His political activities and the involvement of several family members had marked him firmly as a Ross supporter. This is not surprising considering his association with Ross in the East. Yet how much did he profit from his association with Ross, and to what extent did he participate from a sense of public service? Without a doubt, he helped to bridge the gap between Eastern and Western Cherokees. But neither is there indication that Bushyhead accumulated great wealth from public life in Indian Territory. He drew an appreciable sum as a detachment leader, but the responsibilities of a detachment leader proved heavy. Moreover, he received a salary for service on the national court. Yet, in an atmosphere of civil unrest and assassinations, such service was risky. And he only served for four sessions. His work as an interpreter provided intermittent income, but this service was not new. He had also been in periodic demand as a translator in the East. Bushyhead allegedly had made recriminatory remarks against the Treaty party in Kentucky. But after arriving in the West, he did not personally encourage or participate in assassinations. Perhaps one of the greatest assessments of Bushyhead came from Butler. In his official capacity as Cherokee agent, Butler reported on conditions in the Cherokee Nation on 30 September 1843. He lauded Bushyhead as "a man of piety, decision, and intelligence, and, both as a preacher and magistrate exerses [*sic*] a salutary influence over the government and morals of the people."[119]

[118] Congress, Senate Document 140, *Report of the Secretary of War*, 126.

[119] Congress, Senate Committee on Indian Affairs, Senate Document 229, *Report of the Secretary of War, communicating (in compliance with a resolution of the Senate) a copy of a report made by P. M. Butler, United States agent for the Cherokee Indians,* report prepared by William Wilkins, 28th Cong., 2nd sess., 9 (LexisNexis Academic, 2006) Serial Set ID: 434 S.doc. 229.

CHAPTER 7

Ministry in the New Nation

Organized as a territory in 1819, Arkansas extended forty miles into present eastern Oklahoma. Seeking to encourage the removal of the Southeastern tribes, in 1828, the United States severed this strip from Arkansas and made it part of Indian Territory. This addition provided the tribes a larger domain and more valuable assets. The new territory contained salt springs, forested areas, and prairies suitable for hunting, herding, and farming. Yet there remained the issue of American squatters in what had been part of Arkansas Territory. Some were refugees from justice. But most were trappers, traders, merchants, small farmers, and perhaps a few African slaves.[1] These early settlers had entered following the War of 1812. Hoping to avoid conflicts with newly arriving Native peoples, the United States government offered the squatters liberal amounts of land in the newly defined Arkansas Territory. For most squatters, this resulted in a peaceful evacuation.[2]

Yet, at times, violence erupted between white settlers and Native peoples. This friction stirred ill will and hindered the propagation of Christianity. Indeed, the presence of churches in this part of Indian Territory was virtually nonexistent. In 1819, Thomas Nuttall, an English explorer and botanist, explored the area. He noted that jeal-

[1] Thomas Nuttall, *A Journal of Travels into the Arkansa Territory* (Philadelphia: Thos. M. Palmer, 1821; rep., Ann Arbor: University Microfilms, 1966) 158–80, 214.

[2] Arrell M. Gibson, *Oklahoma: A History of Five Centuries* (Norman: Harlow Publishing, 1965) 70–71.

ousy and suspicion of whites made indigenous Native peoples "cold and cautious in the adoption of Christianity."[3] Among early Europeans, the spread of Christianity likewise had faced challenges. During the 1600s and 1700s, both Spain and France at times had claimed the area. Spanish explorers and French fur traders were Roman Catholics. But their small numbers had not warranted the expense of establishing missions. When American squatters first arrived, most were from Protestant backgrounds. But the lack of ministers and unsettled conditions had discouraged the organization of churches.

Early on, there were some feeble attempts to plant Protestant missions among Native peoples. In 1821, Presbyterian and Dutch Reformed missionaries from the United Foreign Missionary Society of New York City organized the Union Mission at Mazie in modern Wagoner County. In 1829 and 1830, the ABCFM established the New Dwight Mission near present Sallisaw and another station fifteen miles north near present Stilwell.[4] But once the emigration of Native peoples increased, more missionaries also arrived. In 1832, Presbyterians organized the Wheelock Church among the Choctaws in present McCurtain County.[5] The same year marked the birth of Baptist churches in the territory.

After the delineation of Indian Territory in 1830, government policies also forced Northwestern tribes to emigrate. Baptist missionary Isaac McCoy followed Native peoples west and settled near what is now Kansas City. McCoy was an experienced missionary. Shortly after the War of 1812, he had been a leader in mission work among Native tribes in western Indiana. Working as a government surveyor, McCoy made brief visits from Kansas to the area near Fort Gibson.

[3] Nuttall, *A Journal of Travels*, 195.

[4] Dianna Everett et al., eds., *Encyclopedia of Oklahoma History and Culture* (Oklahoma City OK: Oklahoma Historical Society, 2009) s.v. "Oklahoma Religion," by Alvin O. Turner; Gibson, *Oklahoma: A History of Five Centuries,* 149.

[5] W. David Baird and Danney Goble, *Oklahoma: A History* (Norman: University of Oklahoma, 2008) 100.

On 9 September 1832, McCoy organized a Baptist church among Creeks at present Muscogee. Besides McCoy, Baptist minister Duncan O'Bryant labored among the Cherokees. As mentioned in a previous chapter, O'Bryant and his family had accompanied most of his congregation from Tinsawattee, Georgia, to Indian Territory. Almost two months to the day after the organization of the McCoy congregation, remnants of the Tinsawattee church, composed of whites, Cherokees, and a few African slaves, formally organized the Liberty Baptist Church in present Adair County. On Saturday, 8 June 1833, members held services in their new meetinghouse about a mile from the Arkansas border. Challenged by excessive rains, there were few in attendance. O'Bryant nevertheless opened the services with Psalm 122: "I was glad when they said unto me, Let us go into the house of the Lord." O'Bryant then preached from 1 Peter 2:7, appropriately choosing a passage that mentioned construction: "Unto you therefore which believe he is precious: but unto them which be disobedient, the stone which the builders disallowed, the same is made the head of the corner." Unfortunately, the ministry of O'Bryant among the Western Cherokees was brief, for illness claimed his life on 25 August 1834. Lacking sufficient financial support and local leadership, the mission soon ceased to function.[6]

Other than McCoy and O'Bryant, no other Baptist ministers are known to have held services among emigrant Native peoples in the area. And little support came from fledgling Baptist congregations in Arkansas. As in Tennessee, many of these ministers had sided with the opponents of missionary societies. In 1838, the Washington Baptist Association in northwestern Arkansas plainly declared "an un-

[6] Gardner, "Duncan O'Bryant: Georgia Missionary to the Eastern Cherokees," 39–62; Robert G. Gardner, "Duncan O'Bryant: Pioneer Baptist Missionary to the Western Cherokees," *Baptist History and Heritage* 43 (Spring 2008): 21–31.

fellowship with the board of missions."[7] Coupled with this isolation was the smoldering strife associated with removal and the New Echota Treaty. Some Cherokees even manifested resentment against white missionaries who had opposed removal.[8] But even after the travails of removal, other Cherokees still clung to their Christian faith. And upon arrival in Indian Territory, Jones assured the Baptist Board that most of "our members" had remained faithful.[9]

Jones and Bushyhead soon initiated evangelistic outreach and sought to stabilize the remnants of the Amohee and Valley Towns congregations. The two ministers assessed needs and determined permanent locations for the congregations.[10] The Amohee congregation held services near the line separating the Going Snake and Flint districts, about thirteen miles south of Bushyhead's home and near Stilwell.[11] Forty or fifty miles north of the Amohee site, the Valley Towns congregants gathered at Delaware Town, two miles south of modern Eucha, Oklahoma.[12] The site was about twenty-five miles north of Bushyhead's home. Other scattered remnants held services at Breadtown. This group later became the nucleus for the Baptist Mission Church just north of present Westville. As these congregations became more established, other satellite congregations and preaching sites developed around them.

At first, almost insurmountable physical needs challenged efforts to renew churches. Illness and death had reduced the numbers of

[7] Minutes of the Washington Baptist Association (1838) 6, Washington County Archives, Special Collections, David W. Mullins Library, University of Arkansas, Fayetteville, typewritten copy.

[8] *Observer* (New York), 2 May 1840, typewritten copy in Grant Foreman Collection, box 7, folder 8, OHSL.

[9] *Baptist Missionary Magazine* 20 (March 1840): 58.

[10] *Baptist Missionary Magazine* 9 (July 1839): 179.

[11] J. R. Stogsdill, "Jesse Bushyhead: Cherokee Preacher-Statesman with a Bible for His Shield," *The Oklahoma Baptist Chronicle* 30 (Autumn 1987): 17.

[12] Everett et al., eds., *Encyclopedia of Oklahoma*, s.v. "Delaware County," by Rose Stauber.

congregational leaders. And the difficulties of building shelters and clearing fields interrupted corporate worship. As late as December 1839, many emigrants still had not found permanent dwellings. Instead of finding their own suitable parcels of land, they remained in temporary shelters near army garrisons or ration distribution centers.[13] Also, white whiskey traders threatened the stability of families and communities.[14] Jones feared that "vicious habits have been introduced or extended, which will require the faithful efforts of Christians and the influence of the Divine Spirit to eradicate."[15] Yet the efforts of Bushyhead and Jones bore fruit. The relocated Amohee and Valley Towns churches served as a viable means for enlisting converts,[16] for during the first six months in the new land, 130 Cherokees joined Baptist congregations.[17]

Bushyhead and Jones also expressed interest in other Native peoples besides Cherokees. In spring 1839, the two visited an Osage camp. Jones wrote:

> And I have no doubt the Osages could be profitably approached, with judicious management, through the Cherokees. Br. Bushyhead and myself visited a large encampment of them.... They were somewhat alarmed at our first approach, but no learning who we were, and our employment among the Cherokees, we were invited into the chief's tent, and all the principal men came in to salute us, and to hear the conversation.[18]

This meeting was significant, for in the past, Cherokees and Osages had been enemies. In order to facilitate Cherokee relocation, in 1825, the government had persuaded the Osage to cede their land in what is now eastern Oklahoma. Most had relocated to what would

[13] *Baptist Missionary Magazine* 20 (March 1840): 57.
[14] *Athens* (TN) *Courier*, 14 January 1842.
[15] *Baptist Missionary Magazine* 20 (March 1840): 58.
[16] Ibid., 57.
[17] McLoughlin, *Champions of the Cherokees*, 201.
[18] *Baptist Missionary Magazine* 20 (June 1840): 129.

become Kansas. Yet not all tribal members chose to cooperate. By 1839, some still lived or hunted in present northeastern Oklahoma. Thus, their presence consequently offended some Cherokees and encouraged renewed violence. No doubt, Bushyhead and Jones hoped that missionary endeavors among the Osages would help defuse tribal rivalries.

The two ministers also made cooperative overtures to non-Baptist missionaries. About three weeks after arriving in Indian Territory, Jones, Bushyhead, and Stephen Foreman traveled to Park Hill. On 17 March 1839, they worshiped with Samuel Worcester and his Park Hill mission congregation. Worcester and family had arrived in the Western Cherokee Nation in May 1835. By December 1836, Worcester had settled at Park Hill and soon established printing operations.[19] Desiring to resume Bible translation and publishing projects initiated in Tennessee, Jones wanted to discuss cooperative printing projects with Worcester. Jones and Worcester were not strangers. As early as 1830, Jones had visited Worcester at New Echota and "met a very friendly reception."[20] And Bushyhead and Foreman remembered Worcester from his visits to the Candy's Creek mission. The cooperation between Jones and Worcester was essential. Because Jones and Bushyhead lacked a press, they remained acutely aware that a means of producing appropriate literature was vital to evangelism and moral instruction.

The three visitors spent several cordial days with Worcester. However, Jones remained cautious not to appear overly close to Worcester, for Worcester had lost favor among some emigrant Cherokees. First, Worcester had chosen voluntarily to exit the Eastern Cherokee Nation. Because of this action, some Cherokees blamed him for abandoning his Georgia flock and capitulating to removal.

[19] Althea Bass, *Cherokee Messenger* (Norman: University of Oklahoma, 1936) 177, 206.

[20] Evan Jones Journal, 12 July 1830, ABHS, FM-98.

Second, Worcester still relied on the translation skills of Elias Boudinot, who also lived at Park Hill. Again, these ties linked Worcester to the Treaty party. With this in mind, Jones needed Bushyhead and Foreman to support him in any arrangements with Worcester. Otherwise, some Cherokees may have assumed that any collaborative efforts between Jones and Worcester also may have involved removal. And if Ross followers soured on Jones, the Baptist missionary risked banishment from the Western Cherokee Nation.[21]

Cooperation between denominations often was vital to the success of frontier missions. There were nevertheless doctrinal differences between the Baptist Board and churches aligned with the ABCFM. The main difference concerned the manner of baptism and the eligibility of candidates for the rite. Unlike churches composing Worcester's denominational support, Baptists rejected infant baptism. Baptists also practiced immersion of converts rather than effusion or sprinkling. Thus, Jones had to be careful to maintain a Baptist identity. Otherwise, there was the danger of losing financial support from the Baptist Board. Jones was willing to accept some materials printed by a non-Baptist press, but was unwilling to take an overly "active part in their distribution."[22] Earlier in Georgia, Jones had encountered a theological dispute when he had confronted a Methodist missionary over the correct interpretation of *baptizo*, the Greek word for the rite.[23] Jones also knew that Cherokee Baptist preachers and lay leaders lacked theological training. If influenced by non-Baptist literature, Cherokee Baptist work risked compromise. Yet, at this point, Bushyhead and Foreman seemed not to evidence sectarian concerns. Worcester recorded a favorable impression of Bushyhead and lauded him as the "right hand man" of Jones. Worcester also attested to the

[21] *Baptist Missionary Magazine* 20 (March 1840): 58.

[22] Samuel A. Worcester to David Greene, 19 March 1839, ABCFM 18.3.1, vol. 10; McLoughlin, *Champions of the Cherokees*, 215.

[23] Evan Jones Journal, 29 May 1830, ABHS.

"very good repute" of Bushyhead "as a Christian and a preacher."[24] He also noted that Bushyhead and Foreman had no objections to "circulating our books."[25]

But enemies of Jones did not long permit him to remain in the nation. Popular among mountain Cherokees, Jones was key to the organization of what Treaty party and some Western Cherokees perceived as pro-Ross congregations. And pro-Ross assemblies harbored trouble for the Ridge faction. On 26 April 1839, Jones had sought the assistance of Bushyhead in quelling rumors involving Situakee and the mountain Cherokees in the alleged attack on Camp Illinois. Occurrences such as these evidenced the influence of Jones and troubled certain Treaty party members. Four days after Jones visited Bushyhead, John A. Bell penned a damaging letter about Jones to Acting Commissioner of Indian Affairs Daniel Kurtz. Bell resurrected the accusations against Jones surrounding the questionable death of the newborn at Valley Towns. Bell furthermore characterized Jones as "Dispised [*sic*] & abhorred." Wishing to neutralize Jones, Bell appealed to government authorities to oust Jones from Indian Territory.[26] The revived accusations resulted in the exile of Jones from the nation. By September 1839, Jones had departed and did not return to the Cherokee Nation until late June 1841.[27] The absence of Jones was critical, for Jones had provided much of the impetus for Bushyhead's ministry. Although Bushyhead maintained communication with Jones via mail, his departure placed more responsibility on Bushyhead and other Cherokee ministers.

During the absence of Jones, affairs of state also occupied Bushyhead. Yet he did not neglect his pastoral duties. He attended to

[24] S[amuel] A. Worchester to David Greene, 19 March 1839, ABCFM 18.3.1, vol. 10.

[25] Ibid.

[26] J[ohn] A. Bell to D[aniel] Kurtz, 30 April 1839, Letters to Cherokee Agency East, 1839, microfilm 83, National Archives, Fort Worth.

[27] McLoughlin, *Champions of the Cherokees*, 197–202.

services at the Amohee congregation on the first Saturday and Sunday of each month. At first, members erected a temporary shed as a meeting place. But difficulties soon developed. By summer 1840, a whiskey shop had opened a few yards from the crude shelter. The possibilities for disturbances, violence, and vice threatened services. But even so, attendance increased. In 1842, the congregation relocated to a new structure, a 70x30-foot shed, two miles from the original site. Although primitive, the building resembled the type of structures used as council houses. More spacious than the previous meeting site, the edifice accommodated larger audiences.[28] Bushyhead continued to shepherd this congregation until his death. The membership seemed to support Bushyhead in his efforts to better conditions for Cherokees. When Bushyhead traveled to Washington in 1842, he was part of a delegation intent on negotiating delicate matters vital to the future of the nation. In his absence, the church met for a special series of services. No doubt, the success of the diplomacy remained on the minds of members. And regular services continued as Cherokee ministers Beaver Carrier and Lewis Downing filled the pulpit.[29] Even as Amohee stabilized, other preachers oversaw Baptist work elsewhere. The Valley Towns congregation established satellite congregations at Honey Creek and Beattie's Prairie. Native preachers John Wickliffe, Oganaya, and Kaneeda preached regularly at these locations.[30]

Fortunately, Commissioner of Indian Affairs Thomas Hartley Crawford had judged the charges against Jones as baseless, and allowed him to reenter Indian Territory in 1841. Following the return of Jones, the ministerial involvement of Bushyhead increased. From late summer through fall, Jones visited the churches from which he had been absent for almost two years. And as was so often the case,

[28] Evan Jones, 19 July 1842, ABHS.

[29] Evan Jones to Solomon Peck, 3 June and 6 August 1844, American Baptist Foreign Mission Society Records, 1817–1959, Mercer University, Atlanta, Georgia.

[30] McLoughlin, *Champions of the Cherokees*, 210.

Bushyhead accompanied him as interpreter. These activities taxed Bushyhead physically and fiscally. On 2 November 1841, Jones described his "numerous" and "urgent" preaching engagements, adding that "Bro. Bushyhead and myself have seldom remained at home more than a day or two, at a time, for the past three months."[31] But the increased ministry also strained Bushyhead's financial resources. Responsibility for a farm and a large family demanded his time and money. Jones was the financial link with the Baptist Board. And while Jones had been absent, Native preachers looked to Bushyhead for monetary advances. These amounts were not great. The board usually supplied no more than ten dollars a month to Native ministers.[32] But even so, the financial demands became a steady drain on Bushyhead's resources.

Bushyhead also extended aid to missionaries other than Baptists. By early 1840, a school had opened near the Bushyhead community. In spring that year, Butrick and his wife, still associated with the Congregationalist-Presbyterian missionary society, learned of a short-term opening for a teacher at the school. The Butricks left Fairfield mission, twenty-eight miles south of the Bushyhead settlement, and arrived at Bushyhead's home on 4 May. They lodged in Bushyhead's crowded home for eleven days before moving into a nearby cabin. But the Butricks soon experienced a physical attack. On the morning of 26 June, as the couple prepared to leave for school, a man came to the door and assaulted Ms. Butrick. Although she was only lightly injured, the encounter alarmed the couple. Accordingly, they sought refuge in Bushyhead's household for the next four weeks until the end of the school term.[33] As his stay extended, Butrick became concerned over the expense incurred by Bushyhead. Four days after the attack, he penned a letter to David Greene, corresponding secretary of the

[31] Evan Jones, 2 November 1841, ABHS, FM 98.

[32] McLoughlin, *Champions of the Cherokees*, 207.

[33] Butrick Journal, 26 June 1840.

ABCFM. Butrick referred to Bushyhead as "a minister of the Baptist church," devoting "much time & property to his people." In light of this, Butrick protested that "we cannot consistently ask him to board us for nothing."[34]

Indeed, Bushyhead did not have the resources to continue subsidizing mission work indefinitely. By September 1841, the financial strain of removal apparently had drained Bushyhead. Making his impecunious plight known to Jones, Bushyhead complained about the lack of recompense from the Baptist Board. He stressed that he had not received any payment from Baptist headquarters since arriving in Indian Territory. So strapped was Bushyhead that he offered to sell his farm to the board for $500, an amount less than its worth.[35] If the board approved the transaction, Bushyhead planned to relocate about half a mile from the site. Jones also agreed with the proposal. He viewed it as a very desirable opportunity to utilize the property for mission purposes. Accordingly, he envisioned the establishment of a printing center, training institution for Cherokee ministers, and a secondary school for Cherokee females. The next step was to convince the Baptist Board to purchase the Bushyhead property.

As part of his ministerial activities, Bushyhead found time for other benevolent causes. One of these involved the Cherokee Temperance Society. Often whites received blame for introducing the curse of drunkenness. Yet some Cherokees also shared the guilt. For example, certain temperance society leaders accused Cherokee peacekeepers for ignoring the whiskey trade, for some peacekeepers considered prohibition as unconstitutional. Yet availability of alcohol threatened a stable society. At one temperance meeting, Thomas Foreman pointed to a nearby gallows. Foreman cited the execution of sixteen Cherokees within the last five years as a result of liquor-induced

[34] Daniel S. Butrick to David Greene, 30 June 1840, ABCFM: 18.3.1, vol. 10.

[35] Evan Jones to Lucius Bolles, 13 September 1841, ABHS.

crimes.[36] Abuse of alcohol also had been a problem for some of Bushyhead's siblings. At times, brothers Charles and Isaac had been overly fond of liquor.[37] Admitting his proclivity for alcohol, Charles had taken the temperance oath. And while living in the Western Cherokee Nation, in 1837, Isaac also had felt the need to join a temperance society.[38] Yet his sobriety wavered. On 14 July 1840, two days after interpreting for a church service, Isaac suffered two head gashes in a severe beating. Isaac's excessive drinking had contributed to the affair.[39]

The promotion of temperance had appeared among Western Cherokees before the Trail of Tears. Worcester had organized the Cherokee Temperance Society in 1836. Four years later, 700 members had enrolled.[40] As in the East, Bushyhead took an active role in the society. In 1840, Bushyhead served as one of its six vice-presidents. By that time, society chapters had been organized in different districts of the nation. Meetings opened with prayer and provided opportunities for members to speak concerning the violence and debauchery associated with liquor. At the end of the meetings, those present who had not taken the temperance oath or wavered in their commitment received an invitation to publicly renounce intemperance. Enrollees, including whites, Africans, and Cherokees, repeated the following promise in unison: "We hereby solemnly pledge ourselves that we will never use, nor buy, nor sell, nor give, nor receive, as a drink, any whiskey, brandy, rum, gin, wine, fermented cider, strong beer, or any kind of intoxicating liquor."[41]

[36] *The Cherokee Messenger* 1 (August 1844): 16.

[37] Ibid.

[38] Moulton, *The Papers of Chief John Ross*, 1:550.

[39] Butrick Journal, 15 July 1840.

[40] Cherokee Almanac: For the year of our Lord, 1840, 20, Gilcrease Museum, 1840.

[41] Ibid.

Another means of ministry concerned the unfulfilled need for a Baptist printing press and schools. Jones still lacked a press, and there were few schools. The visit of Bushyhead to New York City in 1842 proved critical to the achievement of these goals. Jones still hoped for the establishment of an independent Baptist press. As an interpreter, Bushyhead played a vital role in his plan. But the nearest Baptist press with Sequoyan characters was at the Shawnee Baptist mission near present Kansas City, Kansas. Baptist missionary Jotham Meeker had operated a press in that vicinity since March 1834.[42] Separated from Meeker by at least 250 miles, Jones realized the difficulties involved in any cooperative efforts. Jones therefore appealed to the Baptist Board for a press. As Bushyhead prepared to depart for Washington in March 1842, Jones urged him to include time for a visit to the annual meeting of the board in New York City. He implored Bushyhead to explain the problems of long-distance printing and lobby Solomon Peck, the corresponding secretary, for a press.

While in Washington, Bushyhead took the opportunity to travel to New York City. As Jones had requested, he informed the board of denominational developments among Cherokees. He especially emphasized the need for a Baptist-owned printing press and funding for schools and teachers.[43] While in the city and sometime before 17 May, Bushyhead made a public address. He justified the request of Jones for a press and reminded the audience of the need to provide publications that aligned with Baptist doctrines. As an example, he referred to Worcester's translation of "baptize." Bushyhead maintained that the Cherokee word for "baptize" "always meant dip and nothing else."[44] This, of course, implied immersion rather than effusion. After learning of Bushyhead's remarks, the corresponding secre-

[42] Martha B. Caldwell, comp., *Annals of Shawnee Methodist Mission and Indian Manual Labor School* (Topeka: Kansas State Historical Society, 1977) 16.

[43] McLoughlin, *Champions of the Cherokees*, 216.

[44] S. A. Worcester to David Greene, 13 July 1842, ABCFM: 18.3.1, vol. 10.

tary of the ABCFM quickly sent a letter to Worcester and asked for a definition of the Cherokee term. Worcester clearly disagreed with Bushyhead's remarks. Worcester explained that the Cherokee word meant "to wash," but not necessarily to immerse. Thus, the difficulty concerned the "technical signification" of the act rather than the interpretation.[45] On this occasion, Bushyhead demonstrated a more sectarian stance than he had in the presence of Worcester at Park Hill and maintained a more staunch position as he petitioned the board. Otherwise, he risked losing support, for among some Baptist leaders, doctrinally sound translations had become an issue. In Missouri, some Baptists already had censured the American Bible Society for refusing to distribute "translations made by Baptist missionaries."[46] Yet Bushyhead convinced the board. Complying with his request, in September 1842, the board approved funding for a press and salaried printer.

By early October 1842, Bushyhead had returned from Washington and resumed an active preaching ministry. For example, on 14 November, he attended the formal organization of the Taquohee church, six to ten miles southwest of Beattie's Prairie. Yet most of the responsibility of procuring a press and type still rested with Jones. The Shawnee mission had the correct fonts, but not all of them were available for immediate shipment. Although Jones was able to purchase a printing press in Fayetteville, he still lacked an entire set of Sequoyan characters. As time passed, Jones became more anxious over the delayed shipments.[47] Jones and Hervey Upham, the board-

[45] Ibid.

[46] [The Seventh Annual Meeting of the?] Minutes of Franklin Association (1838) 5 (Upper Alton, IL: Pioneer, 1838) Partee Center for Baptist Historical Studies Charles F. Curry Library, William Jewell College, Liberty, Missouri.

[47] Evan Jones to Solomon Peck, 23 November 1843, American Baptist Foreign Mission Society American Indian Correspondence, 1800–1900, FM-99, OHSL; Evan Jones, 14 November 1842, ABFM Society, 1817–1959; McLoughlin, *Champions of the Cherokees*, 210, 224.

salaried printer, finally had to journey to the Shawnee mission to acquire the missing fonts. And still, all of the fonts did not arrive until 1844. It was not until August of that year that *The Cherokee Messenger*, the first periodical published in the Western Cherokee Nation, came off the press. Published in Cherokee and English, each edition numbered 1,000 copies. The first edition included portions of Genesis and Luke, translated by Jones and Bushyhead. Other articles were selections from *Pilgrim's Progress*, chapters from a world history book, and an essay by Jones on Cherokee grammar and syntax.[48]

As important as publications were, they were virtually useless without an educated population. But the frontier posed special challenges to teachers. In 1836, Pennsylvanian Lowell Truxton taught in the Cherokee Nation for three months. He viewed some students as "dull," but considered others to be very intelligent. One challenge was merely keeping students in class, for on one occasion during the lunch period, they went for a dip in the nearest stream.[49] There nevertheless existed a great demand for schools in the nation. In October 1841, the tribal government voted to fund eleven public schools. Accordingly, the plan designated two schools for each of the three larger districts and one school for each of the five smaller districts. But although eleven schools were too few, the most formidable challenge was the lack of qualified teachers.

Jones recommended a partial solution to the Baptist Board. His plan promised to provide more teachers but also advance the denominational presence of Baptists. Jones urged denominational headquarters to recruit teachers for national schools from Baptist ranks. In turn, he suggested that the Cherokee Nation fund their salaries from annuity sources reserved for education. And because most students at

[48] Evan Jones to Solomon Peck, 18 May 1843, ABFM Society Records, 1817–1959; McLoughlin, *Champions of the Cherokees*, 228.

[49] Truxton Lowell to James Lowell, 1 October 1836, Special Collections, Mullins Library, University of Arkansas, Fayetteville.

national schools were male, Jones realized the need for a board-funded secondary school for females. Known as a seminary, such an institution promised to elevate young Cherokee women and provide a future pool of teachers. Stephen Foreman, the newly appointed superintendent of education for the Cherokee Nation, consented. Moreover, he likewise agreed that teacher salaries at national schools should come from the Cherokee treasury. As Bushyhead was preparing to depart for his visit to Washington, Foreman had encouraged him to prevail upon the board for two teachers. While in New York, Bushyhead approached the board with Foreman's request and requested funding for the seminary. Bushyhead secured a positive response. In fact, the number of promised teachers and financial support exceeded the request. The board sponsored four teachers, two for the national schools and two for the seminary.[50] At the September 1842 meeting, the board also approved funds for the purchase of Bushyhead's farm. In addition, it agreed to provide a monthly stipend to Bushyhead and salaries for four more Cherokee ministers.

The board fairly quickly recruited three competent New England teachers. They arrived in the Cherokee Nation on the last day of 1842. Elizabeth Morse and Sarah Hale Hibbard were only in their early twenties, but were experienced teachers. Besides having teaching credentials, Thomas Frye, about thirty, also had some formal medical training. Frye and Hibbard boarded with Jones in the Bushyhead settlement. Hibbard took charge of the newly constructed seminary near the post office at Cherokee, and Frye received an appointment to the local national school. Morse located at Delaware Town, where she taught full-bloods and boarded with Oganaya. Within a year of Bushyhead's visit to New York, the board had met most of the requests of Jones and Bushyhead. Yet Bushyhead personally continued to sustain some of the financial responsibility for the expenses of

[50] McLoughlin, *Champions of the Cherokees*, 219–22.

teachers. As late as November 1843, he still supplied rations to Morse in the form of meat, flour, meal, sugar, and coffee.[51]

By the early 1840s, Bushyhead had gained recognition among supporters of the national Baptist missionary society. His appearance before the board and occasional entries in the *Baptist Missionary Magazine* had stirred hearts and loosened purse strings. Yet the interest of others in the ministry of Bushyhead had negative repercussions. Joel Bacon, president of Columbia Baptist College in Washington, D.C., had accompanied Hibbard, Morse, and Frye to the Cherokee Nation. While touring the mission field, Bacon conversed with church members and preached at almost all Cherokee Baptist churches, including Bushyhead's pastorate.[52] In so doing, he became aware of the presence of African slaves among some of the congregations. Bacon arrived in Boston on 5 February 1843.[53] His reports highlighted the blossoming Baptist work, but also drew attention to Bushyhead as a slaveholder. Unfortunately, this news placed Bushyhead under scrutiny, especially among the growing ranks of abolitionists.

As in the old Eastern Cherokee Nation, slavery was common in the new nation among Cherokee mixed-bloods and white residents. This trend was consistent with the Bushyhead family. As mentioned in a previous chapter, Eliza had inherited a female slave early on in her marriage to Jesse. And at the time of removal, the Bushyheads owned five slaves. Some, if not all, of the slaves may have been part of the family of Eliza's servant. In 1840, Butrick likewise mentioned a slave in the Bushyhead household. While he and his wife boarded with "dear br[other]" Bushyhead, Butrick wrote that a black woman in the home did the washing.[54] The labor of the slave woman and her family no doubt was important to carving out a new farm, for slave-

[51] Ibid., 223; Evan Jones to Solomon Peck, 27 November 1843, American Baptist Foreign Mission Society Correspondence, 1800–1900.

[52] Evan Jones, 28 March 1844, ABFM Society Records, 1817–1859.

[53] McLoughlin, *Champions of the Cherokees*, 224.

[54] Butrick Journal, 26 June 1840.

holders held an advantage over non-slaveholders. After all, slave labor made possible the cultivation and fencing of more acres.[55]

However, the institution of slavery did not prevent the evangelism of African bondmen. The McCoy and O'Bryant congregations included African members. On 6 February 1842, the Amohee Church, approximately eight miles west of the inactive O'Bryant mission, received two black women as members. Both had held membership in O'Bryant's congregation.[56] And from 2 April 1843 through the following October, Jones reported sixty-one baptisms. These converts totaled fifty-two Cherokees, one white, and eight Africans. The latter, presumably all slaves, lived in the Bushyhead settlement. Remarking on the addition of blacks, Jones lauded the ministry of an African preacher who lived in the Bushyhead settlement: "The colored persons baptized at this place are the fruits of the preaching of a Blackman, a slave who devotes the Sabbath and frequently week evenings to tell the love of Jesus to others of his own color, and God has helped his labors."[57] The following July, Jones again mentioned the "considerable attention to religion" among blacks along the Arkansas border "through the instrumentality of a Black man who resides in this vicinity."[58]

Before the 1830s, slavery had not divided Baptists at the national level. And in the early part of that decade, when Bushyhead had become actively engaged with Jones, the abolitionist movement only recently had coalesced. But by the end of the decade, abolitionists had gained more traction. In 1840, the abolitionist wing of the Triennial Convention assembled an antislavery convention in New York City. The attendees purposed to force the national denomination to take a definitive stance against slavery. When the convention remained neu-

[55] William G. McLoughlin, *After the Trail of Tears: The Cherokee Struggle for Sovereignty, 1839–1880* (Chapel Hill: University of North Carolina, 1993) 125.

[56] Evan Jones, 29 March 1842, ABHS FM-98.

[57] Evan Jones, 3 November 1843, ABHS FM-98.

[58] Evan Jones, 10 July 1844, ABFM Society Records, 1817–1859.

tral, delegates organized an abolitionist missionary agency known as the Free Mission Society (FMS). Instead of funding the Baptist Board of Foreign Missions, the FMS provided antislavery Baptists an option to donate to its coffers. And in order to goad the Baptist Board away from neutrality, the *Free Missionary*, thc official publication of the FMS, targeted Bushyhead and other slaveholding missionaries employed by the Baptist Board.

An article in the January 1844 edition alleged the miserable condition of slaves owned by Bushyhead. As such, the story juxtaposed the moral dilemma of a board-supported missionary who simultaneously owned slaves. When the Triennial Convention still failed to alter its neutral position, the *Free Missionary* pushed harder. In August 1844, the journal indicated that the Executive Committee of the BBFM had asked for the discreet resignation of Bushyhead. This may or may not have been true, for there is no record that the Baptist Board ever transmitted such a message. But even if the BBFM mailed the request, Bushyhead likely never received the letter. And even if he did, time prevented a response, for he died on 17 July 1844. Yet rumors of his forced resignation nevertheless disturbed Baptists in the South.[59]

Southern Baptists resented the perceived encroachment in the affairs of a slaveholding missionary. This was understandable. Many Baptists in the slave states did not regard slave ownership as a moral disqualification for ministry. Furthermore, they perceived the censure of Bushyhead by New Englanders as an unjustified moral condemnation of slaveholding Baptists in general. In response, Alabama Baptists threatened to withhold any contributions to the BBFM until the board provided a satisfactory answer. Backed into a corner, the board

[59] William G. McLoughlin, "The Cherokee Baptist Preacher and the Great Schism of 1844–45: A Footnote to Baptist History," *Foundations: A Baptist Journal of History, Theology, and Ministry* (April–June 1981): 139–44.

reached a decision. On 17 December 1844, it declared firm opposition to the appointment of any slaveholder as a missionary.

As a result, Baptists across the South felt impelled to form a sectional denomination permitting the participation of slaveholders in missionary endeavors. Meeting in Augusta, Georgia, the second week of May 1845, delegates organized the Southern Baptist Convention. Justifying their actions, the delegates issued a declaration expressing opposition to the "Autocratical Interdict of the North," which "would first drive us from our beloved colored people...and from the much-wronged Aborigines of the country...."[60] Thus, the delegates blamed abolitionists for discouraging evangelism among slaves and Native peoples. Yet the division among Baptists only exacerbated increasing sectional differences over slavery. Methodists had also split a year earlier, and Presbyterians fractured on the eve of the Civil War. On the political stage, the fissures presaged the breakdown of Whigs and Democrats into sectional rather than national political parties in the 1850s. Unfortunately, the loosening of political and denominational ties jeopardized national union and fueled the secession crisis of 1860.

News of the rift soon reached the Cherokee Nation. Because Bushyhead had remained essential for translation, publishing, and evangelistic purposes, the rupture directly threatened the work of Jones. Real or rumored repudiation of Bushyhead on the part of the Baptist Board threatened to turn Cherokees against the Baptist presence, for many Cherokees still esteemed Bushyhead. Realizing this danger, Jones quickly defended Bushyhead to the Baptist Board. Jones argued that the slave woman was the inherited property of Eliza. Over time, the slave had given birth to at least one child, a daughter. Thus, Bushyhead could not claim this slave or her offspring as his acquired personal property. Yet this explanation did not absolve Bushyhead from blame. Jones also had to address the presence of

[60] *Proceedings of the Southern Baptist Convention, 8 May–12 May 1845* (Richmond: H. K. Ellyson, 1845) 19.

slaves purchased by Bushyhead, for in 1840 or 1841, Bushyhead had purchased a slave family composed of a husband, wife, and child. Bolstering his defense, Jones justified the transaction. Jones claimed that Bushyhead had bought the black man, a Baptist preacher, primarily as a means to evangelize Africans. Bushyhead allowed the preacher considerable liberty and the use of a horse for ministerial travels. Jones also painted Bushyhead as a benevolent master who meted out humane treatment to his slaves. As proof, Jones mentioned that Bushyhead had released Eliza's slave "from all claims on her labor," though providing her with board and clothing.[61] The daughter of Eliza's slave likewise had been permitted to marry a free herdsman and travel extended distances. Jones furthermore stressed that Bushyhead favored emancipation, for he intended on setting the black preacher free. Thus, Bushyhead's bondmen remained legally enslaved but had a degree of freedom.

Other than complete emancipation and transportation to a free state, this arrangement may have been the most tolerable for the Bushyhead slaves under existing circumstances in the Cherokee Nation. Although escape was an option, it was risky, for neighboring Arkansas, Missouri, Louisiana, and Texas formed a phalanx of proslavery governments. Runaways were likely to be apprehended and returned to their masters. Sadly, fugitives were virtually helpless in the court systems. And if they seemed to be a flight risk, owners had the option to sell them in slave markets out of Indian Territory. If this occurred, escapees faced permanent separation from their families.

Also, freedmen in the Cherokee Nation faced significant economic difficulties. Historically, Cherokee slave laws had denied citizenship to most blacks. This partially was done in the interest of preserving the institution of slavery. In the Eastern Cherokee Nation, freedmen had been prohibited from voting and holding office. Although the 1827 Cherokee Constitution extended citizenship to the

[61] Ibid.

children of Cherokee women and black partners, these offspring could not hold political office.[62] Also, freed slaves had to secure permission from the national legislature in order to reside in the nation. In 1840, the reorganized Cherokee legislature adopted a similar policy. It prohibited any free black or mulatto from owning a farm. The regulation proposed to keep free persons of African descent out of the Cherokee Nation and discourage the potential for insurrections. But the law severely limited the opportunities of Africans for economic independence. Moreover, an unsuccessful slave uprising in November 1842 had resulted in even more draconian ordinances. The affair had left one white and one Delaware dead. It also heightened fears of future rebellions. As a result, the Cherokee government required emancipators to post guaranty bonds and thus encourage the good conduct of freedmen.[63]

Bushyhead may have had enough wealth to post bond but seems not to have done so. The reason may have been related to his economic circumstances and work as a smith. Around 1844, he had contracted his services to the tribal government as a blacksmith and wheelwright. According to treaty arrangements, the United States government was responsible for funding blacksmiths and wheelwrights in the Cherokee Nation. In December 1843, the Cherokee legislature had authorized tribal agent Pierce Butler to select the smiths and wrights. Accordingly, Butler oversaw the hiring of four blacksmiths and two wheelwrights and specified the locations of their shops. The council recommended one shop for each district. Located near district courthouses, the shops provided repairs and implements to Cherokees during the farming season and employment for Cherokee workmen.[64] Although it is not known whether Bushyhead re-

[62] Yarbrough, *Race and the Cherokee Nation*, 27, 33, 41.

[63] McLoughlin, *After the Trail of Tears*, 127–28, 134.

[64] John Ross to P. M. Butler, 20 January 1844, Letters Received by the Office of Indian Affairs, 1824–1881, National Archives, M234, roll 115; John Ross to P. M. Butler, 20 January 1844, Letters Received by the Office of Indian Af-

quired the slave evangelist to contribute labor to his smithy, he may have extended some liberty in return for labor necessary to fulfill his contracts. But even if the preacher did not possess the appropriate skills, he still may have had the ability to help with some of the operations.

Bushyhead surely was aware of the difficulties associated with slavery. Yet other issues likely seemed more pressing. Civil unrest and political turmoil remained a constant challenge. For example, recent lawlessness had discouraged the assembling of evangelistic and temperance meetings. In June 1843, Butrick requested that Bushyhead call a meeting of the Temperance Society. The gathering was to convene on Wednesday, 16 August, at Maysville. Yet Maysville was not an ideal location for such a meeting, for it still harbored whiskey traders. And the recent murder of Isaac Bushyhead heightened tensions. In light of these developments, Butrick felt it wise to change the meeting site. Instead of Maysville, the society met at Mount Zion, Butrick's mission at Beattie's Prairie.[65] Jones also lamented the interruptions of Baptist meetings. During most of summer and fall 1843, annual evangelistic gatherings, called "protracted meetings," did not assemble. The impediment was a result of the involvement of male church members in peacekeeping activities.[66] Jones had planned to establish a preaching circuit. If it materialized, the plan provided opportunities for him to preach at all Baptist mission stations on a regular basis. Very likely, he meant to include Bushyhead in some of these appointments. However, his aim did not develop. The threat of vio-

fairs, 1824–1881, National Archives, M234, roll 88; Congress, Department of the Treasury, House Document 91, *Disbursements to the Indians*, report prepared by John M. McCalla, 29th Cong., 4th sess., 140 (LexisNexis Academic, 2006) Serial Set ID: 483 H.doc. 91.

[65] Daniel Butrick to David Greene, 11 September 1843, ABCFM: 18.3.1, vol. 10.

[66] Evan Jones to [Solomon Peck], 28 March 1843, ABFM Society Records, 1817–1959.

lence simply made travel too dangerous. Jones wrote, "The commotions in the Nation, which have intervened, have disappointed us in carrying that plan into effect…."[67]

Moreover, the rigors of the frontier often sapped strength and claimed lives prematurely. In spring and summer 1844, residents throughout the Mississippi Valley experienced excessive downpours and high water. By early June, travel and plowing had become difficult. And as the summer progressed, the mercury also rose. Such conditions favored an abundance of mosquitoes and the resultant spread of malaria.[68] In a letter to Solomon Peck, Jones reported that illness was common and deaths occurred "in great numbers."[69] Unfortunately, one of the victims was Bushyhead.

In spite of swollen tributaries and oppressive heat, Bushyhead attempted to maintain his busy ministerial schedule. He served as president of the Cherokee Temperance Society and the Cherokee Bible Society. As president of the Bible Society, he was one of thirteen who had been entrusted with distributing scriptures in Cherokee.[70] On Sunday, 12 May, four Africans received baptism at Bushyhead's pastorate. Three weeks later, on 2 June, four Cherokee converts entered the baptismal waters at Amohee. The following Friday, Bushyhead attended the Going Snake Temperance Society, which convened at the crude Going Snake District courthouse near Bushyhead's home. On Saturday, 29 June, Bushyhead visited Jones and sent what became his last greeting to the Baptist Board. He likely participated in his last baptismal service eight days later on Sunday, 7 July. Assisted by Lewis Downing, Bushyhead administered the rite to two Cherokees and one African at Amohee. The following Thursday,

[67] Ibid.

[68] Caldwell, *Annals of Shawnee Methodist Mission and Indian Manual Labor School*, 53.

[69] Evan Jones Letters, 26 August 1844, ABFM Society Records, 1817–1959.

[70] *Cherokee Advocate*, 26 October 1844.

he presided over a meeting of the Cherokee National Temperance Society. This may have been his last ministerial function, for death claimed him a week later.[71]

During the first two weeks in July, daily temperatures at Cane Hill soared into the upper 90s. And on 10 July, the thermometer registered 103 degrees.[72] On Saturday, 13 July, Bushyhead set out to attend a "sacramental meeting" at one of the missions, but fell ill with a fever and returned home.[73] Although with limited medical experience, Frye was the nearest person with some formal medical knowledge. Frye cared for the stricken over a ten-mile radius and successfully had treated Bushyhead for fevers before. But this time his illness was more severe. Upon examining Bushyhead on Sunday, Frye solemnly disclosed that recovery appeared unlikely. Bushyhead stoically agreed. The prognosis proved true, for Bushyhead continued to weaken. The next day, Bushyhead's fever remained unabated. Feeling the need for more experienced physicians, riders left the Bushyhead home to summon other doctors. Two physicians arrived in response to the appeal around 1 P.M. on Wednesday, July 17. In accordance with accepted medical practice of the day, they bled Bushyhead. Consequently, the loss of blood only enfeebled him more. Although sinking, Bushyhead faced death calmly. In his last hours, Bushyhead admitted to being "in a very happy state of mind."[74] As life ebbed, he became delirious. He briefly revived and rose from the bed, but collapsed. Death came about an hour after sunset that evening.[75] On the

[71] Evan Jones Letters, 28 May, 29 June, and 10 July 1844, ABFM Society Records, 1817–1959; Butrick Journal, 19 July 1844, ABCFM: 18.3.1, vol. 10.

[72] Jacob M. K. Smith Diary, Special Collections, Mullins Library, University of Arkansas, Fayetteville.

[73] Evan Jones Letters, 26 August 1844, ABFM Society Records, 1817–1959.

[74] "Death of Rev. Jesse Bushyhead," *The Cherokee Messenger* 1 (August 1844): 16.

[75] Thomas Frye to Solomon Peck, 26 October 1844, ABHS, FM-98.

frontier, the preparation of corpses took place at home. The process included washing and dressing the body and building a crude coffin. Because of the hot weather and lack of embalming services, the burial of Bushyhead almost certainly occurred the following day.

Word of Bushyhead's death quickly spread locally and nationally. On 19 July, Butrick received the news at Beattie's Prairie. That same day, Jones penned a notice to the Baptist Board. As these events occurred, Jones was preparing to publish the first edition of his long-anticipated *The Cherokee Messenger*. By 6 August, the first edition was being circulated and carried the death notice. Three days before, the Amohee congregation had met and mourned the passing of their pastor. They also appointed Lewis Downing to succeed Bushyhead as pastor.[76] In August, Elijah Hicks, a Cherokee delegate in Washington, notified John Ross, then in New York, about Bushyhead. Hicks also wrote an obituary and sent it to the widely read *National Intelligencer.*[77] William P. Ross, editor of the *Cherokee Advocate*, reprinted the Hicks announcement from the *Intelligencer* in the 26 September 1844 edition of the *Advocate*. The article praised Bushyhead as a "self-made man," faithful to his duties, and an able interpreter and translator. It also included a personal assessment. The paper described Bushyhead as "a man of good natural sense, upright in his dealings, exemplary in conduct, kind in feeling, independent in character, and one who had deeply at heart the welfare of his whole people, among whom he sought to inculcate the principles of order, industry, and religion."[78] On 18 August, Solomon Peck also extolled Bushyhead in a letter to Jones. Although the status of Bushyhead as a slaveholder was about to spark a denominational fracture, Peck's panegyric omit-

[76] Butrick Journal, 19 July 1844; "Death of Rev. Jesse Bushyhead," *Cherokee Messenger*, August 1844, 1; Evan Jones Letters, 26 August 1844, ABFM Society Records, 1817–1959.

[77] Moulton, *The Papers of Chief John Ross*, 2:243.

[78] *Cherokee Advocate*, 26 September 1844.

ted such accusations. Jones reprinted the letter in the December 1844 edition of *The Cherokee Messenger*:

> *No one* of our native preachers was more highly valued than brother Bushy-head, none whose service seemed so useful and so indispensable. His mature piety, his sound, judgment, his perfect mastery of the Cherokee language, as well as familiar acquaintance with our own, the confidence reposed in him by his countrymen and by us, and the ripeness of preparation in *all* respects to do a great work for his people, both in preaching and translating the word of God, all seemed to mark him as *the one* chosen of God, to carry on the work of evangelizing the Nation to its completion.[79]

Bushyhead's death also left a void concerning relations between the United States government and Cherokees. Cherokee agent Butler clearly noted the vacuum. In his annual report, Butler considered Bushyhead as one "who occupied that middle ground between the Cherokees and the whites, which rendered his intervention most important and influential in all their intercourses; and who exercised his influences in a manner uniformly beneficial, that we may not soon find another competent to supply his place."[80]

Bushyhead's survivors included his mother, widow, several siblings, and nine children. The ages of his children ranged from a son, about twenty, to a one-year-old daughter.[81] With such a large family and his eldest son away at school in New Jersey, Bushyhead must have left debts. Eliza realized the need for income and placed a notice in the August edition of *The Cherokee Messenger*. She offered to take in boarders attending the Cherokee Female Seminary for $1.25 per

[79] "Extract of a Letter from the Rev. S. Peck," *The Cherokee Messenger* 1 (December 1844): 47–48.

[80] P[ierce] M. Butler to T. Hartley Crawford, 30 September 1844, Letters Received by the Office of Indian Affairs, 1824–1881, National Archives, M234, roll 88.

[81] Bell, *Genealogy*, 92–93; L[uther] W[hitfield] Marks, "The Story of Oklahoma Baptists," unpublished typewritten manuscript, 88.

day. Stephen Foreman served as the legal administrator for Eliza. An October edition of the *Cherokee Advocate* contained Foreman's announcement concerning the financial affairs of Bushyhead. The notification carried a sense of urgency: "All persons that are indebted to the estate of Jesse Bushyhead, deceased, either by note or otherwise, are hereby notified to come forward and make payment immediately...."[82]

By the time Bushyhead died, Baptists had made significant gains in the Cherokee Nation. In a little over five years, four churches and three mission stations had been established. Five Native preachers, two ordained and three licensed, held services. Also, several teachers, one printer, a printing press, and one Native interpreter supported the ministry. These efforts resulted in membership gains. Although Methodist communicants numbered 1,300, the Baptist presence was strong as well. In 1844, there were 800 Baptists. And two years later, much of the New Testament and Genesis had been published in Cherokee.[83] Without a doubt, a major part of the progress was due to Jones. Jones supervised the work and served as the liaison between the mission field and the Baptist Board. He also trained Native ministers as much as possible. But without Bushyhead, progress would not have been as great. Serving as translator and orator, Bushyhead provided a lasting foundation for Cherokee Baptist work.

[82] Cherokee Advocate, 26 October 1844.

[83] "Summary of Baptist Work at Present," *The Cherokee Messenger* 1 (September 1844): 29; P. M. Butler to T. Hartley Crawford, 30 September 1844.

Conclusion

The Legacy

The grave of Bushyhead is in the Baptist Mission Cemetery, about three miles north of Westville, Oklahoma. The site is on the east side of U.S. Highway 59 and directly across the highway from the Baptist Mission Church. Sometime before Oklahoma statehood in 1907, a grateful public placed an imposing tombstone. Inscriptions in Cherokee and English memorialize Bushyhead as a noble servant of God and Cherokees. The English version reads:

> Rev. Jesse Bushyhead was a man noble in
> person, and noble in heart: His choice
> was to be a true and faithful minister of his
> Lord and master, rather than any high
> worldly position: He loved his country
> and people, serving them from time to time
> in many important offices and missions:
> He united with the Baptist church in his
> early manhood and died as he had lived
> a devoted christian [*sic*].

In Sequoyan characters, the Cherokee lauds Bushyhead as a noble man and minister who served and loved his people.[1]

The Bushyhead legacy of public service endured. Two of his surviving nine children, a son and a daughter, rose to prominent posi-

[1] Cherokee translation provided by Betty Smith of Bartlesville, Oklahoma.

tions of leadership. From 1871 through 1887, Dennis served as treasurer and then principal chief of the Cherokee Nation. Eliza Missouri Bushyhead taught school for several years before becoming a successful businesswoman at Tahlequah. In later years, she was influential in establishing the institutional antecedent of Northeastern State Oklahoma University at Tahlequah. She lived until 1919.[2]

An assessment of Bushyhead includes political and religious aspects. As is often the case with historical figures, an element of legend has developed around his life. Doctor Emmet Starr, an early twentieth-century Cherokee historian, was partially responsible for creating the legend. Starr erroneously characterized Bushyhead as lacking interest in the "feudal and political troubles among his people." He somewhat naively extolled him as "being the only man of any consequence among the Cherokees who habitually traveled among his people...unarmed, except as he said, with his Bible."[3] Others such as Grant Foreman built upon this misconception. But against the backdrop of legend, Bushyhead merits a closer look. The political significance of Bushyhead is apparent. Historians Grant Foreman and Stan Hoig also have credited George Guess and Bushyhead with spearheading the compromise that ultimately influenced most Western Cherokees and Ross supporters to agree on the Act of Union. Without the influence of the newcomer Bushyhead and the Old Settler Guess, unrest may have resulted in full-blown civil war and prompted more aggressive interference by the United States military. Such a conflict may have doomed hopes for self-government among Cherokee nationalists. And if Cherokees had been denied a degree of autonomy, the same result may have befallen the other four Southeastern tribes after their arrival in Indian Territory. Yet, fortunately, over

[2] Meserve, "Chief Dennis Bushyhead," 352–54; Carolyn Thomas Foreman, "Aunt Eliza of Tahlequah," 48–54.

[3] Starr, *History of the Cherokee Indians and Their Legends and Folk Lore*, 256.

the next decade, all of the five tribes developed or perfected some type of self-government.

Even from his early days in Tennessee, Bushyhead's social and economic standing in white society provided advantages. Both he and his wife were mixed-bloods. And marriage into a slaveholding family marked Bushyhead as a member of the rising upper-middle class of Cherokees. Reaching early manhood at Candy's Creek, he was near the Cherokee agency and Ross's Landing, centers of Cherokee economic and political activities. This location offered opportunities to form acquaintances with tribal leaders, white missionaries, and United States authorities. He also knew or had kinship ties with other influential mixed-bloods such as the Fieldses, Foremans, Springstons, Bigsbys, Martins, and Walkers. Furthermore, his skill as a translator allowed him to gain additional prominence. And as some other mixed-bloods, he had converted to Christianity. In this vein, his position as a minister provided a measure of notice among whites, mixed-bloods, and full-bloods, for his pulpit responsibilities and oratory allowed him to demonstrate his public-speaking skills. Through this means, he garnered respect as a supporter of missions and benevolent causes among some white audiences. Furthermore, his oratorical abilities likewise accorded him esteem among full-bloods.

During his early manhood, removal had become a divisive issue. Some middle-class Cherokees such as Elias Boudinot, Stand Watie, and the Ridges came to support the removal policies of the Jackson administration. Yet, at first, even Bushyhead and some of his family did not take a definitive position against removal. Before the 1838 exodus, two of his brothers freely had chosen to move to Indian Territory. And it seems that Bushyhead had expressed interest in voluntarily relocating to Texas. At the time Bushyhead held these sentiments, Texas was under a government that had shown favor to Cherokees. Even Jack Walker, Jr., the pro-Jackson schemer, was in the social circle of Jesse and Isaac Bushyhead. And there were additional links with Walker. Nannie Bushyhead was the mother of two of Walker's children. And at times, Isaac Bushyhead cooperated with Walker in financial ventures. Why, then, did Bushyhead reject the influence of Walker and Boudinot and oppose removal? Part of the weakening of the Walker link related to the erosion of family ties. Walker put aside Nannie and married a white bride. Also, the assassination of Walker reinforced the serious nature of Cherokee blood law to those who dared to thwart tribal policies.

But there were other influences besides Walker. Two ministerial associates, Evan Jones and Stephen Foreman, also had a marked effect. Foreman, a relative and an acquaintance of Bushyhead from his youth, remained a lifelong friend. Foreman served as an assistant detachment conductor on the trail west and was an early leader in the Western Cherokee Nation. Foreman had professed Christianity and joined Candy's Creek mission in 1825, some four years before the conversion of Bushyhead. Serving as interpreter and preacher, Foreman became an integral part of the mission work at Candy's Creek. Considering the success of Foreman, one may surmise that Bushyhead realized the financial opportunities open to those who entered the ministry, for the path to ordination among Baptists did not require the formal theological training required by Congregationalist and Presbyterians. This may have influenced Bushyhead to align with Baptist ranks rather than remain within Congregationalist-Presbyterian circles. After all, Foreman's preparation was extensive. Foreman had begun to prepare for the ministry six to eight years before the ordination of Bushyhead. He also had received at least three years of seminary education before being licensed. But unlike Foreman, Bushyhead received licensure without any formal education, other than a few years of rudimentary studies at Candy's Creek. Moreover, he was ordained near the same time as Foreman. Thus, Baptist alignment provided a fast track to ministerial credentials and the possibility for a salaried position as a missionary/translator.

Besides Foreman, Jones provided the additional impetus. Jones may not have been the primary influence on the initial alignment of

Bushyhead with Baptists. Nevertheless, above other Baptist ministers, the influence of Jones cannot go unnoticed. Bushyhead ministered only for a total of twelve years. And during this period, affairs of state consumed much of his time. Although Bushyhead aided in the establishment or support of several mission stations, he personally organized only the Amohee congregation. Without Jones, he may not have remained active in the ministry. Inarguably, Jones provided the encouragement, opportunities, and links to financial support necessary for success. From Valley Towns to Georgia and on to the Western Cherokee Nation, Bushyhead and Jones were companions in the ministry. They traveled together and shared pulpits. Although unsuccessful in preventing removal, they ameliorated its effects. Thus, Bushyhead saw in Jones a white spokesman for Cherokee self-determination. And without Bushyhead, Jones may not have had as much influence among Cherokees.

Another question remains concerning Bushyhead's affiliation with Baptists. Did Bushyhead align with Baptists because Tennessee Baptists generally supported slavery? By the time Bushyhead joined a Baptist congregation, he had kept at least one slave in his household for at least five years. It is true that Baptists in the South had more relaxed attitudes toward slavery, whereas New England-rooted Congregationalist-Presbyterian missionaries were less open to ministers holding slaves. Yet, at the time of Bushyhead's entrance to Baptist circles, the abolitionist movement had not coalesced. Moreover, there are several other reasons that lessen the slavery issue as a primary reason for affiliation with Baptists. Even Jones, a New Englander, held antislavery views. During the Civil War, his antislavery views forced him to exodus the Western Cherokee Nation. His antislavery stance could have alienated Bushyhead but, apparently, did not. And even among southern Presbyterians, slavery existed. It is unknown whether or not Stephen Foreman owned slaves in Tennessee. But after reaching Indian Territory, he was a slaveholder.[4] Although missionaries under the auspices of the American Board of Commissioners for Foreign Missions opposed slavery, there is no evidence that slave ownership had become a bar to membership in Congregationalist-Presbyterian chruches around the Cleveland area. So, slavery itself does not appear to have been a determinant in denominational preferences.

Although educational requirements may have been a factor in Bushyhead's choice of denominations, it does not explain entirely the ultimate affiliation of Bushyhead. If Bushyhead simply had desired additional recognition, it would have been more convenient to remain in Congregationalist-Presbyterian circles. Already, even Foreman had been employed in this capacity before his licensure and ordination. And Bushyhead's skill as a superior translator, so valuable to missionaries, already had been acknowledged. Moreover, participation with Baptists carried definite negative aspects. Distance and denominational polity were barriers. The Valley Towns mission was more than seventy miles away. And although more Baptist than Presbyterian churches existed in southeastern Tennessee, many Baptist congregations harbored strong sentiments against salaried missionaries. If one wanted to ensure some type of income through missionary endeavors, better opportunities existed among groups other than Baptists. Finally, life as a preacher involved financial and personal sacrifices. Attending denominational meetings and riding to distant preaching appointments took time away from one's family and livelihood. It also meant exposure to inclement weather and perils of travel. With this in mind, there were easier ways to profit other than receiving a missionary's salary.

Aside from the ministry, another contribution of Bushyhead came as a political figure. From his days in Tennessee to his death in

[4] Celia E. Naylor, *African Cherokees in Indian Territory: From Chattel to Citizens* (Chapel Hill: University of North Carolina, 2008) 139.

Indian Territory, Bushyhead was a significant figure in the Ross faction. By December 1835, he had been drawn into the Ross circle and journeyed to Washington to mediate removal with the Jackson administration. Two years later, he served as an emissary to the Seminoles at the request of Ross. And receiving an appointment as a detachment leader, he retained the confidence of Ross. As a detachment captain, he was a recipient of funds managed by Ross. Once in the West, Bushyhead continued to support Ross. And in 1842, Bushyhead and Ross made one more journey to Washington in an effort to renegotiate the New Echota Treaty. But his political life in the new land at times provoked strong opposition. Unlike the accolades of nonpartisanship offered by some, he risked assassination at the hands of enemies. Bushyhead may have traveled armed only with a Bible, yet he had every right to carry firearms. One of his foes was the noted manslayer Archilla Smith. Ultimately, Smith stood before Bushyhead and heard the chief justice condemn him to death. The involvement of Bushyhead in this matter stirred more resentment among his enemies. Even Jones admitted that Bushyhead was not beloved by all. Jones alluded to several assassination attempts. Upon Bushyhead's death, Jones attempted to console mourners. Jones speculated that "perhaps, God has taken away br. B., and permitted him to die peacefully in the bosom of his family, to save him from a more violent death."[5]

While in Tennessee, Bushyhead became aware of the loss of personal economic and political advantages should the Eastern Cherokees remove to Indian Territory, for reports from Arkansas had been negative, and the messages from Isaac Bushyhead only confirmed these forebodings. Jesse, therefore, worked within and without the system to halt or delay removal and the threatened disintegration of the Eastern Cherokee Nation. And having arrived in Indian Territory, he continued to be an instrument for national unity, for

[5] *Baptist Missionary Magazine* 24 (October 1844): 310.

Bushyhead realized that violence and disorder posed a serious challenge to national survival.

The association of Bushyhead with Ross and Jones raises another question. Was Bushyhead simply a tool of Ross and Jones? Did Jones utilize Bushyhead partially for political purposes—that is, to organize pro-Ross groups in the form of Baptist churches, temperance movement chapters, and the Cherokee Bible Society? Certain Treaty party supporters, especially Jack Bell, viewed Jones as a political threat. On one occasion, their antipathy was strong enough to cause his exile from Indian Territory. It remains clear that many of the associates of Bushyhead in church and benevolent organs did share his political leanings. For example, some fellow members of the Cherokee Temperance Society and Cherokee Bible Society had opposed the New Echota Treaty and supported the Ross administration in the new Cherokee Nation.[6] But this does not necessarily point to a cabal among these organizations, for the great majority of Cherokees opposed the treaty almost from the beginning. And although the congregations of Bushyhead and Jones were composed of mountain Cherokees and remnants of the Amohee Church, part of the justification centered on factors other than political alignment. Church planting on the frontier was difficult at best. Usually, only those willing to support such efforts with funds, time, and labor became members of struggling congregations. It is logical that only those who felt some manner of sympathy for the minister chose to attend services. Thus, Ross opponents did not feel comfortable among congregations led by Bushyhead and Jones. Yet this does not mean that the worship groups were strictly political enclaves.

[6] *Cherokee Advocate*, 26 September 1844; *The Cherokee Messenger* 1 (August 1844): 15–16; Moulton, *The Papers of Chief John Ross*, 1:21, 378, 382–83, 391, 410, 474, 504, 516, 605, 676, 697; and 2:24, 106, 114, 162–63, 172, 205, 380, 716, 730; Franks, *Stand Watie and the Agony of the Cherokee Nation*, 62.

Although significant, Bushyhead should not obscure the early work of other denominations and church planters among the Southeastern tribes. Butler, Butrick, and Worcester all made major contributions to Cherokee evangelism. Congregationalists, Presbyterians, and Methodists continued to labor among all of the Southeastern tribes in future Oklahoma. And Roman Catholic clergy ministered to the Osage in Missouri and later in Oklahoma. Among Cherokees, Lewis Downing and Stephen Foreman gained recognition as ministers and tribal leaders. Downing followed Bushyhead as a congregational shepherd and served briefly as chief of the Cherokee Nation.[7] And Foreman became invaluable to Worcester as an interpreter and translator. As a result of his assistance, Worcester was able to publish a translation of the New Testament and other portions of the Bible. On the political level, Foreman signed the national constitution and helped to heal factional differences. In addition, he held important national positions, including a Supreme Court seat and the first superintendent of education.[8]

Bushyhead represents an important bridge in the conversion of the Cherokees to Christianity. Although not the first Cherokee Christian, he was among the first generation of converts and ministers. Faced with nontraditional customs and religion, Cherokees, especially full-bloods, had to grapple with change. Yet Bushyhead proved invaluable in helping them to do so. His linguistic skills and association with Jones allowed him to function in white and Cherokee worlds. His stance against removal wrought a favorable position among most full- and mixed-bloods. And this position allowed him to become a more effective evangelist and statesman. Through his alliance with Ross, Bushyhead gained the political support and re-

[7] John Bartlett Meserve, "Chief Lewis Downing and Chief Charles Thompson (Oochalata)," *Chronicles of Oklahoma* 16 (September 1938): 317–22.

[8] Minta Ross Foreman, "Reverend Stephen Foreman, Cherokee Missionary," *Chronicles of Oklahoma* 18 (September 1940): 235–36.

spect necessary to be an effective leader. Sadly, these political ties also garnered enemies. Finally, Bushyhead sparked controversy over slavery and became a lightning rod for abolitionists. Given his contributions, it is unfortunate that he touched off a sectional division among Baptists, which foreshadowed the rupture of the United States. This is part of the legacy of Bushyhead and the accompanying controversies in the Cherokee Nation.

Bibliography

Primary

Manuscripts

American Baptist Foreign Mission Society Records, 1817–1959. Mercer University, Atlanta, Georgia. Microfilm.

B. B. Cannon Journal, 1837. Western Historical Manuscript Collection, Ellis Library, University of Missouri, Columbia.

Daniel S. Butrick Journal, American Board of Commissioners for Foreign Missions (ABCFM).

E. C. Boudinot Papers. Oklahoma Historical Society Library (OHSL), Oklahoma City, Oklahoma.

Evan Jones Letters, Indian Correspondence, 1800–1900. Baptist Foreign Mission Board, American Baptist Historical Society (ABHS), FM-98, Mercer University, Atlanta, Georgia.

Gary Moulton Papers. OHSL.

Grant Foreman Papers, Cherokee Notes. Gilcrease Museum, Tulsa, Oklahoma.

Jacob M. K. Smith Diary. Special Collections, Mullins Library, University of Arkansas, Fayetteville.

John Cocke Papers. Oklahoma Trail of Tears Association Collection, Sequoyah Center, University of Arkansas at Little Rock. Photocopied.

John Howard Payne Papers, Ayer MS. Newberry Library, Chicago, Illinois. Typewritten CD copy.

John Ross Papers. Gilcrease Museum.

Journal and Letters of Stephen Foreman. Western Heritage Collections, University of Oklahoma, Norman. Typewritten copy.

Letter Books. Special Collections, McFarlin Library, University of Tulsa, Tulsa, Oklahoma.

"Ludovic Grant." Bushyhead Folder, Special Collections, OHSL.

Poinsett Papers. Pennsylvania Historical Society, Philadelphia.

Records of American Board of Commissioners for Foreign Missions (ABCFM). Microfilm at OHSL.

Schermerhorn Papers. Western Historical Manuscript Collection, Ellis Library, University of Missouri, Columbia.

Will of John Walker, Jr. John Walker, Jr. File, Cleveland (TN) Public Library. Typewritten copy.

Letters

Buckner, Daniel, to R[obert] S[amuel] Duncan, 17 September 1875. Partee Center for Baptist Historical Studies, William Jewell College, Liberty, Missouri.

Bushyhead, Jane, to Martha Thompson, 10 March 1838. Cleveland Public Library. Photocopy.

Lowell, Truxton, to James Lowell, 1 October 1836. Special Collections, Mullins Library, University of Arkansas, Fayetteville.

Ross, Lewis to John Ross, 18 February 1837. Penelope Johnson Allen Cherokee Collection, box 1, folder 24. Tennessee State Library, Nashville.

United States Legislative Publications

U.S. Congress. House Document 91. *Disbursements to the Indians.* Report prepared by John M. McCalla. 29th Cong., 4th sess. LexisNexis Academic, 2006. Serial Set ID: 483 H.doc. 91.

———. House Document 129. Committee on Indian Affairs. *Memorial of the Delegation of the Cherokee Nation.* Report prepared by George Hicks. 26th Cong., 1st sess. LexisNexis Academic, 2006. Serial Set ID: 365 H.doc. 129.

———. House Document 219. Committee on Indian Affairs. *The Report of Lieutenant Colonel Hitchcock, respecting the affairs of the Cherokee Indians.* 27th Cong., 3rd sess. LexisNexis Academic, 2006. Serial Set ID: 425 H.doc. 219.

———. House Report 271. Committee on Indian Affairs. *Frauds upon Indians.* Report prepared by James Cooper. 27th Cong., 3rd sess. LexisNexis Academic, 2006. Serial Set ID: 428 H.rp. 271.

———. House Document 285. Committee on Indian Affairs. *Memorial of the Cherokee Mediators.* Report prepared by Major Polecat and others. 25th Cong., 2nd sess. LexisNexis Academic, 2006. Serial Set ID: 328 H.doc. 285.

———. House Document 286. Committee of the Whole. *Memorial of the Cherokee Representatives, submitting the protest of the Cherokee Nation against the ratification, execution, and enforcement of the treaty negotiated at New Echota, in December 1835.* 24th Cong., 1st sess. LexisNexis Academic, 2006. Serial Set ID: H.doc. 292.

———. House Document 288. Committee on Indian Affairs. *Removal of Cherokees*. Report prepared by James Cooper. 27th Cong., 3rd sess. LexisNexis Academic, 2006. Serial Set ID: 429 H.doc. 288.

———. House Report 1098. Committee on Indian Affairs. *Removal of the Cherokees West of the Mississippi*. Report prepared by William Alexander Harris. 27th Cong., 2nd sess. LexisNexis Academic, 2006. Serial Set ID: 411 H.rp. 1098.

———. Senate Document 1/6. *Report of the Commissioner of Indian Affairs*. Report prepared by Thomas Hartley Crawford. 26th Cong., 1st sess. LexisNexis Academic, 2006. Serial Set ID: 354 S.doc. 1/6.

———. Senate Document 140. *Report of the Secretary of War, communicating (in compliance with a resolution of the Senate) the report and correspondence of the board of inquiry, to prosecute an examination into the causes and extent of the discontents and difficulties among the Cherokee Indians*. Report prepared by William Wilkins. 28th Cong., 2nd sess. LexisNexis Academic, 2006. Serial Set ID: 457 S.doc. 140.

———. Senate Document 229. Committee on Indian Affairs. *Report of the Secretary of War, communicating (in compliance with a resolution of the Senate) a copy of a report made by P. M. Butler, United States agent for the Cherokee Indians*. Report prepared by William Wilkins. 28th Cong., 2nd sess. LexisNexis Academic, 2006. Serial Set ID: 434 S.doc. 229.

———. Senate Document 298. Committee on Indian Affairs. *Message of the President of the United States, relative to the internal feuds among the Cherokees*. Report prepared by James Knox Polk. 29th Cong., 1st sess. LexisNexis Academic, 2006. Serial Set ID: 474 S.doc. 298.

———. Senate Report 744. Committee on Territories. [Untitled] Report prepared by George Washington Patterson. 45th Cong., 3rd sess. LexisNexis Academic, 2006. Serial Set ID: 1839 S.rp. 744.

National Archives

Correspondence of the Eastern Division Pertaining to Cherokee Removal, April–December 1838. National Archives. M1475, rolls 1–2.

Letters Received by the Office of Indian Affairs, 1824–1881. M234, rolls 75, 83–84, 87–89, 115.

Muster Roll of Cherokee Indians to Emigrate West of the Mississippi. Microfilm A-42.

Records of Headquarters, Army of the Southwestern Frontier, and Headquarters, Second and Seventh Military Departments, 1835–1853.

M1302. Accessed at Arkansas History Commission, ML0602, ML0604.

Special Files of the Office of Indian Affairs, 1807–1904. M574, roll 25.

Special Files

A Record Book of the Proceedings of the Supreme Court of the Cherokee Nation, 9 October 1829. Cherokee Supreme Court Minutes, vol. 1, 1823–1835. Cherokee Collection, 1775–1878. M-815, box 10, file 10. Tennessee State Library.

Tennessee

State v. Anderson Springston and James Foreman. East Tennessee Supreme Court, box 245. Tennessee State Library.

Published

Anderson, Rufus. *Memoir of Catharine Brown: A Cherokee Indian of the Cherokee Nation*. Cincinnati: Morgan, Fisher and L'Hommedieu, 1827; reprint, n.p.: Our Christian Heritage Foundation, 2012.

Baker, Jack D., transcriber. *Cherokee Emigration Rolls, 1817–1835*. Oklahoma City OK: Baker Publishing, 1977.

Bassett, John Spencer, editor. *Correspondence of Andrew Jackson*. Nashville: Carnegie Institution, 1931.

Caldwell, Martha B., compiler. *Annals of Shawnee Methodist Mission and Indian Manual Labor School*. Topeka: Kansas State Historical Society, 1977.

Census Roll, 1835 of the Cherokee Indians East of the Mississippi and Index to the Roll. National Archives: Washington, D.C., 1960.

Chase, Marybelle W., transcriber. *Records of the Cherokee Agency in Tennessee, 1801–1835*. n.p., 1990.

Cherokee Almanac. Tulsa OK: Gilcrease Museum, 1840.

Constitution and Laws of the Cherokee Nation. St. Louis: R. & T. A. Ennis, 1875.

Foreman, Grant, editor. *A Traveler in Indian Territory: The Journal of Ethan Allen Hitchcock, Late Major-General in the United States Army*. Cedar Rapids IA: Torch Press, 1930.

Hoskins, Shirley Coats, editor. *Cherokee Property Valuations in Tennessee, 1836*. n.p.: By the author, 1984.

Moulton, Gary E., editor. *The Papers of Chief John Ross*. 2 volumes. Norman: University of Oklahoma, 1985.

Nuttall, Thomas. *A Journal of Travels into the Arkansa Territory*. Philadelphia: Thos. M. Palmer, 1821; reprint, Ann Arbor: University Microfilms, 1966.

Payne, John Howard. *Indian Justice: A Cherokee Murder Trial at Tahlequah in 1840*, ed. Grant Foreman. Harlow Publishing, ; reprint, n.p.: Red River Books. Norman: University of Oklahoma, 2002.

Proceedings of the Southern Baptist Convention, 8 May–12 May 1845. Richmond: H. K. Ellyson, 1845.

Sherrill, Charles A., editor. *Bradley County, Tennessee Circuit Court Case File Abstracts, 1836–1860*. Cleveland TN: Cleveland Public Library, 1988.

Whitmire, Mildred, editor. *Noland's Cherokee Diary: A U.S. Soldier's Story from Inside the Cherokee Nation*. Spartanburg SC: Reprint Company, 1990.

Church Records

"Big Pigeon Church Minutes, 1787–1874." Transcribed by Glen R. Bayless. Courtesy of Stokely Memorial Library, Newport, Tennessee. Typewritten copy.

Minutes of the Fifth Session of the Sweet-Water Baptist Association (1835). N.p. Monitor, [1835?].

Minutes of the Fourth Session of the Sweet-Water Baptist Association (1834). Madisonville: Tennessean, [1834?].

Minutes of the Seventh Annual Meeting of the Franklin Association (1838). Upper Alton, Illinois: Pioneer, 1838. Courtesy of Partee Center of Baptist Historical Studies, Charles F. Curry Library, William Jewell College, Liberty, Missouri.

Minutes of the Hiwassee Association (1830). N.p.: F. S. Heiskell, [1830].

Minutes of the Hiwassee United Baptist Association (1834; 1836). Athens, Tennessee: John M. Gibbs, [1834?].

Minutes of the Washington Baptist Association (1838). Typewritten copy. Washington County Archives, Special Collections, David W. Mullins Library, University of Arkansas at Fayetteville.

Religious Periodicals

The Baptist. 1 August 1837; 4 November 1838.

Baptist and Reflector. 15 June 1837.

Baptist Missionary Magazine. 1832–1833; 1836–1840; 1844.

Latter Day Luminary. 3 July 1822.

Missionary Herald. 1825–1826; 1828–1829; 1832–1833.

Newspapers

Arkansas Intelligencer. 18 March–4 November 1843.

Athens (TN) Courier. 14 January 1842.

Atkinson's Evening Post. 6 July 1839.

Cherokee Advocate. 26 September, 26 October 1844.

The Cherokee Messenger. August–December 1844.

Cleveland Daily Banner, 10 September 1973.

Hamilton (TN) Gazette. 26 July 1838.

Secondary Materials

Unpublished

Conner, John B. "Materials Toward a History of the Baptists of Cleveland, Tennessee." Unpublished typewritten manuscript.

Marks, L[uther] W[hitfield]. "The Story of Oklahoma Baptists." Unpublished typewritten manuscript.

Reed, Gerald Alexander. "The Ross-Watie Conflict: Cherokee Factionalism in the Cherokee Nation, 1839–1865," PhD. dissertation, University of Oklahoma, 1967.

Wooten, John Morgan. "Chief Jack Walker," John Wooten Scrapbook. Chattanooga Public Library. M-54.

Books

Ahlstrom, Sydney E. *A Religious History of the American People*. New Haven: Yale, 1972.

Alden, John Richard. *John Stuart and the Southern Colonial Frontier*. New York: Gordian, 1966.

Ashton, Sharron Standifer, compiler. *Indians and Intruders*. Norman: Ashton Books, 1997.

Baird, W. David, and Danney Goble. *Oklahoma: A History*. Norman: University of Oklahoma, 2008.

Bass, Althea. *Cherokee Messenger*. Norman: University of Oklahoma, 1936.

Bell, George Morrison, Sr. *Genealogy of "Old & New Cherokee Indian Families*." Bartlesville OK: By the author, 1972.

Bordewich, Fergus M. *Killing the White Man's Indian: Reinventing Native Americans at the End of the Twentieth Century*. New York: Anchor Books, 1997.

Broyles, Bettye J. *Churches and Schools of Rhea County, Tennessee*. Dayton: Rhea County Historical and Genealogical Society, 1992.

Calvert, Robert A., and Arnoldo De Leon. *The History of Texas*. Arlington Heights IL: Harland Davidson, 1990.

Corn, James Franklin. *Red Clay and Rattlesnake Springs*. Cleveland TN: By the author, 1959.

Denson, Andrew. *Demanding the Cherokee Nation: Indian Autonomy and American Culture, 1830–1900*. Lincoln: University of Nebraska, 2004.

Ehle, John. *Trail of Tears: The Rise and Fall of the Cherokee Nation*. New York: Anchor Books, 1988.

Foreman, Grant. *The Five Civilized Tribes*. Norman: University of Oklahoma, 1934.

———. *Sequoyah*. Norman: University of Oklahoma, 1938.

Franks, Kenny A. *Stand Watie and the Agony of the Cherokee Nation*. Memphis: Memphis State University, 1979.

Gardner, Robert G. *Cherokees and Baptists in Georgia*. Atlanta: Georgia Baptist Historical Society, 1989.

Gibson, Arrell M. *The American Indian: Prehistory to the Present*. Lexington MA: D. C. Heath, 1980.

———. *Oklahoma: A History of Five Centuries*. Norman: Harlow Publishing, 1965.

Gilbert, Joan. *The Trail of Tears across Missouri*. Columbia: University of Missouri, 1996.

Hampton, David Keith. *Cherokee Mixed Bloods*. Lincoln, Arkansas: ARC Press, 2005.

History of Benton, Washington, Carroll, Madison, Crawford, Franklin, and Sebastian Counties, Arkansas. Chicago: Goodspeed Publishing, 1889; reprint, Greenville SC: Southern Historical Press, 2002.

Hughes, William W. *Archibald Yell*. Fayetteville: University of Arkansas, 1988.

Kieffer, Charles L. *Maligned General: A Biography of Thomas S. Jesup*. San Rafael CA: Presidio, 1979.

King, Duane H., editor. *The Cherokee Indian Nation: A Troubled History*. Knoxville: University of Tennessee, 1979.

Littlefield, Daniel F., and James W. Parins, editors. *Encyclopedia of American Indian Removal*. Santa Barbara CA: Greenwood, 2011. S.v. "Cherokee Removal," by Daniel F. Littlefied, Jr.

Mahon, John K. *History of the Second Seminole War, 1835–1842*. Revised edition. Gainesville: University of Florida, 1985.

McLoughlin, William G. *After the Trail of Tears: The Cherokee Struggle for Sovereignty, 1839–1880*. Chapel Hill: University of North Carolina, 1993.

———. *Champions of the Cherokees: Evan and John B. Jones*. Princeton: Princeton University, 1990.

———. *Cherokees and Missionaries, 1789–1839*. Norman: University of Oklahoma, 1995.

______. *Cherokee Renascence in the New Republic*. Princeton: Princeton University Press, 1986.

Moulton, Gary E. *John Ross: Cherokee Chief*. Athens: University of Georgia, 1978.

Murrow, J. S. *Rev. Jesse Bushyhead: Cherokee Indian and Missionary*. Privately published, 2015.

Naylor, Celia E. *African Cherokees in Indian Territory: From Chattel to Citizens*. Chapel Hill: University of North Carolina, 2008.

Nelson, Joshua B. *Progressive Traditions: Identity in Cherokee Literature and Culture*. Norman: University of Oklahoma, 2014.

Parins, James W. *Literacy and Intellectual Life in the Cherokee Nation, 1820–1906*. Norman: University of Oklahoma, 2013.

Perdue, Theda. *"Mixed Blood" Indians: Racial Construction in the Early South*. Athens: University of Georgia, 2003.

Perdue, Theda, and Michael D. Green. *The Cherokee Nation and the Trail of Tears*. New York: Viking, 2007.

Perrin, Henry William, editor. *County of Christian, Kentucky*. Chicago and Louisville: F. A. Battey Publishing, 1884; reprint, Easley SC: Southern Historical Press, 1979.

Reid, John Phillip. *A Law of Blood: The Primitive Law of the Cherokee Nation*. DeKalb IL: Northern Illinois University, 2006.

Remini, Robert V. *Andrew Jackson and His Indian Wars*. New York: Penguin, 2001.

———. *The Life of Andrew Jackson*. New York: Penguin, 1988.

Royce, Charles C. *The Cherokee Nation of Indians*. Chicago: Aldine Publishing, 1975.

Schroeder, A. E., Rebecca B. Schroeder, and Donald M. Lance, compilers. *Remembering Eliza Missouri Bushyhead*. n.p.: Missouri Chapter of the Trail of Tears Association, 2001.

Snell, William R. *Cleveland the Beautiful: A History of Cleveland, Tennessee, 1842–1931*. Cleveland TN: First American National Bank, 1986.

Starr, Emmet. *History of the Cherokees and Their Legends and Folklore*. Oklahoma City OK: Warden, 1921; reprint, Millwood NY: Kraus Reprint, 1977.

Strickland, Rennard. *Fire and the Spirits: Cherokee Law from Clan to Court*. Norman: University of Oklahoma, 1975.

Torbet, Robert G. *A History of the Baptists*. 3rd edition. Valley Forge: Judson, 1973.

Tyner, James W., editor. *Those Who Cried: The 16,000*. n.p.: Chi-ga-u Inc., 1974.

Walker, Robert Sparks. *Torchlights to the Cherokees: The Brainerd Mission*. New York: MacMillan, 1931; reprint, Johnson City TN: Overmountain Press, 1993.

Wardell, Morris L. *A Political History of the Cherokee Nation, 1838–1907*. Norman: University of Oklahoma, 1938; second printing, 1977.

Wilkins, Thurman. *Cherokee Tragedy: The Ridge Family and the Decimation of a People*. 2nd edition, revised. Norman: University of Oklahoma, 1986.

Wimberly, Dan B. *Frontier Religion: Elder Daniel Parker, His Religious and Political Life*. Austin TX: Eakin Press, 2002.

Woodward, Grace Steele. *The Cherokees*. Norman: University of Oklahoma, 1963.

Yarbrough, Fay A. *Race and the Cherokee Nation: Sovereignty in the Nineteenth Century*. Philadelphia: University of Pennsylvania, 2008.

Journals and Articles

Boyd, Mark F. "Asi-Yaholo or Osceola." *The Florida Historical Quarterly* 33 (January–April 1955): 249–305.

Brown, John P. "Eastern Cherokee Chiefs." *Chronicles of Oklahoma* 16 (March 1938): 3–35.

Chase, Marybelle W., transcriber. "Cherokee Removal Records." *Cherokee Tracer* 10 (Summer 2000): 68-72.

———. "1838 Cherokee Claims." *Cherokee Tracer* 9 (Spring 1999): 36–40.

Everett, Dianna, Linda D. Wilson, Larry O'Dell, and Jon D. May, editors. *Encyclopedia of Oklahoma History and Culture*. Oklahoma City OK: Oklahoma Historical Society, 2009. S.v. "Delaware County," by Rose Stauber; and "Oklahoma Religion," by Alvin O. Turner.

Fiorato, Jacqueline. "The Cherokee Mediation in Florida." *Journal of Cherokee Studies* (Spring 1978): 111–19.

Foreman, Carolyn Thomas. "Aunt Eliza of Tahlequah." *Chronicles of Oklahoma* 9 (March 1931): 43–55.

———. "An Early Account of the Cherokees." *Chronicles of Oklahoma* 34 (Summer 1956): 141–58.

———. "General Richard Barnes Mason." *Chronicles of Oklahoma* 19 (March 1941): 14–36.

Foreman, Grant. "Notes and Documents." *Mississippi Valley Historical Review* 18 (September 1931): 232–45.

Foreman, Minta Ross. "Reverend Stephen Foreman, Cherokee Missionary." *Chronicles of Oklahoma* 18 (September 1940): 229–42.

Gardner, Robert G. "Duncan O'Bryant: Georgia Missionary to the Eastern Cherokees." *Viewpoints: Georgia Baptist History* 11 (1988): 39–62.

McLoughlin, William G. "The Cherokee Baptist Preacher and the Great Schism of 1844–45: A Footnote to Baptist History." *Foundations: A Baptist Journal of History, Theology, and Ministry* (April–June 1981): 137–47.

Meserve, John Bartlett. "Chief Dennis Bushyhead." *Chronicles of Oklahoma* 14 (September 1936): 349–59.

———. "Chief Lewis Downing and Chief Charles Thompson (Oochalata)." *Chronicles of Oklahoma* 16 (September 1938): 317–22.

Moffitt, James W. "Early Baptist Missionary Work among the Cherokees." *The East Tennessee Historical Society's Publications* 12 (1940): 16–27.

Moulton, Gary E. "Cherokees and the Second Seminole War." *The Florida Historical Quarterly* (January 1975): 296–305.

Perdue, Theda. "The Conflict Within: The Cherokee Power Structure and Removal." *The Georgia Historical Quarterly* 73 (Fall 1989): 467–91.

Routh, E. C. "Early Missionaries to the Cherokees." *Chronicles of Oklahoma* 15 (December 1937): 449–65.

Snell, William R. "Candy's Creek Mission Station, 1824–1837." *Journal of Cherokee Studies* 4 (Summer 1979): 163–85.

———. "The Councils at Red Clay Council Ground, Bradley County, Tennessee, 1832–1837." *Journal of Cherokee Studies* 2 (Fall 1977): 344–55.

Stogsdill, J. R. "Jesse Bushyhead: Cherokee Preacher-Statesman with a Bible for His Shield." *The Oklahoma Baptist Chronicle* 30 (Autumn 1987): 9–27.

Thornton, Russell. "Cherokee Population Losses During the Trail of Tears: A New Perspective and a New Estimate." *Ethnohistory* 31 (Autumn 1984): 289–300.

White, Frank L., Jr. "The Journals of Lieutenant John Pickell, 1836–1837." *The Florida Historical Quarterly* 38 (October 1959): 142–71.

Unpublished Interviews

Bagby, Margaret Sixkiller. Interview by J. W. Tyner, 31 March 1970. History Materials of Northeast Adair County, Oklahoma, vol. 10, transcript ID: T-559-3, Western History Collections, University of Oklahoma.

Conner, John B. Telephone interview by Dan B. Wimberly, 19 August 2006.

Index

Achaia Baptist Church, 26-29, 37, 40
Act of Union, 136, 141, 152, 191
Adair, George Washington: 67, 143, 148
Adair, Walter Scott, 122, 124, 139, 152
Adams, Joseph B., 44
African slavery xiii, xix, 28, 36, 178-79, 182, 184, 194-95, 199
Ahtzthee, 109
American Board of Commissioners for Foreign Missions (ABCFM), xxi, 13-14, 16, 18, 44, 163, 168, 172, 175, 195
Amohee Baptist Church, 37- 40 42, 43, 45-46, 65, 67, 165-66, 170, 179, 185,187, 194, 197
Antislavery and slavery, xvi, xviii-xix, 18, 28, 36, 178-80, 182, 184, 194-95, 199
Antitreaty party also Patriot party, xvii, 40-41, 43, 49, 57, 59-60, 69, 72
Aquohee, 65, 96
Arch, John, 14, 24-25
Atkinson's Evening Post, 132-33
Baldridge, John F., 65n43
Baptist Board of Foreign Missions (BBFM), xxi, 21-22, 29, 30-31, 33, 40, 43-44, 48, 115, 165, 168, 171-72, 174, 176 181, 185, 187, 189
Baptist Missionary Magazine, 42, 178
Baptist settlement, 119
Baptists Cherokee, xi, 45, 48, 109, 168, 178, 189
Beanstick, Joseph also Beanstalk, 130
Beaver Carrier also Beaver Toter, 42, 101, 122, 170
Bell, John Adair (Jack), 67, 126, 140, 143, 169, 197
Bell, Samuel W., 153
Beattie's Prairie, 121- 22, 130, 151, 170, 175, 184, 187
Betsy Walker v David Vann, 11
Bigby, James, Jr., 101n42
Blackburn, Gideon, 12
Blythe's Ferry, 102-03, 104
Boudinot, Elias also Buck Watie, 41, 50-51, 54, 65n45, 67, 69, 94, 126, 128n28, 130, 131,135 138, 141, 146, 154, 168, 192-93
Brainerd Mission, 13-14, 24, 34, 48, 57
Breadtown, 119, 165
Brown, John, 118, 137, 153
Buchanan, Andrew, 126
Buckner, Burrow, 25-28, 40
Buckner, Daniel, 26, 39
Buckner, James F., 111
Bushyhead also Oo-no-du-tu, 7-10, 101, 111-12, 139
Bushyhead, Caroline Elizabeth, 33
Bushyhead, Dennis Wolfe, 150, 191
Bushyhead, Eliza Missouri, 114, 191
Bushyhead, Eliza Wilkerson, xiii, 10-11, 19, 33, 91, 113, 178, 182, 188-89
Bushyhead, George, 15, 34, 53, 57, 126, 138

Bushyhead, Isaac, xv, xviii, 11, 51, 53-54, 57-59, 62, 101, 138, 142, 146, 152-53
Bushyhead, Jacob, 62
Bushyhead, Jane, 11
Bushyhead, Jesse also Tas-ke-ket-chee: alleged threat against Treaty party, 112-13; ancestry, 7-9; birth, 9-10; census taker, 63; chief justice, xi, 143-49, 157-58; conversion, 16-17, 24, 35; death of, 185-88, 196; delegate to Washington, 42, 65n45, 68-70, 149-50, 170, 174-75; detachment leader, 100-102, 103-16; Double Springs compromise, 127-28; early ministry of, 28-34; economic challenges in Indian Territory,172; emissary to Seminoles, 73-74, 77-87; Evan Jones and infanticide accusation, 30-32; Georgia preaching tour, 45-47; Illinois Camp Ground convention, 134; John Walker, Jr. involvement with and murder trial, 50-53, 56-57, 162; linguistic skills of, xi, xv, 17, 28, 32-33, 48, 56, 73, 120 147,150 161, 187, 189, 192-95, 198; oratorical skill, xv, 47-48; 189, 192, property in Tennessee, xiii, 70; Red Clay conference, 67; salt works assessor, 158-61; slaveholder, 10, 101, 178-182, 184; threats on life, 145, 196; wheelwright, 183
Bushyhead, Nancy also Nannie (sister of Jesse Bushyhead), 34, 51-52, 56, 114, 192-93
Bushyhead Nancy Foreman (mother of Jesse Bushyhead), 7, 9, 56
Bushyhead settlement in Indian Territory, 119
Bushyhead settlement in Tennessee, 14
Bushyhead, Susan, 111-12
Butler, Elizur, 15, 97, 116,
Butler, Pierce Mason, 160-61, 183, 188, 198
Butrick, Daniel Sabin, xxi, 48, 97, 100, 112, 116, 145, 171- 72, 184, 187, 198,
Butterfield, Leonard, 32-33
Calhoun, John C., xiv
Camp Hetzel, 93-94, 99
Camp Illinois, 124, 169
Candy's Creek, 3, 14-17, 20-21, 24-28, 34, 36, 48, 56, 97, 112, 131, 167, 192-93
Cane Hill, Arkansas, 102, 124, 126, 186
Cane Hill Independent Regulators, 126
Cannon, B. B., 102, 105
Car-soo-taw-day, 102
Cass, Lewis, 53, 60, 69
Chambers, George, 67
Cherokee Constitution (1827), xiii, 4-5, 18, 55, 182
Cherokee Constitutional Convention (1839). 131, 135-39
Cherokee Messenger, 176, 187-88
Cherokee Phoenix, 18, 46
Cherokee religion, xiii, 5, 23, 109
Cherokee Temperance Society (Indian Territory), 172-73, 185, 197
Chestua Baptist Church, 26
Christie, John, 62
Chunalusky, 107
Coahajo, 79, 82
Cocke, John, 50-51
Colston, Daniel, 130, 138n57
Conrad, Hair, 68, 73, 76-77, 101, 102
Coodey, William Shorey, 108, 150, 156-57
Creeks, 35, 71, 96, 134, 144, 164

Crawford, Thomas Hartley, 154, 170
Cunningham, Cynthia, 30-31
Currey, Benjamin F., 55, 58, 66-68
Daniel, James, 65n45
Daniel, Moses, 111
Davie, Anna, 113
Davie, Winstead, 113
del Castillo y Lanzas, Joaquin Maria, 57
Doublehead, Bird, 101n33, 131, 135
Double Springs Campground also Takatokah, 126, 141
Downing, Lewis, 170, 185, 187, 198
Duck-wa, 130
Ellsworth, J. C., 57
Emory, Susannah, 7
Eustis, Abraham, 98
Fairfield Mission, 171
Fields, Richard (English immigrant), 7
Fields Richard (Bushyhead associate), 65n45, 73, 75-77, 79, 86
Fly Smith, 111-12
Foreman, Charles, 67
Foreman, Grant, xx, 8n11, 191
Foreman, James, 11, 55-57, 131, 151
Foreman, Samuel, 122
Foreman, Stephen, 16, 27-28, 34, 36, 89, 91, 94-95, 111. 122, 124, 128, 129n31, 140, 167, 177, 189, 193, 195, 198
Foreman, Thomas, 36, 54, 65n45, 101n33, 172
Fort Butler, 98
Fort Marion, 79, 81, 84
Fort Mellon, 81-86
Fort Wayne, 119
Foster, 101n33, 115
Foster, James, 67
Free Mission Society (FMS), 180
Free Missionary, 180
Frye, Thomas, 177-78, 186
Gilmer, George, 92
Glasgow and Harrison, 120
Grant, Ludovic, 7
Guess, George also Sequoyah, 18, 127-29, 134, 138, 191
Gunter, Edward, 62, 96, 128, 130, 135, 138
Gunter, John, 67
Gunter, Samuel, 96
Hair, James, 101n33, 131
Hair, Jefferson, 131
Half-breed, Jesse, 67
Hammond, C. M., 124
Henderson, Daniel, 63
Herring, Elbert, 69
Hibbard, Sarah Hale, 177-78
Hicks, Charles, 45
Hicks, Elijah, 54, 65n45, 96, 110, 154, 156-57, 187
Hicks, George, 139, 159
Hitchcock, Ethan Allen, 122, 151
Hiwassee United Baptist Association, 25-27, 36, 37, 39-40
Hog, 98-99, 106-07
Hoig, Stan, 191
Holland, Electra, 13, 27
Holland William, 9, 14-17, 21, 27-28, 34
Holt, William, 146, 148
Honey Creek, 130, 151, 170
Hopkinsville, Kentucky: 102, 110-11
Hunter, 130
Huss, John, 65
Illinois Camp Ground, 128-29, 131-32, 134
Jackson, Andrew, xiv, 41-43, 47, 52-56, 59-61, 64, 67, 69-70, 192, 196
Jefferson, Thomas, 6
Jenny, 10
Jesup, Thomas Sidney, 75, 77-87, 112-13
Jones, Elizabeth, 23

Jones, Evan, xi, xvi, xix, xxi, 9, 23-24, 29-33, 38, 42-49, 58, 66, 68, 74, 91, 94, 97-99, 103, 106-07, 109, 114, 119, 125, 148, 165-72, 174-77, 179, 182, 184, 185, 188-89, 193-94, 196-98
Jones, Pauline, 30-31
Jones, Sam, 80, 82-86
Katihee, 67
Kurtz, Daniel, 169
Lassley, William, 67
Lincoln, Heman, 30-32
Lowrey, George, 128, 129n31, 142, 152-53
Lyon, Castillion, 121
Macedonia Baptist Church, 25
MacIntosh, John, 144-47
Martin, John, 4, 41, 62, 65n45, 122, 139, 142-43
Martin, Joseph, 7
Mason, Richard Barnes, 160
Mayfield, Jesse, 102
Maysville, Arkansas, 151-52, 184
McCall, George A., 124
McCoy, Daniel, 69n58, 122
McCoy, Isaac, 44, 163-64, 179
McLoughlin, William G., xxi
Meigs, Emily, 51-52, 55
Meigs, Return J., 51
Mikanopy, 82-83, 87, 89
M'Junkin, Samuel, 11
Money Taker, 130
Moore, Charles, 67
Moravians, 12, 18
Moseley, John, 123-24
Moulton, Gary E., xxi
Nashville, Tennessee, 46, 55, 102, 108-10
National Gazette, 132
New Dwight Mission, 163
Nicholson, John R., 123-26, 131, 134-35
Noland, Charles Fenten Mercer, 66,
O'Bryant, Duncan, 44, 164, 179
Oganaya, 101, 170, 177
Old Fields, 125
Old Settlers, xvii, 117, 127, 129, 139, 149, 191
Opothleyoholo, 134
Order 34, 93
Order 25, 92-93
Osages, 166-67, 198
Osceola, 71, 73-74, 79-81, 88,
Page, John, 96
Payne, James M., 159-60,
Payne, John Howard, 144
Perdue, Theda, xii
Peter of Aquohee, 65n45,
Pilgrim's Progress, 176
Poinsett, Joel Roberts, 73-74, 79, 87, 89-90, 140-43
Polecat, Major, 73, 73n6, 76-78, 80, 84-86, 101
Porter, James Madison, 154, 160,
Posey, Humphrey, 22-23,
Powell, J., 99, 104, 107, 111
Price, Looney, 136, 139 40, 145-46,
Proctor, William, 122
Raincrow, Sarah, 10
Red Clay, 41-42, 47, 54-55, 63, 65-68, 69n58, 72, 97
Ridge-Boudinot-Watie faction, 41, 61, 117
Ridge, John, 41, 50-51, 60-62, 65, 68-69, 126, 130
Ridge, Major, xiv, 40-41, 54, 67, 112, 126, 131, 144, 151, 159
Rogers, John, 118, 137-38, 141, 155, 159-60
Rogers, Lovely, 159
Rogers, Robert, 67
Rogers, William, 52, 67
Roman Nose, 68, 72, 99, 101n33,
Ross, Andrew, 67
Ross, John: alleged complicity in death of John Walker, Jr, 55; alleged conspiracy in Boudinot-Ridge murders, 130, 141; alleged influence on Baptist

congregations in Indian Territory, 168-69; Antitreaty party and, xvii, Archilla Smith trial, 144-45, 147-48; attempts on life, 143, 157; 40, 59; brother-in-law of Jesse Bushyhead, 10; business interests in Tennessee, 5; death of Jesse Bushyhead, 187; delegate to Washington, 65n45, 140, 150; discussions with Tyler government, 149; Double Springs convention, 128-30; early influence on Jesse Bushyhead, xviii, xx-xxi, 41, 62, 161, 196-98; election of 1843, 152-54; Illinois Camp Ground convention, 131; Isaac Bushyhead murder and, 155-57; investigates possible emigration to Texas, 57; kinship ties to William Shorey Coodey, 108; legal defense for Anderson Springston and James Foreman; 57; lineage of, 41; negotiations with Andrew Jackson, 59-60, 124-26, 132; New Echota convention and, 67-68; opposition from John Ridge over New Echota Treaty, 68-69; overtures by John Walker, Jr. to, 50; papers of, xxi; Park Hill home, 130; political alignment in Tennessee, 41; political influence in Indian Territory, 117-18, 127, 135-40, 142; principal chief, xxv; protests poor rations, 122; relations with William Carroll and/or John Freeman Schermerhorn, 63-64, 67; requests a delay for emigrant departures, 95, 100-01; role in removal, 96, 100, 102n34, 103, 106-08, 116; Running Waters convention and, 61; salt works assessments and, 158-60; Seminole mission and, 73-75, 77-78, 82-83, 87-89; supported by Thomas Foreman, 54; temperance support of in Tennessee, 21; Tennessee home, 13; unrest in Indian Territory, 134, 151
Ross, Lewis, 5, 65n45, 96, 103, 143
Ross's Landing, 93, 144, 192
Ross faction also party, xviii, 54, 60-61, 64, 68, 117-18, 128-29,135-36, 138, 143, 153-54, 196
Running Waters conventions, 60-63
Sarepta Baptist Association, 22
Schermerhorn, John Freeman, 61-69
Scott, H. S., 107
Scott, Winfield, 92-96, 98-101, 103-04, 107-08
Second Seminole War, 71
Sherburne, John H., 73-77, 79-81, 83, 87-88, 90
Situakee, 68, 96, 103, 106, 113, 115, 124-25, 169
Sleeping Rabbit, 65
Smith, Archilla, xviii, 61-62, 67, 143-49, 196
Smith, Cabbin, 144
Smith, Nathaniel (census taker), 62
Smith, Nathaniel (general), 97
Smith, Sam, 99
Soft-shelled Turtle, 138n57
Southern Baptist Convention, 180
Spears, Archibald, 130
Spears, James, 68, 130, 138n57
Spears, John, 138n57
Spears, Joseph, 51, 130
Springplace, 12
Springston, Anderson, 55-57, 131
Springston, Isaac, 131
Starr, Emmet, 191
Starr, James, 67, 155
Stuart, John, 7-9

Sweetwater Baptist Association, 39
Taquohee Church 175,
Tayeskee, 67
Taylor Richard, 65n45, 96, 111-12, 128-29
Taylor, Zackary, 155
Teasteskee, 67
Tekaheskee, 67
temperance societies, 36-37
Texas Cherokees, 58, 133-34
Thompson, Benjamin F., 121
Thompson, James Allen, 121-22, 153
Thompson, Matthew, 153-54
Timson, John, 24, 29, 33, 63, 68
Treaty of Cusseta, 71
Treaty of New Echota, 43, 47, 67-73, 75, 89, 91, 112, 117, 120, 126, 129, 135, 144, 147, 151, 153, 196
Treaty of Payne's Landing, 71, 78, 80
Treaty party, xvii, 41, 59-61, 112, 117-18, 127, 129, 135-36, 139-43, 145, 150, 161, 168-69, 197
Triennial Convention, 21-22, 36, 179-80
Trott, James J., 67
Truxton, Lowell, 179
Upham, Hervey, 175
Valley Towns, 22-25, 28-33, 38, 43, 46-47, 56, 66, 98, 103, 165-66, 169-70, 194-95
Vann, Charles, 56, 65n45
Vann, David, 11, 54, 150, 152
Vann, Joseph, 41, 65n45, 139, 152
Van Buren, Martin, 47, 73-74, 92, 141
Walker, John (Jack), Jr., xv, 11, 50-56, 112, 114n73, 126, 154, 192-93
Walker, Major John, 50
Wallace, Isaac, 123
Washington Baptist Association, 164-65
Watie, Stand, 41, 54, 65n45, 68-69. 126, 135-36, 140, 146-48, 151, 154, 192
West, Bluford, 159
West, Ellis, 153, 155
West, George, 152-56
West, Jacob, 153, 156, 159
West, John, 54, 153-54, 156
White Path, 18, 96, 111-12
Wildcat, 79, 80, 84
Wilkerson, Edward, 10
Woodward, Thomas, 73, 76-77
Wool, John E., 43, 45-46, 72
Worcester, Samuel, 15, 33, 44, 167-68, 173-75, 198
Worcester v Georgia, 20
Work, John, 153-56
Yell, Archibald, 123, 125
Young Wolf, 147-48